Iron Curtain Memoirs

Irene Kucholick

Three Kings Publishing

Princeton, Kentucky

2013

To Mother and Nadja, without them, us kids would have not survived.

Acknowledgements

With many thanks to my good friend Sam Cooper, who spent much time helping me greatly with research and general detail work. Also many thanks to my good friend Phyllis Hole who helped and worked with me to start this enormous amount of labor and urged me to go on when I wanted to give up. I want to thank my good neighbor Merlin Berry, who gave me many good tips and helped me greatly over the last year of writing. Thanks so much to my brothers Hartmut and Claus, (Ortwin died in 1961) who were able to dedicate their time and helped me with details. But above all, I want to thank my husband Walter P. Kucholick, who always gave me great encouragement.

Copyright © 1996 by Irene Kucholick (previously published under Irene L. Emmerich-Kucholick)

Previously self-published in manuscript format as "Survive Little Buddy" by Revere Printing Inc.

All rights reserved, including the right to reproduce this book or portions thereof in any form whatsoever. For information address Three Kings Publishing, 115 Canterbury Court, Princeton, KY 42445.

For information about special discounts for bulk purchases, please contact ThreeKingsPublishing@gmail.com.

Design by Ryan King

ISBN-13: 978-0615894928 (Three Kings Publishing)

ISBN-10: 0615894925

Publisher's Foreword

As incredible as it is, everything you are about to read really happened. This is the true story of Irene Kucholick, a woman I have come to know and respect through the process of helping her tell this fantastic story. If not for the unlikely circumstances of our meeting, her story might have been lost to the world forever. I am honored to be a part of telling the tale of this amazing woman and her survival against all odds. This is her story in her words.

Kristin King
Founder of Three Kings Publishing
                                            October 1, 2013

Book I

Before the Iron Curtain My WWII Childhood

CHAPTER ONE
HOW IT ALL BEGAN
1929-1938

This is a story about what it was like to grow up in Germany, dominated by Adolf Hitler and the feared Nazis; of what civilian life was like during a war that Hitler thrust upon us with a destructive fury; what it was like in our section of my native land--East Germany--when, after the war, we were released from the hand of the Nazis only to be seized at once by the equally strangling bonds of Communism.

Around the time of my birth in 1929, in the industrial city of Chemnitz, Bolshevism had established itself in Russia. The Nazi Party, catapulted into power, teetered Europe on the brink of great turmoil.

My father, fluent in many languages, worked as a foreign correspondent for industrial firms. During evening hours refugees from Russia--members of the old white Russian nobility (anti red) crowded into his study to learn the German language. His attraction to a Russian countess and subsequent unfaithfulness to my mother caused her to leave him while she was pregnant with me, her first child. She later divorced my father.

Growing up in an atmosphere darkened by informers, by disappearances of Jewish and other friends, by hunger and exploding bombs, I was forced to learn many survival skills. In time, I developed a special kind of cunning in dealing with both Nazis and

Communists. In time too, came a burning desire for the sweetness of freedom out from under the yoke of occupied Germany while being held in check by loyalty to my mother's needs and by her decision to stay in East Germany.

By the time I was three, my mother had remarried. By the time I was five, I had two brothers, Ortwin and Hartmut.

We lived in the center of Chemnitz, which lies about 70 kilometers southwest of Dresden and approximately 95 kilometers north of the Czechoslovakian border. Coal smoke from the factories and from thousands of chimneys above our homes poured a grey mantle over our city.

Slate roofs sheltered our sturdy buildings with walls made thick to accommodate the chimneys. Central heating was a luxury and did not exist in our area.

Our home was a four-room apartment on the second floor of a four story building. Storage rooms filled the fifth floor and an attic provided a place to dry clothes during winter months. A deep basement held more storage rooms and would become our air raid shelter.

Two blocks away, some trees and grass were growing, none in our street. In order to enjoy nature, we owned a garden in a garden colony three miles away. Everyone owned approximately half an acre and people grew everything under the sun. My mother had a green thumb and won many ribbons for the best flowers. There was also a garden hut with a few pieces of old furniture which sheltered us from any occasional showers.

Near the colony was a place called "Planitz Wiese"--Planitz Square--where special summer events brought a merry-go-round, a

Ferris wheel, and sometimes a whole circus. Booths, for selling sweets and beverages, lined the sides of the square. During community activities, park police occupied a building in the center. At other times, soldiers from a nearby barracks kept the ground dusty and bare by their constant marching.

My first experience of evading the police occurred in this square when I was five years old. Although I can recall the incident now with some amusement, it was a painful episode for me then. Perhaps it helped shape my behavior and certainly my attitude towards men in uniform.

One day, as we set out to see the sights, Mama had Ortwin and Hartmut in the baby carriage, and me beside her. Fascinated by a clown tumbling about in the crowds, I followed him. Other sights caught my attention and I wandered on. Some time passed before I realized I was lost, then remembered a cousin of mine named Susanne. Her parents operated a cigarette booth next to one where Italian candy was made and sold. Slowly I worked my way through the crowd. There was deafening noise all around me - music, played by electric automatic organs and manual organ grinders and merchants loudly praising their wares. When I found Susanne she was not particularly pleased to see me. She was much older then I and her boyfriend was with her.

"Go home!" she shouted. "Your mother is looking for you."

She simply was too busy to bother with me. I loved the smell of fresh tobacco and there were cigarette brands from many different countries. As I viewed all the colorful packages which were laid out on a large table, another smell caught my attention. I walked over to the Italian booth to watch a man pouring molten candy out of a big copper kettle. A magnificent golden stream flowed into trays where it was spread out with paddles. How heavenly it smelled.

Suddenly the man's hand slipped and the hot candy shot into my face. I screamed! Oh, the pain! My skin seemed to be on fire. The owners of the booth became very excited and led me to a trailer in the rear. They washed my face with cool water until the pain subsided.

To console me they gave me several big bags of candy--many different kinds, so much I had to be careful not to spill any as they pushed me back into the crowd. I think they wanted me to get lost again. They need not have worried because now all I wanted was to find Mama. My face was beginning to burn and I had an armful of candy to share with her.

Searching through the noisy crowds, I came to the police station in the center of the square. There I opened a sack to sample my sweets. The candy coated almonds looked good but the stuff was so hard it broke my fingernail and when I tried to separate a couple of pieces I cut my finger. With blood running down my hand, I started to cry. I must have looked a mess.

A policeman, spotting me through the station window, motioned for me to come inside. His uniform and large helmet scared me. I thought to ignore him might be best to handle this. He climbed out of the window and came toward me. I got terrified he might take the candy away from me. I turned around and ran as fast as I could.

"Hold that kid!" he shouted.

He ran into the crowd which parted unwillingly. It was much easier for a small person to slip through the crowd than for a big man to chase me so I got away. After all, maybe he thought I had stolen the candy. Why would a dirty little kid have all those expensive sweets?

I walked farther in one direction and soon heard bells above the noise of the music and crowd. Streetcars! By walking toward the sound I found the main street. I hurried around the outside of the square and down the street. I found our garden and there was Mama. What a relief! My next encounter with the police would not occur until I was about eleven.

One year later my education began. It was 1935 and school began at Easter time. A picture still in my possession recalls memories of that first day in school. I wore a dark green pleated dress with silver buttons and a white collar. Clipped to my hair right in the middle of my head was a large white ribbon bow which was then big in fashion.

Also I now owned a *schulranzen*, the leather knapsack all German children used to carry books. The high point of my first day in school was the same as with other beginning students, a *zuckertuete*, which is a large colorful cardboard cone filled with candies, cookies and school supplies, a gift from our family, immediate and extended, on the first day of school.

Our school stood in the business section of Chemnitz and the playground was a small brick-fenced courtyard. Boys' and girls' classrooms occupied different sections of the building with separate gymnasiums and a locked door between. Girls joined the boys only during programs in the auditorium. Even there boys sat on one side, girls on the other. Doors were locked when school started and late corners had to ring the bell to be admitted. Punishment for tardiness was certain. The school had no social life, it was learning only and above all, we had to be always very quiet. The teacher was not satisfied unless he could hear a small pin fall to the ground. Hot lunches were never served and of course, we had half a day school on Saturday.

Although my stepfather treated me as if I was his own, I knew that I had a father who lived somewhere else. As a still single parent, he had no visiting rights. German law forbade a single divorced father from having his child spend a full day in his bachelor home. Visiting days became permissible only if he remarried. Mama refused to let Father come near her home. I was in her custody and Father paid for my support.

But he made sneak visits anyway. He often drove his car to school just to see me. I looked forward to his visits.

Especially the short automobile rides. His car, a DKW-German model, was more exciting than the Dreirad, a modified motorcycle with three wheels that my stepfather drove.

Father told me how he loved Mama. Even after she remarried and had two children he was sorry for what happened in the past. It was through his eyes I saw Mama as a brown-eyed beauty. She combed her brown hair in soft waves and knotted it loosely in back. Little curls fringed her face and she rarely used cosmetics. Her smile revealed even white teeth.

Mama liked to wear an apron. This was big fashion for all housewives then and I remember a store which specialized in nothing but selling aprons, any size and with very beautiful patterns. Papa Walter teased her sometimes about her shapely legs. She'd tilt her head, smile and wink, then do a little skip and whirl. She wore high heels only when "going out."

My real father, Basil, was taller than Papa Walter. He had a trustworthy face, rather square with full eyebrows over large brown eyes and his smile showed teeth yellowed by much cigar smoking. He was slightly bald and though clean shaven could have had a heavy beard. I remember his broad shoulders and muscular build. His big hands had much hair on the back of them. He wore dark suits and white shirts and carried a pocket watch on a chain he removed from a special little pocket.

By contrast Papa Walter was of slighter build and very active. Mama called him a "tinkerer" since he was usually working with his special radio equipment when at home. His blue eyes contrasted with the rest of the family and his curly brown hair was passed on to his sons.

Papa Walter had a rich singing voice and he always encouraged us to sing along with him. He indulged his athletic interests in bike racing and occasionally he entered racing events. During my seventh year Father Basil married again. This gave me the opportunity to visit him in his home. One day after school he came for me in his DKW. As we drove away I waved proudly to my admiring classmates.

I remember fairly well what was said and will try to reconstruct this and other conversations as my story proceeds. "I am going to take you to my new home, Irene," he said. "I hope you like it."

He drove to a different section of the city while I bounced on the cushions and gazed loftily out on the passing world. Every time a car passed us he explained to me what make it was. Then he drove to the westside of the city up West Street and turned right into a street which was renamed by the Nazis Franz Selte Strasse. The corner building of West and Bergstrasse was a villa with a beautiful lawn. There were more buildings like that around. Then I gazed at a row of three story apartment buildings set well back on landscaped lawns. In front, along the sidewalk, a two-foot thick brick wall was topped by an ornate fence. In contrast, Mama's house was next to the sidewalk with no garden in front.

We walked hand in hand up the steps and through a large door into a small vestibule. The mosaic tile floor had a circular design of flowers. In front of us were double doors with stained glass panes and more stained glass windows beside the doors and above them.

Through these doors we walked on a highly polished tile floor and up a broad stairway to a second floor apartment. Ornate lamps topped the stair posts at the bottom and on each landing above. It was a grand looking stairway.

"These stairs would be good for jumping." I said.

"I don't think you will be allowed to do that." His voice sounded stern.

A door opened and a tall well-dressed lady with short black hair smiled at us.

"This is your Aunt Johanna."

"Come in Irene," she invited me pleasantly.

Father hugged me and said, "We are going to be a very happy family, Irene."

I looked at Aunt Johanna, and I felt she was looking me over carefully. Thinking of what surprises I would bring into her well organized existence.

"Come on, Irene, I'll show you your room." she said.

A room just for me? At home I shared a room with my brothers. This was a medium-sized bedroom with new ruffled curtains at the window and a yellow silk spread on a high bed.

The closet door was partly open and I could see a few dresses, just my size.

"Get washed, change your clothes and come to dinner," she commanded as she walked to the door. I was too amazed at the things I was seeing to answer her.

I opened drawers that held new stockings and underwear. I tried on a white blouse and a blue jumper. As I looked in the mirror I could see it fit just right. Mama would like this one, I thought.

What about Mama? I hurried back to Father.

"Did Mama know I was coming here?" I asked.

"I am lonely to see you, Irene. My, you look nice in that dress." His big warm hand around mine was reassuring.

Dinner was good and served in a fancy manner with much silver and many dishes. At home we ate from bowls and plates, never both at the same time. Here they put the bowl on the plate and changed to other dishes later in the meal. The tablecloth was white and of fine material,

At home I helped wash the dishes--here a lady washed them after serving dinner. I was not to go in the kitchen unless asked. Feeling out of place, I went into the living room, and sat on a chair.

After dinner, strange people in elegant clothes began to arrive. Father took them immediately into his study. They spoke harsh-sounding words I could not understand.

"Russian," Father told me.

When they took off their coats, I saw fashionable dresses of fine wool. They wore jewelry and I saw large rings reflecting bright colored lights from moving hands. Long earrings and necklaces held brilliant jewels.

"This is the wealth they brought from Russia," Father said, "and they keep much of it on them. They are slow to trust others." When the men removed their coats, I noticed medals of rank and honor, awarded by the Czar, across the fronts of their jackets.

Although I was told emphatically to "Stay away from the study" while Father was teaching, my curiosity to meet his royal students stayed with me.

Within a short time I learned there was to be a custody suit between my parents. In the meantime I was to stay with Father until things were settled.

When Father went to work all day, Aunt Johanna worked on me.

When in the garden it was, "A lady cuts flowers this way." In the house it was, "Don't whip your legs when you sit on a chair," and "Handle your napkin this way." "Don't say that." "Wash your hands if you touch this or that and comb your hair."

Unfortunately, I wore a bow ribbon that had to be tied, then clipped in my hair so it would sit on top of my head.

Mama had always fastened the ribbon in my hair. Those days were filled with frustrations.

Aunt Johanna's statement that "Maybe she could make a human being out of me yet," let me know I had a long way to go before I could measure up to her expectations.

One day she slapped me when I told her that Mama was prettier than she. She shook her finger, bent her face toward me and said, "I had money before I married your father, young lady and don't you forget it. I did not ask to have you live here." Her arched black eyebrows emphasized her anger.

Aunt Johanna was an affluent lady and she wore pretty clothes but she could not equal Mama.

I stood at the window and looked down on their flower gardens. At home, we had a courtyard in back of our building with a big washhouse where I helped Mama sort the clothes. I missed hearing the fire crackle under the big kettle where she boiled our white sheets. I missed the smell of soap and how we laughed when I helped her prop up the clotheslines with poles after the laundry was hung to dry. We kids played in our courtyard. Out in our garden, we had vegetables and fruit. It was almost time right now to pick gooseberries, Mama used to make delicious desserts out of them. I missed Ortwin and Hartmut and the lively play after school.

I did not succeed with Aunt Johanna but Father and I spent many happy hours together. I remember the little gifts he brought when he came home. He'd sit and watch me unwrap them and I'd give him a hug. We laughed and talked but it was not the same as home. I longed for Mama's comforting voice and understanding smile.

Extremely curious to see and talk to my father's Russian guests, I knocked on the door of his study one evening.

"Please let me come in," I pleaded. "I'll recite a poem and then I'll go away."

Finally the door opened and I slipped into the study. I curtsied as I recited and studied Father's guests, a couple and their son, who must have been just a little older than I. He was absolutely interesting with his dark hair but very pale face. He looked like he studied a lot. Father declined my request to "stay and watch." I was told to leave and close the door behind me. Sadly I obeyed. This couple and their son came only once a week.

There was a young girl in the neighborhood, named Eleonore. The way she spoke her name was as if she was singing the high C. She was about my age but her disdain for my unsophisticated ways discouraged me from having a real friendship with her. She thought she knew everything since her Father was the Chief surgeon at the City Hospital. I just thought she was silly and she was just no fun to be with. I wished that my girlfriend Esther could have been here with me.

Once, Eleonore's parents gave her a birthday party. I had to bring a gift that Aunt Johanna picked and wrapped. There were no more than about eight children, carefully selected. There was a lot of food and games. But the girl received so many gifts as if it was Christmas. How can she have a joyful Christmas when she already received so much for a simple birthday? I wondered.

I never liked the Russian language and I was horrified when I heard my father speak it. Maybe it was because I connected Stalin, deportation and Siberia with the language. Mama used to say, it is a language people curse with.

During the evening hours, Father told me many stories about his former home in Galicia, Poland (later Russian territory). I learned, that after WWI, the Russians had their bloody revolution, which sometime in the years after that war spilled over into Eastern Poland and the Polish forces fought gallantly and successfully in those battles against Bolshevism. If it had not been for the strong Polish defenses, Bolshevism would have easily taken over all the countries that had been weakened by WWI and European history would have been written quite differently.

Father's books from Galicia contained pictures of beautiful countrysides but his recollections of his family were filled with sorrow.

"Irene, you should have known your grandmother. You would have loved her. Her name was Irina."

"But Irina sounds like a Russian name, Father."

He didn't seem to hear my question and his face saddened. He leaned forward, removed his cigar and said, "My brother Alexander fought fiercely in the war against Bolshevism. He died on the battle field and Mother and Father and many other people were captured and deported to Siberia. I never saw them again.

"Since I was the youngest, my parents had sent me to the University of Krakow to study language. I eventually finished my studies and had not been able to go back home, I took a position here in Germany." He bowed his head in his hands and wept. When Father raised his head he put his arms around me and held me close. After a few moments he went on. "Germany is my home now and you are my daughter, Irene, the only real part of my family."

His eyes were sad. I loved my father but I missed Mama and my brothers.

A retired school teacher was my private tutor while I lived with Father. She lived close by and I was her only pupil. I learned quickly, since she made learning a game and the hours I spent with her were always pleasant.

Once she invited me for dinner. Her home was dark with heavily carved furniture and Persian rugs. Precious looking books were kept behind glass doors lined with fabric to protect them from the light. We ate fish covered with a thick sweet sauce and sipped Seltzer with a drop of white wine for me and wine for her from stemmed glasses. We laughed and I felt warm friendliness as she walked me home in the evening.

When the day came for the custody hearing, I was dressed in fancy clothes, "so everyone would think I was well taken care of." The charge that it is "illegal to take a child from school" was satisfied since I had two tutors, Father and Mrs. Hanson, a certified teacher in retirement. The judge from the *Jugendamt* (Department for the Youth) sat in front of a large desk and asked me to step forward. I stood and walked toward him. My legs felt shaky. In great anguish, I looked at Mama's tear filled eyes.

"Irene, you must choose the parent with whom you want to live." Without hesitation I ran to Mama. Her arms felt strong around me. And so it was decided.

Although my mother now had custody again over me, my father and I remained good friends and with liberal visiting rights, it was the best for the both of us. He never had any other children and on Sunday afternoons I often took the streetcar to his home. Our friendship was to prove good for us in the later years of the war.

* * *

Home again! It felt so good, so comfortable to be with Mama and Papa and my brothers.

Our big live-in-kitchen, the white stove and the large sturdy table where we ate and studied looked like old friends welcoming me home. I could be here in the kitchen while Mama cooked all the things we liked and she let me help too. I could go out on the balcony and talk to our neighbors.

We kept our hardwood floors heavily waxed and the rug in our seldom used living room was made to look like an Oriental. Our furniture was made from dark finished wood. The closet Mama bought from the owners of the building was so large it had to be taken apart to be moved into our apartment. The lower section contained a chest that held all the family shoes.

We could build a small fire in a heater under the water tank in the bathroom. It heated water for our baths and I remember Papa had to install a flush toilet himself with a water closet high on the wall. Ours was one of the few in the neighborhood.

The bedroom I shared with my brothers was a place where we could talk when sent to bed. After we snuggled down in our featherbeds I had to tell them bedtime stories otherwise they would not fall asleep.

A picture of Jesus walking on the water still hung in Mama's bedroom. This gave me another "welcome home" feeling.

"Mama, that is one of the best pictures I ever saw."

The best thing about our clean home was the feeling of love we all had for one another. I did not miss Aunt Johanna but I felt sad about my father.

We lived in the inner city. I knew it inside out. It was my part of town. Everything exciting happened in our neighborhood, which was near the stores and the railroad station. We could go "big shopping" in the large Jewish department stores. I played with the kids on the Jakobstreet and we called ourselves the Jakobstreet Band.

Our favorite playground was the iron railroad bridge. It crossed about a dozen tracks a few blocks from the railroad station. Massive steel cross-structures with huge bolts and nuts made adventurous climbing for us. We scaled the iron struts over the wide span, playing those great imaginative childhood games.

Our play area was constantly challenged by the Tammstreet Kid's band who came from the other side of the tracks. We lost some of our battles because our members were younger and fists were our only weapons but when Esther Goldberg led our fist fights, we always won. Esther, tall and lanky with dark brown hair and eyes, was warmhearted and shared everything with us but she demanded our loyalty in return. All members in our band, including the boys, pledged our staunch support to her.

Some afternoons Esther brought a big sheet cake. I loved that cake her mother baked. She even shared it with some of the Tammstreet Kids when they were behaving.

Our pretend-to-be-grownup game was called the dating game. It consisted of choosing partners and walking arm in arm, imitating grownups.

Esther liked Karl-Heinz and she chose him for her partner. He was her age and the most handsome boy in our band. All the girls liked him. According to Esther, Luzie must walk with Eberhardt, Gisela had to take Gunther, and I had to walk arm in arm with Alfons, whom I disliked.

On one such occasion, Alfons played with his nose and I hit him over the head. Alfons cried and Eberhardt, who didn't like the game anyway, hit Alfons too. This made Luzie cry. Then Esther ordered, "Peace."

Gunther and Gisela quit in disgust. While Esther was trying to calm things down, Karl-Heinz took my arm and started to flirt with me. Esther didn't like this because she was really fond of Karl. It was a fiasco.

Another of our pastimes was to lie on the cobblestones and hang our heads through the open basement windows of the Kaiser Coffee store. We watched them stir the coffee beans in the copper kettles and sniffed the aroma of roasting coffee.

Gerda Weirs, the shortest and prettiest girl in our band, liked to tap dance. Her father was a professional comic and clown. Gerda planned to "go into show biz" when she grew up. I'd play the harmonica while she danced at the Dresdner Square, this also was another favorite place where we played, since Papa's store was there nearby.

Another game we played was cowboys and Indians, right out of Karl May's books. His works are classical literature in Germany.

Before the Nazi uprising came boiling into our lives we enjoyed many family excursions to Dresden, just an hour's drive from Chemnitz. This spectacular city housed the history of art in nearly all its fields. The past King of Saxony had priceless masterpieces in splendid buildings of German baroque architecture which are now museums.

These one-day trips were made in Papa's Dreidad. This vehicle, originally a motorcycle, had one small wheel in front and two large wheels in back. Over these wheels Papa had built a wooden structure, narrow in front where he sat and steered with the motorcycle handlebars.

We entered through a little door in the back and sat on wooden benches along each side. A frame over our heads held a canvas roof with roll-down sides to protect us when it rained. We felt the heavy jolts from the potholes and were thrown around a bit by the big bumps but we always laughed and straightened ourselves out. This was all part of the fun. The nearer we got to Dresden the cleaner the air seemed. Industrial factories in Chemnitz kept our air smoky and full of odors.

The Zwinger Museum, built by King Augustus II (August the Strong) and his son King August III in the early 1700's, consisted of six pavilions connected by arcaded galleries. These galleries enclosed a courtyard called the "festival room." The sky was the ceiling. Gardens, graced with sculpture and fountains, surrounded the buildings.

Museums displayed paintings by Duerer, Cranach, Vermeer, Rubens, Rembrandt, Raphael, Jan van Eyck, Titian, Lucas von Leyden and Tintoretto.

As we stood admiring the Sistine Madonna by Raphael, Mama recounted, "It is said that when this painting arrived, King Augustus III was so proud of it he wanted it hung in a place for all to see. He pushed his throne aside with his own hands and shouted, 'Make room for the great Raphael!'"

Mama's stories made our visits to Dresden an exciting experience. There was so much to see we visited only parts of this great display of art each trip.

We saw Chinese and Japanese porcelain as well as our own German Meissen porcelain. Meissen porcelain was developed by Boettger in 1710. When King Augustus saw its potential for both profit and prestige, he started the Royal Saxon Porcelain manufacturing in Meissen. The official signature for these prized pieces is the crossed swords on the bottom of each piece.

The Green Vault, deep under the Royal Castle, had walls 80 inches thick. Under its arched ceilings the most priceless treasures were displayed. Five of the original eight rooms of the Green Vault were not destroyed in the war, although the Royal Castle was burned out.

Of all the treasures in Dresden, the one most beautiful to me was the little blackamoor in the Green Vault. His happy face was topped by a crown of gold set with jewels. The big stone he held was full of uncut emeralds. The best gift a king could ever have, I thought. Everything he wore was set in precious stones.

We took boat trips on the Elbe River to see Pillnitz, a summer castle built in 1720 by Augustus the Strong.

"The Elbe River," Papa explained, "begins in the southern hills of Czechoslovakia and runs right down through the middle of Germany to Hamburg in the far north. Hundreds of barges move freight up and down this river. They survey this stream twice monthly. They close her about four weeks every year for drifting ice, too low water level or flood stage water."

Mama told us about many famous people such as Richard Wagner, Friedrich Schiller, Johann Wolfgang von Goethe, Wilhelm von Kuegelgen and Ludwig Richter.

"Wolfgang Amadeus Mozart gave concerts here for the King," Mama said. "Heinrich von Kleist, Hans Thoma, all of them have been here. All those famous poets and musicians have come here to be inspired by this beautiful river."

Mama's voice was soft as she spoke about our homeland. We were sitting together on the upper deck enjoying the river sounds and the sunshine. People were quiet. Children were not permitted to run around but we didn't mind. We enjoyed sitting like grownups watching the view.

As the Water Palace came into view it appeared to be suspended in air above the water. The river mirrored the pale yellow walls of this graceful oriental structure. The Hill Palace was built near a park, away from the river. In one building a row of high tile stoves lined one side of a long hall, windows lined the other.

"There is a row of bedrooms on the other side of these walls," Papa explained. "Hot air from these stoves blows right into the rooms. Even though this is a summer castle the nights are often chilly."

Outside, beds of colorful flowers captured and held the sunshine. "It was the wish of the King," the gardener said, "to have fig trees, the finest apples and pears as well as melons, artichokes and berries. We have many foods here which do not ordinarily grow in Germany."

Our tour always ended back by the river. Standing at the river's edge, Papa would say to Ortwin and Hartmut, "Spit in it!" They would lean their curly brown heads as far out as possible and spit.

"It will take nine days for that to reach Hamburg," Papa predicted. We all laughed.

After a picnic lunch we'd travel home, bumping along in our Dreirad, singing songs and talking about the beautiful things we saw in Dresden.

CHAPTER TWO
GATHERING CLOUDS
1938 - 1939

My memory is that I was eight or nine when I became aware of the frequency with which the grownups listened to Hitler's radio speeches. His voice was commanding, no matter what he said. Speaking about WWI, he kept saying "Germany must be avenged." He talked about *lebensraum*, a word Hitler used in all his speeches. "*Lebensraum*," Mama explained, "means that Hitler thinks Germany needs to expand so the people can have more living space." We laughed and said, "Why does he not build up skyscrapers like the Americans, then we don't need to go into other countries territory."

The hate propaganda, instigated by Goebbels, Hitler's Propaganda Minister, blared from our radios and headlined the newspapers. Along with the feeling of hate, an emotion of fear began to arise.

Some neighbors turned into informers. We had to be careful about whom we were speaking to and what we said. The Nazi party had ears everywhere. National Socialistsche Deursche Arbeiter Partei called in short NSDAP.

My parents never accepted the Nazis and they continually cautioned me and my brothers to be careful of what we said in the presence of anyone outside our immediate family. As children we learned early to keep our beliefs to ourselves.

Each month Herr Heinrich, wearing a Nazi Party pin, came to our home. This stoutly built man with a churlish manner held out a long list of names and threatened Papa.

"If you want to get along in this town you'd better join the Nazi Party!"

Papa always refused. One time after our threatening visitor left, Papa said, "Next time that Nazi fascist comes back, I'll kick him down the stairs!"

We prayed in church, pleading for protection. Papa told us of gangs of men in brown shirts who were roaming the streets, unhampered by the police. They carried clubs and beat up many innocent people. Papa pointed out the dance hall near our home where men were stripped of their clothes and whipped, some beaten very badly. These brutal acts took place just before the Nazi Party was coming into full power.

He remembered when street fighting had started, people locked their doors. Uncle Helmut, Papa's sister's husband, was caught once as he walked in the street wearing checkered knickerbockers from America. Locked out of a building when the fighting began, he was captured, called a capitalist, and beaten with clubs.

Mama did not believe the German people really voted for Hitler. Listening to our parents, we children soon came to think Hitler and Stalin were the biggest villains Europe had ever produced. Many in our neighborhood said, "He who votes for Hitler, votes for war."

Kristallnacht or Crystal Night came November 9-10, 1938. Our teachers warned us earlier that day not to go near the Jewish department stores. The nicest one, Schockens, was near our school. It was a six story building with windows on all sides.

When we walked to school the next morning I saw lots of broken glass on the street in front of the store. All the windows were broken and emptied of merchandise. Sturm Abteilung or SA men in brown uniforms with swastikas on their arms were supervising the cleanup.

During morning classes we heard hammering in the distance. By noon all the store windows were covered with wooden panels. Papa told us that Jewish stores all over Germany had been broken into and things carried away.

SA men guarded the front doors of the Jewish stores, warning people they would 'write down the names of anyone who shopped there.' The SA men disappeared in a few weeks and people walked in and tried to do their shopping, but merchandise was not as available anymore as it was before.

"We got good quality for less money," Mama would say.

These statements angered those owning Aryan, or non-Jewish stores. They posted signs on the entrances reading "We are Aryan" or "This store is Arisch." Some store owners put "Aryan" signs on their doors because they were afraid they would be mistaken for Jewish stores and vandalized.

Upon returning home from school one day, I heard someone crying through our half open door. Fearing for Mama, I burst into the room. Frau Wabra, our neighbor, was talking and crying at the same time; her hands twisting her apron into a knot. The dark shawl that always covered her hair had fallen back, revealing graying hair and a bony face in utter despair. She and her family moved into our neighborhood from Czechoslovakia some years ago. She was now a widow living with her son in one of the apartments in our building.

The Geheime Staatspolizei or Gestapo, the secret State Police, had arrested her 25 year old son, Stachu and taken him away.

Mama explained later, "They dragged Stachu from their home. Frau Wabra clung to him until they kicked her aside." Mama stared at the door Frau Wabra had just closed. Her face revealed fright as she pushed her hands through her hair and pulled it back into a tight knot.

"What terrible thing has Stachu done, Mama?"

"He has done nothing wrong, child, nothing! The Gestapo just picks up whoever they want, for God knows what reason." Mama's voice was angry. "We must pray they won't pick us up too."

On another day, Frau Taume came running to Mama. "Have you heard? Have you heard?" She was crying. "They picked up Herr Ottmann, Herr Fischer and Herr Nolte. What are we getting into?"

Despite these incidents, my life went on much the same at school, play, and church but little by little troubles became more frequent. Our fears increased. People's faces looked tense and a feeling of apprehension about the future clouded conversations. Teenage boys in brown uniforms stomped their feet to stout-hearted singing and marched in groups through our neighborhood streets. They carried a red flag with the swastika on it and pennants with the large letter S." Flag bearers, flanked by drummers and trumpeters, led them in their rousing songs. Leather encased knives swung from their belts, some even carried wooden clubs.

When they marched by, we were required to salute and keep our arms in this position until their flags passed by. For those unfortunate people who did not salute, a dozen rowdies in brown uniforms would break ranks and attack them, while their leader fired them on to do so. I saw children run away quickly, but old men and women, who did not salute, were beaten about the head and shoulders in a cruel, and vicious manner.

On one occasion a group of older men stood stunned as these young bullies came at them. In utter disbelief those men just stood there as the brown uniformed youth plunged into the crowd and beat them with unrelenting fury. I saw it all from the inside of a large store window.

These occurrences caused two kinds of reactions among us. Some simply left the scene of the marchers, paying no heed to their proud strutting. Others stayed but felt inside, "This is my street! Who do those young scoundrels think they are?"

One evening Papa came home and banged the door shut, he was apparently very exasperated.

"Walter, what happened? Here, sit down." Mama pushed a chair toward him.

"It's those boys! Those kids in their black uniforms are absolutely fanatic about their importance. They think they're going to take the whole world by storm. I've never seen anything like it. Hitler is using them to whip up an evil force. I can feel it in the air when I hear them. Have you looked at their faces while they're singing?"

"Thank God, Ortwin and Hartmut are too young to get caught up in this marching," Mama said. "Any attempt to discipline these boys is only bringing contempt. Parents are helpless."

Some of the marching songs were romantic in thought. The music to "Oh, du schoener Westerwald," a popular song with a strong marching rhythm was an example. This song is also a very old folksong and still a favorite today. The translation is about like this:

Marching we will go today

and a new march it will be

into the beautiful Westerwald

where the wind does blow so cold.

Oh, you beautiful Westerwald,

over your hills the wind is whistling so cold,

although the smallest sparkle of sunshine,

penetrates deep into our hearts.

Other marching songs kindled feelings of destruction and force. Such a song about conquering and revenge was written by a fanatical 16-year old Nazi youth, Hans Baumann. It was so inflammatory that people resented the words and forbade it to be sung in their homes, yet we heard it over and over as the youth marched in the streets. Part of this song went:

See the rotten bones are shaking

as if before a total war.

We have overcome our fear.

We have victory.

On and on we shall march now

let everything fall apart.

Today we rule our country

and tomorrow the whole world

and if the old ones scold us

let them shout and rage

and if the whole world is against us

We shall continue marching

Let everything fall apart.

Today we rule our country

and tomorrow the whole world.

This rousing march music, created for Hitler's use, whipped emotions of the Hitler youth into believing they were supreme.

History has recorded well the hate wave instigated by Joseph Goebbels, Hitler's propaganda minister. For several years Julius Streicher in Nuremberg had published a notorious anti-Semitic paper, Der Stuermer. Goebbels circulated it.

Very few people in our neighborhood would buy it so Goebbels' people built wooden stands with windows and hung pages from this biased paper in them. We were encouraged to look at the lurid pictures and read the filthy ravings against the Jews.

Mama forbade me and my brothers to read it, saying, "It's spiteful and full of hate. Decent Christians know those pictures and words are untrue."

Many whispered jokes were made about Goebbels, who had what we supposed to be a clubfoot. Imagine, in a Nazi society where they claimed everyone to be perfect, yet our government minister had a clubfoot.

At the age of ten I was required to go to the Bund Deutscher Maedchen or BDM, a Hitler youth organization for girls. The meeting house was just two blocks from home.

All ten year olds were to assemble at the Schlageter Square in full uniform which we were required to buy ourselves. Mama said sternly "No! You will not have a uniform," which consisted of a black skirt, white blouse, black scarf, pulled through a leather knot and a BDM pin.

Most mothers accompanied their children and I saw that at least half of the 45 girls had no uniform. This was our initiation. The purpose was to see how much we could endure. Some mothers, suspicious of what was happening, did not leave as they were told, but followed us. Mama was pregnant and unable to join them. For hours we were ordered to run, walk fast, turn left, march, turn right, then repeat all this to the shouted commands and loud whistles of some older girls, our leaders.

Just as we reached the technical high school, it started to rain. We were ordered to stand at attention while the leaders went into the building entrance. Thunder and lightning brought rain that fell in sheets until the street was running with water. We were drenched to the skin.

As we stood shivering from the cold rain, mothers watching us became angry and ordered all of us to go home. The leaders tried to stop them but the mothers would have none of it. We ran as fast as we could to get home and out of our wet clothes.

Within a week another notice came to attend the BDM meeting.

I went to church instead. I felt more comfortable in church than in a meeting where they shouted orders.

A few days later when another meeting was scheduled, a policeman was sent to fetch me. Not knowing who they were, he asked my brothers where I lived.

Ortwin ran upstairs to warn me. "Hide! Hide!" he whispered loudly. "A policeman is looking for you!"

Frantically I searched for a safe place to hide. There was no time, no place to go! The closet! Quickly I crawled under all the family shoes and closed the door just as we heard the commotion outside.

Our bell, which did not always work, rang loudly. Everyone knew how they punish people caught lying.

"Where is Irene and why isn't she at the BDM meeting?"

"Irene?" asked Mama. "I sent her off to the meeting. She must be there."

The policeman went into all the rooms. I held my breath and remained motionless when he came into the bedroom. He opened all the closets, even the one where I was hiding, but it was too dark inside to see me and he closed the door again. He wrote in his little black notebook and said, "When she returns send her to the meeting."

Before the next scheduled BDM meeting, school authorities asked us to bring a record of our family tree. This was not to show how large our family was but to show if we were "Aryans" and for how many generations back.

Mama's line was all German. Her parents had owned a glove factory in Koethensdorf near Rochlitz. Her parents had died young and the three children, Mama, her sister Martha, and her brother Albert were raised by relatives while the factory was run by other family members. I remember when I was much smaller I had a visit with Mama's aunt and I didn't like the place, it smelled of treated leather. That smell had made me cough. Now it was gone. It had been lost already to the terrible inflation after WWI. There were still some relatives working there.

Father, although born in Galizia, had become a naturalized German citizen in 1938.

When the kids at school learned I was part Polish, they taunted, "Polack! Polack!" This name calling was painful for me and on one occasion I started a terrible fight. Even kids who didn't know what it was all about got into it and some kids were on my side. We drove our fists into jeering faces, punching noses, chins and eyes. We hit kids in the belly and swung at every piece of flesh we could reach. We really felt good after that fight.

When my Galicia-Polish ancestry became known, I was considered undesirable for the BDM. That suited me just fine. What I didn't know was that the Polish blood on my father's side would bring us much trouble in the future.

Our band leader, Esther Goldberg, came to play one day wearing a large yellow star. When I asked her where she got it from, she quickly explained, "That yellow star is a mark of identification, Irene. All Jewish people are required to wear them."

At that time my childhood friendships with the Cohens, Blausteins and the Goldberg kids far outweighed any racial differences the government might have--yellow stars or not. They had fought with me when I was taunted as a Polack and we were friends.

At our home, potato pancakes were a special treat. Everyone made his own. Mama gave each of us four or five potatoes and an onion to peel and grate very fine. We added salt and pepper, then an egg. Once all this was thoroughly mixed, we were ready to fry our pancakes. We all crowded around the stove to watch our cakes fry in the pan until they were golden brown and crisp on the outside. They smelled so good. We sprinkled them with a sugar-cinnamon mixture or spread on some applesauce and ate them with much gusto.

One evening, while enjoying our potato pancake feast, our laughter almost drowned out a knock on the door. Curiously we all looked toward the opening door to see who was calling. It was Herr Heinrich with his long list again. He insisted that Papa join the Nazi Party.

"I must have one of the families from this building join the NSDAP tonight," he insisted.

He threatened that we would lose our store if Papa did not sign up. This infuriated Papa.

"I had my store before you Nazis came along. I don't owe you anything!" Angrily, Papa pushed him out the door and down the steps. The scuffling and yelling brought neighbors out of their apartments.

Papa shouted, "Don't you ever come back here again!"

Herr Heinrich limped away. We returned to our potato pancakes but things were not the same. Papa's anger did not subside and his concern for all of us became the topic of conversation.

"If it's necessary," he told Mama, "I'll go to England. They won't touch you and the kids here."

Mama was pregnant and fairly large. She pushed her hair back in that nervous gesture that told me she was worried.

Life went on as usual for a while then came another dreadful day. The Gestapo picked up Papa from the store. We did not know until someone came to our home to tell Mama. Few homes had telephones, only stores and some places of business. We could not find out where he had been taken. No one would talk to us, not even our neighbors. Everyone seemed to harbor this deep fear of what would happen to them. I could see it in their eyes. We thought Uncle Helmut would come, but he had been beaten up by the Nazis before and he was as afraid as our neighbors.

We spent a tense and sleepless night. Mama paced back and forth, holding her apron tight around her as though it would shield her from harm. My brothers kept saying, "Where is Papa? Will they let him come back?'

Our store, a radio and repair shop, stayed closed. Mama was unable to go out so I was sent on errands. No one would talk to me. Finally Mama sent me to Herr Reuter, owner of the general store across the Street. He seemed to understand our plight and gave us everything we needed, not even knowing whether we could repay him.

A few days later a black ugly car stopped in front of our building. Papa was thrown out into the street and the car roared off. He could not get up. He had a large cast on one of his legs.

"Oh, God almighty! What have they done to him?" Mama ran down the steps and into the Street. We kids followed.

"They've broken your leg? Mama screamed. She knelt beside him and cradled his head in her arms. Papa's eyes looked dull. I stood by Mama, and we cried. Tears running down our faces.

Men who were at home did not come out to help for fear they would be reported, but some women came. They helped Mama carry him upstairs and lay him on the bed. His face was like gray stone. He answered no questions, just turned his face to the wall and lay silent.

After the women left, us kids were asked to leave the room. We could hear Mama and Papa sobbing. We put our arms around each other and cried. We were glad to have him home but we wept for his condition and we were afraid. After many weeks of rest, Papa's leg healed enough so that he could reopen the store. At the age of ten, I was now considered old enough to help in the shop after school. I waited on customers while Papa sat and repaired radios.

Recharging batteries for radios was a tedious chore that Ortwin and I helped with in the store. Such batteries were then as large as the modern car battery. Papa attached a generator to one or more batteries, after which Ortwin or I climbed up and sat high above this homemade contraption and pumped a wheel bicycle to make the generator work.

As the months went by electrical power extended to more streets in Chemnitz, including ours. It brought many changes. The man who lit the gas lights in the streets each evening stopped coming around. Electricity provided much more light in our home.

With no more calls for recharged batteries, Ortwin and I gladly gave up the task of pumping the generator wheel. Papa's business slowly changed to selling and repairing electric radios and other kinds of equipment. Papa was pleased with the changes electricity brought. He talked about how he thought radios would be in the future. He even predicted television or what he called "movies in the home," if we lived that long. Of course people had not heard of this so they did not believe him. This prediction was just as strange as his prediction of a man on the moon, but we believed him and both came true.

He put loudspeakers in every room of our home and entertained us with our own private humorous radio broadcast of music and make-believe events. My parents' bedroom had a lot of radio equipment in it and we were not allowed to handle any of it.

Papa used his complicated radio equipment for more serious purposes too. He knew much more about the world situation than he would talk about. I am sure he listened to BBC broadcasts from London during the later years of the war.

CHAPTER THREE
WAR
1939 - 1944

September 1, 1939-a bright Sunday morning! Papa had just finished polishing the large kitchen floor that Mama waxed every week. He was listening to the radio. I was in the bathtub and Mama was scrubbing my back.

Ortwin and Hartmut were sitting on the balcony shining everyone's shoes. This was their Sunday chore. Boys on other balconies were doing the same, calling back and forth making Sunday afternoon plans, for the usual soccer games. But first we would all attend Sunday school.

Suddenly trumpeted fanfare blared from the radio. A loud excited voice addressed the people of Germany. We stopped what we were doing and focused our attention on the radio. Our concern deepened as we heard.

"Our troops have entered Poland!"

"War!" Mama cried.

Panic gripped me. "Get me out of here Mama! Hurry!" I put my arms around her as she hugged me close with a towel. I saw tears in her eyes and I felt like crying myself.

At church people stood around talking about their future. The terrible news of Germany getting into a war worried everyone deeply. Women worried about their husbands and sons and I was glad to be a girl. Then someone said, "If Germany loses this war, just like we lost

WWI, it will be unbearable for the survivors." The memory of WWI was on everyone's mind. In a war, everybody's life changed dramatically. There was no escape, no matter what was lying ahead. Whether people hated this whole Nazi business or not, they had us over a barrel.

When the Nazi Government declared one of their festivals, people had to hang a flag out of their window. If there was no flag, stones smashed windows until people bought and hung out a flag.

If anyone protested, he disappeared and their family and even their friends were in danger. The Government proclaimed as of now, anyone who opposes Hitler is an enemy of the State and could be punished by death without a proper trial. As one Nazi bellowed in the radio, "This is war, and in a war, everything is allowed."

People working for the defense industry must work all holidays and many Sundays. Slogans like "Wheels must roll for victory" and many others were seen all over the country. Higher taxes had to be paid and we were constantly reminded that "spies" were everywhere and we must inform the Police immediately if we hear or see anything resembling sabotage. People were turned against each other and nobody knew who his friends were now. Just about all the German people were scared to death. It seemed like the stories about that which was already established in Russia under Stalin. The general feeling around our circle was that much suffering lay ahead.

That Sunday an undercurrent of apprehension started to grow among the people. Our family had known the constant fear of reprisals for speaking our disapproval of the Nazi Party activities. Now our fears were multiplied. A feeling of foreboding crept over us and our neighbors like a mantle of gloom. Church remained important to our family. We believed that no matter what was to happen, our belief in God would see us through. We prayed together often.

Suddenly everyone lived in a state of hysteria, people talked in harsh voices. Our Pastor shouted when he talked, his wife was worse. She would not open the door of their home even when we went there for errands. We had to talk through a little window in the door.

"Mama, why does Pastor Jaeckel shout when he talks?"

"Dear child, he is paid by the State. He is as uncertain about the government and the future of this war as we are."

Older boys teased, "The first thing the war is going to do is take all those candy bars away from you kids." Little did we know that this would be the least of the hardships we would endure.

Ration cards for each person were delivered by the block warden. Everything was now rationed: food, clothing, soap, cigarettes, and special permits to buy coal. Each family registered in one grocery store and one butchery. Merchants stamped the names of their businesses on unused coupons to further tighten control on ration coupons. We were not allowed to shop in another store.

Each month ration coupons were issued in different colors to help merchants quickly identify expired ones. People quickly learned how to exchange coupons among themselves; thus, the black market began.

Those people whose work required them to travel were allowed to buy at different places and their ration cards were called "travelers rations." These coupons became desirable items on the black market.

Children under ten, which included my brothers, were allowed one pint of milk each day. Pregnant women got a little more on their coupons. Tobacco cards were issued to men and women, two cigarettes a day. Heavy smokers, always looking for more to smoke, were often eager to trade food coupons for tobacco coupons. Since neither Papa nor Mama smoked, they exchanged their cigarette allotment for food coupons.

Like the blow of a hammer the changes brought about by the war reverberated throughout our neighborhood and all of Germany. Each new regulation further restricted our activities and controlled our lives. One order followed another in rapid succession.

Now, prayers and classes in religion were banned in school. "Heil Hitler" was ordered to be the greeting of the day. No more "Good mornings," it was "Heil Hitler" on the street, in the market place and in the school. Everyone must comply.

*Verdunkelung*s or blackouts began. Special black paper blocked all windows. Each evening the house warden checked all windows from the outside. If the slightest crack of light showed, the family was fined and had to correct the problem immediately.

On September 27, 1939, less than a month after war was declared, my third brother Claus was born.

Defense plans were required of every family in case of a bomb attack. We learned how to use a fire extinguisher, put on gas masks, and where to go when an air attack came. We learned what kinds of bombs to expect and how to deal with them.

"Your life will depend upon your ability to protect yourself," bellowed the block warden.

House wardens hung flat disks, with metal hammers, in the central halls of each apartment building. At the first whine of an air raid siren, these disks were struck. Their earsplitting clang sent us scrambling down into the air raid shelters.

If one family or even one person was missing, the house warden went upstairs immediately and searched for them. The wardens took their jobs very seriously. Families disobeying the alarm were reported to the block warden. If a block warden was mean, he imposed stiff punishment saying, "She wanted to go on the roof and give signals to the enemy." Which, of course, was absurd. Punishment for smaller violations could be to work a day without pay or go to jail on their day off. Parents were responsible for their children and were punished for their acts.

Our air raid shelter was right underneath our apartment building in the front part of the cubicle where we stored our coal, winter potatoes and foods that Mama had canned. There was a partition between the coal and the foodstuff. In front of this wooden door Mama kept first aid supplies, a lantern, blankets, chairs, and buckets of water. We were drilled to descend the long stairway down to the cellar and hurry to our places in front of our cubicles.

Sandbags guarded the basement windows against bombs that could roll in and explode inside. Sections of bricks without mortar were built into supporting walls dividing one basement from another. These mortarless places provided escape hatches to be used in the event of a direct hit. Misuse, that is, going through without permission from one basement to the other, brought also severe punishment, because people had valuables in their cubicles and unauthorized persons might steal them.

Citizen centers were formed. All people in our block, from infants to the very old, were counted. Our names, ages and addresses were registered on official papers.

Then came the work assignments. All fourteen-year old girls with no opportunity for education beyond elementary school were assigned to labor for one year on a farm. It was officially called the "*Pflichtjahr*" or obligation year. Although most girls intended to marry early and have children, a plan much approved by Hitler.

Fourteen-year old boys entered trade schools. Fifteen to eighteen-year old boys and girls continued their education some in school, some in the trades, or some went to do other work. Once they were eighteen, if they did not enter higher education, they were conscripted to do labor for two years in a work program called "*Arbeitsdienst*" or Labor Service. Their uniforms were brown-beige and on their hats they wore a brown spade insignia. I saw trainloads of those girls being sent to the country to help on farms. They were singing the rousing marching songs of Germany as train after train left the railroad station. Later in the chaos of the war, there was hardly anybody without some kind of uniform who worked or fought in some service.

It was unthinkable that people would be without jobs. Although, like in any society, there are people who just don't want to work. They, if found out, were assigned to labor camps where they were taught trade skills and labored under strict discipline and with no pay until released to take a job, mostly in the defense industry. If they stayed away from their assigned job they were arrested and put into labor camps again as enemies of the Third Reich. Later, we learned what those camps really were.

Punishment was harsh and feared. At the same time, women replaced men who were called into military service, all except mothers with more than one small child We began seeing women in long pants. This seemed strange at first but we soon became accustomed to this kind of dress. Some women wore their husbands' suits, some women altered those suits to make them fit better. Apparently they did not expect their husbands to come back? I even thought they acted like men, striding about, talking loudly.

Esther's father was still working as an accountant for a large department store. Frau Goldberg and Esther were ordered to work in the stocking mills. They replaced two men transferred to jobs in the ammunition factories on the other side of the city.

Steel factories belched smoke in an ever mounting fury as the war effort increased. The constant radio message was, "All must work for the great victory of Germany" or "One Nation, one War, one Leader." It was a crime to hide a "work skill" and pay was extremely low. I am sure certain people in that war machine knew how to get rich. But it was not the ordinary person.

Sick leave was out of the question. Mama said that once, when a friend of ours was really sick, the doctor told him, "You'd better pull yourself together, I am not allowed to give sick leave to anyone." Some doctors were rude, some compassionate, but their hands were tied.

Some elderly people were recruited as neighborhood spies. Tension increased and everyone lived in fear of punishment. Mama and Papa talked more and more about the danger of the Gestapo and the rapid growth of the SS. During all our working hours, the fear of talking followed us like an anxious shadow.

One evening Papa came home and said, "I saw Block Warden Heinrich today. I have an uneasy feeling when I look at him, that shifty-eyed Nazi! When the war is over he'll get his punishment.

Those goose-stepping Nazis will lose their war!" Papa sounded very convincing.

Ortwin looked at Papa, his eyes very serious, "Why did the Nazis bring you back alive? Herr Ottman and Hans's father haven't come back."

Papa paused before answering, "Those two are old Communist street fighters, who knows if they ever let them come back." He sat down and drew Ortwin to him, "Son, you know I don't believe in Hitler and his group. I told them there is no way they can last. They beat me and others with clubs and forced me out of a third story window. They wanted it to appear that I was running away so they could shoot me but after those beatings the fall broke my leg. Some men died from that kind of punishment.

"They brought me back because they don't want to support my family. I had to promise to say nothing to anyone, ever. If I do they threatened to punish all of us. We must never talk about this. Promise me."

With tears in our eyes, we solemnly promised Papa we would obey his request.

As the war activity increased the government confiscated cars and even bicycles. They took our Dreirad. Papa had to give it up for a piece of paper saying he would get the same thing back after the war. Now we would have to travel by train. No more family trips. Father's beautiful red DKW was taken too. Only doctors and high officials were allowed to keep a car. As cars were confiscated, horse drawn wagons and carts appeared on the streets. The horses dropped manure, "horse apples" to us kids, an excellent fertilizer for gardens. Papa stuck his nose up in the air, "I'll never in my life pick up a horse apple."

However, we noticed that by evening all of the manure had been picked up. We kids went around like others with our handwagon and small spade and gathered them to use in our gardens.

One day we saw other children playing with horse apples.

"What are you doing?" I asked them.

"We are making big heads, see that one?" the boy whispered to me gleefully. "It looks like Goering!"

"What about Hitler?" I asked back in the same whispered tone. "Oh," he retorted in the same way "We could never find a big enough pile of shit in all of Germany that we could model that one." Thus, we found some humor in this lowly task.

Another order came, teenagers must sell little plastic pins, symbols of the Third Reich. This was a Sunday assignment and everyone was expected to buy one each week. Hundreds of people bought them and in the city, one could see, nobody would dare to walk around in the streets without a pin. The design changed weekly. Those not wearing the current sign were accosted by one youth after another, who shook tin money-cans noisily about the victims face until a pin was purchased.

Other than church and reading, movies were an important pastime for us. However, American movies were banned and libraries were ordered to burn many of their books. Families owning certain books were warned to destroy them.

One little bookstore, a Mom and Pop shop, continued to lend books in defiance of the burning order. For a few pennies I could rent all the forbidden books I wanted. I read Zane Grey westerns and imagined I helped to conquer the West. No one reported this store and it continued to stay open for years although its location was very unfortunate sitting next to a railroad bridge. In 1944 the little bookstore was totally destroyed by bombs. The Allies probably wanted to hit the bridge but missed. The bridge by the way, is still standing to this very day.

Recognition meetings for mothers with large families was one thing the government did that I enjoyed. They served mountains of cake, with coffee made out of wheat. Mothers were awarded beautiful crosses of different sizes and designs. The more children the more valuable the cross. Mama's cross was enameled blue and set with one precious stone. When she was called forward to receive it she was told she had done her duty for Germany. Families with ten or more children received a real gold cross set with a small diamond. There were several families of this size.

When I was not needed in Papa's store after school, I began working in Uncle Albert's butchery, just a few blocks from home. His shop had a few round tables near the entrance of the store where he sold cups of bouillon and potato salads that did not require ration coupons. My job was to fill the cups with hot bouillon. On cold rainy days many people came to get something steaming hot to drink.

I was often sent to a small bakery in the Koenigstrasse to buy fresh buns to sell with our hot dogs. Everything worked better when business people exchanged favors. The baker received a package of uncle Albert's sausage and uncle Albert got baked goods of a better quality and a larger amount. Mama and Aunt Margarete got their season tickets to the opera when the opera singers came to the butchery to select their meat. They trusted no one with their ration cards.

When Mama could not go to the opera I was able to use her tickets. During intermission we mingled with the singers in a cocktail lounge where they greeted friends and influential people. It was exciting to be noticed by the actors and opera singers. The statement, "There is Irene who sells us the delicious liverwurst," gave me much pleasure. It also reflected how highly people valued food.

Some of our neighbors were ordered to come to the SS Headquarters. There, they were arrested by the Gestapo and forced to build camps. Years later we found out what camps. When they were released to come home they were watched and spied upon. But none of them ever talked about their camp-building experiences.

There was one man who had been released from a construction job in a concentration camp. He came into the dairy store near our home and while waiting in line for milk he was heard to say, "What? We have to stand in line for a cup of milk? We never did that in the KZ." KZ was short for *konzentrationslager*, or concentration camp.

"What is the KZ?" The words were spoken almost as a chorus by those who had heard him. Everyone was curious to know more.

Realizing that he had said something he could not explain, he turned pale, shivered uncontrollably, and left the store. That same day he was picked up by the Gestapo and never heard from again.

I knew the terror he felt after saying the wrong words. My tongue slipped the day I delivered meat to the Loeffler's, a "big shot" family who owned a uniform store. I was led through their shop then upstairs to their living quarters. Several people were listening to the radio espousing the usual propaganda.

Hans Fritsche, a radio commentator and official in the Propaganda Ministry, was speaking. "In one week we will be in London. Germany will be victorious." I started to laugh. I couldn't stop. People stared at me.

"When Hans Fritsche speaks, I listen," said Frau Loeffler. "He is my favorite."

Suddenly I hated everyone in that room. They stared at me in disbelief.

"I hate that voice." I shouted. "Don't you know he is lying?" No one spoke, just icy silence.

I went on, "With his phony oily voice, he tells us lies! Our soldiers are dying and he says we are victorious! We don't have enough to eat and he tells us food is plentiful. He says foreign bombs will never reach us. Promises! Lies! Can't you see it?"

There was absolute silence, then the too sweet voice of Frau Loeffler coved. "Well Irene, is that what your mother and father say?"

Ice formed at the back of my neck and poured down my spine. Goose bumps on my arms made my hair stand up. I had blurted out the total beliefs of my family. I was cornered.

Trying to hide the cold fear in me I said, "I have told you MY opinion! Kids can have opinions too. You don't have to be a big person to come to this conclusion. If you listen you will know what is really happening." Then I lied.

"My parents," I screamed, "are just as foolish as you are. They like Hans Fritsche too!" Dear God, I was glad I had thought of that.

Heads were shook and Frau Loeffler said, "You have foolish thoughts girl. Never say things like that again. You had better listen to your mother and father."

"Yes, Ma'am," I said meekly.

I left feeling sick in the pit of my stomach. Had I lost my parents? For days, every knock on the door brought terror that stopped only when the caller turned out to be a friend. Nothing happened and I thanked God with all my heart. From that day on I was more wary than ever.

Although I knew that some elderly people had become informers, I did not suspect Frau Hickman, who lived below us. On my way upstairs one day she called to me.

"Irene, would you come in for a while. I am so lonesome. You know both my boys are in the army and I just need to talk with you."

Feeling sorry for her, I went into her apartment. When she started asking questions I knew immediately what she was up to. Remembering the dreaded incident of talking too much when I had delivered meat, I quickly excused myself and ran upstairs. When I told Mama of my experience she was furious. She went to Frau Hickman's apartment and knocking loudly on her door.

"Of all the low down tricks I've ever heard of, this is the lowest. Trying to trick a kid into saying something that could hurt the whole family."

"I only wanted to hear a young person's voice," Frau Hickman whined. "I'm lonely for my boys."

"Humph!" Mama retorted. We left.

"I have a feeling she wants to get rid of us because she thinks we are making too much noise. She lives right under us and she has always complained."

Mama was angry as she stomped up the stairs. That evening everyone in our family was again warned to be careful about statements made to our nearest neighbors.

Scarcely an hour went by without news broadcasts. Hitler put a call out to German people all over the world to "come home to Germany" (*Heim ins Reich*) to the *Vaterland* (Fatherland), and they came. By the thousands they came from Wollynien Russia, the Black Sea region, southwest Africa, South America and even from Australia. They came from Yugoslavia where they had lived for generations as the *Donauschwaben* or farmers from Germany.

They came by train or covered wagon, anyway possible to avoid the war on different fronts. We had to make room for them. Housing became scarce as families were crowded together.

Our school kept their regular schedules although classrooms became crowded. An application to learn to play a musical instrument was sent home from school. I wanted to learn to play the guitar. Mama, however, liked to hear Uncle Richard play his accordion. She and Papa talked it over and it was decided. "It's the accordion or nothing. With Papa's beautiful voice we need the accordion. First thing Saturday morning we will buy one." Mama was enthusiastic.

After a long search throughout the city, we found an accordion I, however, was not too happy to have to hang such a heavy instrument in front of me. Lessons were taught in the home of the music teacher, next to the school. I lined up with about ten other students on a row of chairs to wait my turn for a lesson.

Our music teacher, Herr Vogelsang, taught students to play a variety of instruments. Slow-learning kids tested his patience but since he was being paid to teach us he could not resort to slapping as did our regular school teachers. He sputtered and talked "wet," spewing spit on our notebooks. He had a carafe of water and a glass on the piano. He sat in front of it and drank frequently when he talked "wet."

Unfortunately, the building where our music teacher lived was one of the very first to be bombed. He was killed in the explosion. The bombing that had begun in northern Germany was now extended to the southern cities. It was scary to walk past the rubble of my music teacher's home where I had been taught more than a dozen lessons. I had only just begun to play some tunes when my music training ended.

"You can play enough for our family singing." Mama said.

I put aside the accordion for a while. Survival quickly became our chief concern as the bombs dropped on Chemnitz.

We stopped playing children's games at the iron bridge because most of us helped our parents or did other work. When we met now, we stood by the fence and watched the trains loaded with soldiers going to war. The soldiers were given flowers in the railroad station. Some of them wrote their names and addresses on cards tied to their bouquets and threw them to girls as their trains slowly drove by.

One day, as we clustered by the fence to watch the soldiers leave, a bouquet fell right on my head. A boyish soldier shouted, 'Hello brunette!" Astonished, I could not believe he meant me. In a moment it was all over; the train rushed by and all we could see were waving arms and friendly shouts. I picked up the flowers and searched for a note. It said "Willi Springmann," along with his address. Gerda, standing by me, said she had written to soldiers and received answers. Since all my relatives lived in our town, I had never written a letter.

That first letter was childish and stiff but since it was my first, Mama helped me write it. Willi's answer came from the Russian front. He wrote that he had been drafted into the army immediately after graduation from a business school. Also that his hometown was Stettin.

We exchanged many letters. My letters were about my family. His letters were sincere and long, telling me what was happening at the front and of his wish to meet us if he had leave. Sometimes a few lines were blocked out, the letter was censored.

* * *

Herr Wabra came back after being gone a long time. He learned of what Papa had gone through in the meantime and secretly told us about the work camps. He talked in a low voice and emphasized that his information could never be repeated. We nodded and gathered close to hear him.

"But when families are picked up," Papa said, "they are told they will be taken to Poland."

"Don't think they send all of them to Poland."

"But the work camps are not large enough to hold all of them. Don't you think? What else could they do with so many?" Papa asked.

"Jewish families and all those arrested can expect only sorrow," he said. He leaned toward Papa and whispered, "I suspect they want them all dead."

We shuddered.

Herr Baustein came back to his non-Jewish wife. Together they owned a tobacco store which was now closed. He had been gone three months but knew he would be picked up again. He was ordered to divorce his wife, otherwise she would have to go into a camp with him. Their son, Jedediah, was arrested and they did not know what happened to him.

"I don't want her to go into a camp. Dear God, help us!"

One morning Mama went out, early as usual, to the dairy store. She came back, shaking all over and crying. All the neighbors in our building came out into the hail.

"The truck!" she cried. "They are at the Zweiniger dance hall. They are loading family after family into them. The Gestapo has been gathering people all night."

Everyone ran to the dance hall.

"Get out of here or we'll put you in these trucks too!" threatened the uniformed and plainclothes men.

People were forced into the trucks by soldiers prodding them with the butt of their rifles. Children were crying as their mothers clutched them close. Fear was on everyone's face.

"Hurry! Hurry!" shouted the men in uniform.

This went on many mornings as they gathered up most of the Jewish families at night and trucked them away. Our neighbors, including the Jewish families, believed they were being taken to Poland, since Poland at that time had the largest Jewish population in Europe.

The police came to the Cohen family who lived in back of their shoe store across the street. Their three sons, Tobias, Simon and Abner were accused of stealing some bicycles right from the police station. But most of us doubted this. The boys were not home. One neighbor said he thought they had gone one way, another neighbor said another way; everyone cooperated in confusing the police. This went on for a few days. When the police asked the Krueger family the whereabouts of the Cohen boys, they threatened, "We are going to pick up the parents if we cannot catch those boys."

This threat shocked us. As many Jewish families were disappearing regularly, some of our neighbors decided to dig caves where such families could hide. They chose to dig under a five story apartment building standing along a 55 foot bank above the rail tracks.

This site had many advantages. The noise from the trains would cover the sound of digging and construction. The Zweiniger dance hall, now used to temporarily house troops, created a constant flow of strangers who did not know what was going on and did not particularly care.

Because of the food shortages, everyone was encouraged by the authorities to dig up any available space to raise vegetables. Thus, the fresh soil taken out through the back of the building from the cave digging did not attract attention. Ortwin and I had overheard the planning and were repeatedly warned, "You'll never get a bite of food again if either of you says anything about this to anyone!"

We realized the danger of this undertaking and were eager to help. This was high adventure for us but of the most serious kind.

The fear of informers was so great, only very few people knew of the plan or were allowed to work on the project.

They dug through the floor of the Winkler apartment since there was no basement under this building. The Cohens worked on the digging and slept in the caves even before they were finished. No dirt could be thrown out on the side of the railroad tracks since any loose soil in that area would bring an investigation. Papa helped brace the ceiling with railroad ties. The vibration from the trains required strong construction. Uncle Helmut installed an electric wire, connecting this wire to the main cable pole that carried electricity to the Zweiniger dance hall area and many other buildings around it. No one paid attention to those electrical wires, and no one discovered this extra line. Papa provided an old radio that required earphones to be heard. A small heater with kerosine was also put in. This provided only a minimum amount of warmth, and because of the smell, they were able to put a small potbelly stove in after a few months. It was connected to the main chimney, although it was extremely hard to find extra coal and wood. Water came in through a water hose and buckets were used for toilets. I heard that during the air raids they went up into the Winkler apartment and took baths in the semi-dark. The Winkler family had three children so there was always someone to keep watch.

One or two friends the hidden people and us could really trust came at nights, they were bartering food for things the hidden families had taken with them. No one else was ever allowed into the Winkler apartment. The Winkler children were between ten and twelve years old. They knew and understood the danger, if they were caught everybody else who helped, including us, would get arrested and the punishment was death. Everybody knew this and everyone was scared, very scared. The blackouts were so complete it became difficult to walk about at night without bumping into obstacles in the street. This made it easier for the hidden people to venture outside when nights were dark and there was no moon out. People wore round disks that glowed for hours after being held near a light. Those disks did not provide any light to see by but helped us walk about without bumping into each other in the pitch dark. Our food rations were continually reduced, especially meat and butter. The amount of food allowed for one week was stretched to a ten day period. Still we all had to share our rations. Rabbit hutches appeared in our back courtyards. The Winklers, we and others raised rabbits for ourselves and to help our hidden friends. It was a way of getting some meat without allotments.

Every other day Mama took some meals late at night to the cave. She covered the food with potato peelings just in case some suspicious person would see her. Those peelings were fed to the rabbits mixed with some grated wheat.

I heard that Esther Goldberg and her family moved into the caves. The hidden people now totaled nine. I sent them books, magazines and newspapers and asked Mama what else I could do. We kids were not allowed to hang around the Winklers' apartment because we had not been seen there in the past.

A letter came from Willi saying he was in the army hospital in Dresden convalescing from Russian typhus. When he recovered, our whole family went to see him. Willi was tall and extremely slender. His blue eyes sparkled when the doctor said he could leave the hospital for a few hours. He seemed like our adopted big brother. We rode the trolley car up to our favorite restaurant on the hill but the restaurant was empty because they were selling nothing but chicory coffee. The guests had to bring the cake themselves. Mama knew this beforehand and had baked her famous coffeecake which we had brought with us. But there was a fee to be paid for them allowing us to eat this cake in their establishment. Everybody got a piece and enjoyed it immensely. We felt it was a festive occasion.

Willi did not want to go back to the front. He thought the war was futile and could not be won. He said the VIP-militaries would spend their leave in Switzerland with their friends and would unknowingly tell them all the secret information. Those friends in turn were passing it on to the Russians. This caused an enormous amount of German casualties, but nobody cared. Everybody wanted to get something out of this war. We little ones were the losers and there was nothing we could do about it.

When we said a tearful goodbye to Willi there was a feeling of real friendship and family love for this young man. He looked so sad when we left him at the hospital and caught the train back to Chemnitz and to our many responsibilities there.

When we washed clothes for the hidden people we could see the fabric was wearing to shreds. Mama got in touch with a *Diakonissennurse* she knew, who managed to bring us a box of used clothing and some soap.

The *Diakonissen* was an organization that worked closely with the protestant church to bring help to the poor and ill. The *Diakonie* existed for hundreds of years. By 1836, Theodor Fliedner of Kaiserswerth, Germany, established the first Mission Motherhouse for *Diakonissen* nurses and helpers. This organization also had a hard time under Hitler, since in his mind, there were no poor people in Germany.

The soap was of poor quality, it was more sand then soap.

Sometimes this soap could scratch our faces like rugged sandpaper. There was another one called "swimsoap." It did not go under in the water and lasted only for one bath. Soap powder was scarce and not a bit better. Mama took the clothes we got from the

Diakonissen sister to the hidden people. One day Papa brought home some "army uniforms" and no one asked him how he got them. All he said was "uniforms are more available then civilian clothing." The Cohen boys were grateful for them.

In the late fall and winter when evenings were quickly dark the ever hungry Cohen boys, dressed in their army uniforms, would slip through the courtyard fence and line up with the soldiers in temporary quarters outside the dance hall where the Army cooks dished out the stew and bread. No one paid attention to them, although the "kitchen bulls" made sure there were no civilians present. The bread was a coarse, whole-wheat moist mass. It was called *commisbrot* by the soldiers.

Our food rations continued to diminish and we received less meat and more starchy foods. Grandmother Thekla, Papa Walter's mother, now ate Sunday dinner with us. Rations for two were hard for her to manage. Grandmother Thekla took care of her future fourth husband, Michael Mason, a Frenchman who had lived in Germany since World War One. It was evident that they both loved and needed each other. Papa Walter's father had died in WWI. Grandmother then married a businessman who helped her raise her three children, Papa, Aunt Martha, and Aunt Lina. He later died of cancer. Grandmother Thekla's third husband, Hermann Schmidt, a younger man, was drafted into the war and was reported to have died for the Vaterland.

Grandmother Thekla was a slender woman and looked much younger than she was. Her clothes were more modern than the dresses worn by other women her age. She had beautifully groomed white hair and usually wore long earrings. Papa worried about her because women involved in love affairs with foreigners were sent without trial into concentration camps. Grandmother and Mike wanted to get married in church but the Pastor was afraid to perform the ceremony. Mike did not have German citizenship yet, although he had lived in Germany for a great number of years. The Pastor promised to marry them once the war was over. Even though Mike was over sixty, he had a job in the leather industry. He was in good health and spirits and Papa felt very uneasy when they came to eat with us. One activity they really enjoyed together was singing, that is, until Papa was called into the service.

Papa was ordered to "man the flack," our term for shooting at planes during air raids. There was no other transportation but the streetcar; using it, he rode to his station on the edge of the city and came home when not on duty.

"Now we dissenters are needed by the army," Papa said. Hamburg, Berlin, Cologne, and other heavy-industry cities in the north were already demolished. Leipzig too, and Chemnitz seemed to be next on the list. Bombs were aimed at the steel factories and defense industries, but of course, the bombs often failed to hit the target and killed civilians. Papa knew from the BBC that English pilots flew the night missions and the American pilots flew by daylight.

One afternoon, when I worked for Uncle Albert, I was carrying my basket of buns from the bakery, and I saw hundreds of women, some with teenage children, marching down the street from the railroad station. Soldiers were encouraging them along, speaking some Russian words to them.

I rushed ahead to the butchery, deposited my basket and ran outside to see what was happening. These people were not German, their clothing was different. Great dark kerchiefs wrapped the women's heads, completely covering their hair, their shoulders, and half their bodies. Some of them were barefoot. Their clothing was dark and some ragged.

There must have been a whole train full of people. They walked along the street and into a large building. Curious, I ran up the sidewalk to see more of them. They looked tired. Angry at my curiosity the soldiers shouted, "You'll be shot if you don't leave!"

I returned to the butchery feeling sorry for those ragged people. We learned they were Ukrainians brought into Germany to work in the ammunition factories or as domestics in German homes and businesses. I was soon to meet one of them. Her name was Tanja.

Tanja came to help Uncle Albert and Aunt Margaret in the butchery. She was a large woman of athletic build, with long brown hair and a pockmarked face. Tanja had a cheerful disposition and we all liked her immediately. She sang a lot but her Russian songs always had a sad melody.

Tanja washed the cups and saucers and made a fire every morning under the big kettle in the sausage house. She helped Uncle Albert pick up the quarters of meat from the slaughter house. Now and then I came along just to be allowed into the slaughter house, which was off limits for people in general. I always was amazed to see all that meat and the people who worked there. Even though it was man's work, Tanja was able to easily load the wagon with the help of my uncle.

Tanja also helped Aunt Margaret in their home above the butchery. In return for her work, Tanja had a room of her own and one day off each week. Uncle Albert and Aunt Margaret provided her with clothes and other necessities and a wage, which was pocket money. Although the NSDAP Party Office warned all the employers not to give foreign workers any money, they did it anyway. Tanja knew she was one of the lucky ones; instead of working in an ammunition factory she worked in a butchery where she had enough food to eat and where she lived with people who appreciated her help. In broken German she said many times, "Stalin no good, Hitler good." We would say "Stalin no good" then with a quick look around to make her understand the situation, we said, "Hitler no good," she would say "A--a--ah, they all no good" and we would laugh.

Once Aunt Margaret baked a birthday cake for Tanja and she said she would like to live with Aunt Margaret for the rest of her life.

* * *

By 1941, two air raids were coming each night and at least one by day. Familiar places became heaps of rubble.

Hannelore's parents had a bookstore where most of the parents bought their children's school books. Hannelore was my age and we occasionally did our homework for school together. I was at her house one afternoon when an air raid started. Being alone in the apartment, we decided not to let the house warden know we were there when he struck the alarms. From the window we watched the planes pass over our building and we tried to count them. They were heading toward the ammunition factories further south of the city. We saw them dropping their bombs, already some overhead, and heard the whistling sound as they were carried by the air to their destination. We heard many close and distant explosions that rocked the building. Smoke and flames boiled up into the sky. Then still another wave of planes came, their wings glistened in the warm afternoon sun.

"They're coming toward us!" we both screamed. Our faces turned white, we crouched down, sure that we would be bombed. Then the sound of the motors diminished and we knew they were flying away. The bombs whistled through the air before they exploded on the steel mills. Shaken and frightened we waited out the alarm. We never disobeyed an air alert again.

While I was on an errand one summer morning, the sirens started howling. With no time to go back, I ran for the nearest shelter. There were about 25 people inside, mostly women, a few children, some older men and one soldier. We waited in silence listening to the blasts. To my surprise, the soldier appeared to be the most frightened. His face was white and his eyes were tense with fear. Suddenly he shouted, "I can't stand here doing nothing while the bombs drop! I'd rather be out there than waiting here to be blown to bits!"

A thunderous explosion let us know a bomb had dropped close to our building and children started to cry. Another deafening blast shook the basement. Some people started to lie down on the floor while others huddled in great fear. We all knew going outside now would be certain death, that is, all but the soldier.

We leaped to restrain him as he jumped up and rushed to the door. It took five people to hold him down. Another bomb hit with such impact that the door frame twisted and the door swung open. There was a smell of fire and destruction in the air. Before I knew it, the metal disk covering the cleanout hole on the large central chimney blew off. Clouds of black soot swelled into the shelter covering all of us. I couldn't breathe. I coughed but got more soot in my throat. I was suffocating. I dug at the soot coating my nostrils and mouth until the panicky feeling of suffocation left me. I wiped my eyes repeatedly, trying to see more clearly. My eyes and hands were black with soot.

More bombs fell. The earth shook as blast after blast let us know the entire neighborhood was under heavy attack. I could dimly see others, crying and coughing all covered with soot and trying to clean their eyes to see.

When the all clear signal came we climbed through the crooked door frame and up the stairs. To our amazement the building above us was still holding together, though badly damaged. The building next to ours was totally destroyed. Bombs had bounced through windows into bomb shelters, killing all inside. Unexploded bombs were lying in the street, sinister promises of death.

What a bloody morning! I saw a hand sticking out of a pile of rubble. We instinctively knew many had suffocated. People started digging and I showed them the hand. All of us dug with our hands for whatever we could find. No one survived and I was told to go home, that adults would do the job.

I walked home, shaky, weak, and covered with soot. Mama gasped when she realized it was me. It took several baths to remove the soot and clean the clothes. I collapsed on the bed to rest.

Our family now faced another sacrifice. Papa was called into the army and left immediately for the Russian front. Uncle Helmut's father offered to help in the shop so we could keep it open. We still had a good supply of merchandise. Our camping equipment was in great demand since many families were living in bomb damaged homes. Mama was having difficulty managing all the work. One rainy day she left me in charge of my brothers, saying "I won't be long. I have some business to do."

After a few hours I saw her coming up the street, walking side by side with another woman. They were hurrying and not talking.

"She has come to help us," Mama announced. "Nadja is her name. She is Ukrainian and doesn't speak much German."

Mama smiled at Nadja and said to us, "We must be good to her because we are now her only family. Hitler's propaganda isn't going to tell me how to treat people in my home."

Nadja had dark blue eyes and brownish blond hair. I liked her pleasant face. She definitely needed some better clothes and shoes. Mama laughed when I told her how they looked coming home. Raising her eyebrows she said, "I couldn't even keep up with her! She is very strong."

Mama went to work in the store and Nadja looked after the house and the boys. She was good for us. She sang her Ukrainian folksongs and kept our home clean. Mama had to tell her about the hidden people and she cheerfully cooked potatoes and meatless stew for them and for us. Although she spoke little German, she knew immediately of the danger we were in as we fed our Jewish friends. We shared everything. She wore some of Mama's clothing and we grew to love her as one of our family.

About once a month Mama had to go to a place to pick up sunflower seeds. These came from the Ukraine, and Mama explained, that the German soldiers had brought a whole trainload full of this stuff to feed the Ukrainian workers. Nadja loved it and she roasted and chewed on them as long as she had some.

Nadja was pleased with the attic room we furnished for her. Through her window she could see many roofs and the church tower.

Birds rested on her window sill and she showed them to me. She let us know she did not want to return to Russia. Nadja and Tanja became friends and spent some of their free days together. Unfortunately, Tanja had a boyfriend and she became pregnant. This was a crime punishable by banishment to a concentration camp. Uncle Albert pleaded with the authorities to let Tanja stay with them. It cost them lots of beef to get Tanja an abortion and permission to stay on.

"I wonder how he was able to manage it," Mama said. "That's a very high price to pay for that girl."

When I saw Tanja again she looked very pale. Her happy look was gone but she was grateful and very devoted to Aunt Margaret and Uncle Albert.

I wanted Nadja to learn the German language and asked Father to teach her. Luckily, I asked beforehand. Papa was already on the eastern front but Father had not been called yet. His job involved translations in foreign languages so apparently they needed him.

"Irene, I wish I could teach her but it is forbidden that we be friends with foreign workers." Father and Aunt Johanna were visibly shocked at my request. So Nadja learned her German in our everyday conversations.

Another family learned of the hidden people and helped provide for them. They were older people and the old man worked for the *Wjnterhilfswerk* or WHW. The *Winterhilfswerk* was something like a good will station, where bombed people could pick up some donated clothes and things. They never saw the hidden people but Mr. Koch brought a lot of stuff which our friends could use. Policemen continually watched the neighborhood for some signs as to the whereabouts of the Jewish families. I just knew there must be more

Jewish people in hiding all over Germany, being protected and helped by friends. Of course we spread a lot of rumors that all the Jewish people had been already picked up, and they ought to get their records straight.

Herr Helbig, another friend who drove a truck for the cities' food supplies, came by our house often to bring sacks of potatoes and sometimes other foods, whatever he could organize. "For them," he used to say.

Mama worried constantly. She cooked up pots of mixed vegetable stew, covered it with potato peelings, and carried it to the hidden people. The families were grateful for anything, but they had not seen meat for a long time. Survival was uppermost in everyone's mind. Many thought the war would not last much longer. "Soon we will wake up and it will all be over" was a frequently heard comment. No one hoped for an end to the war more than the Winklers. The opening to the caves through the floor of their apartment kept them in constant fear for their lives.

The Cohen boys, restless from their confinement, scuffled frequently and occasionally got into a fist fight causing dangerous noise. One day they dug a hole in the wall towards the railroad tracks "just to see more daylight" and loosened a large rock.

Luckily they were stopped in time. Any large rock on the railroad tracks below would have brought an investigation about the source of the break and our hidden people would have been discovered.

Uncle Helmut's lamp shop was located across the bridge in a corner building in view of the critical wall above the railroad tracks. He kept a wary eye on this area and if anything looked disturbed he passed the word to get it fixed.

The hidden people were able to make air holes which were not visible from the outside for better ventilation between the rocks. This also provided more daylight. Illness among the hidden people was feared by all who helped them. Frau Goldberg was the first. Mama cooked some beer soup and different herb teas for her and it seemed to help. When Frau Cohen became ill, she needed some medicine. One of the helping families knew a nurse and was able to get her to bring medicine from the hospital without telling her about the hidden people. Frau Cohen recovered. Fortunately, no one ever needed surgery.

A letter came from Willi Springman saying he had been asked to go to Officer's school. This would take him away from the Russian front. He wrote:

"....I am convinced Germany is fighting for a lost cause. I cannot see myself as a diehard Nazi....I do not believe in Hitler as strongly as they do...."

A few days later another letter came. Willi was given leave to visit his parents in Stettin.

On Saturday evenings the Ukrainian people gathered in nearby *Schlossteichpark* (Castle Lake Park) to visit and relax. Najda and Tanja usually joined this gathering. Nadja's boyfriend worked in the ammunition factory. Mama would send him a big sandwich because he did not get enough to eat. One evening Nadja invited me to go with her to meet her friends. We crossed a bridge into this lovely island park where patches of flowers brightened the shoreline and songbirds fluttered about a large birdhouse.

I was amazed to see so many Ukrainian people. At least several hundred were standing or sitting on the grass. They talked in low voices with occasional soft laughter. Their smiling faces reflected a relaxed group.

"Irene, this is Timothy Roskovich."

I looked into the face of a young man in his mid-twenties. His brown crew-cut hair topped a thin smiling face. We shook hands and his eyes looked longingly at the loosely wrapped sandwich Nadja was holding.

"Irene's mother made this for you, Tim." His thin hands eagerly took the big slices of dark bread with salted lard. He looked so hungry as he half turned away and ate the sandwich.

We sat with some of Timothy's friends and talked about things of the past week. All was peaceful and quiet. As dusk came they began to sing the songs of their homeland. They sang melodies about the tundra and the wide steppe, about the long winters, the wolves and Ukrainian love and folk songs. Nadja had taught me a few of these songs and I joined in the singing. Just as twilight came I noticed men coming over the bridge and onto the island. They were Germans in civilian clothing. No one seemed concerned. They came and sat among us, watching everyone. Just watching and waiting for a signal perhaps. Some stayed on the bridge. They did not look as though they came to join in the fun. More and more of them crossed the bridge to the island.

I looked more closely at the man who appeared to be guarding the bridge. He held a raincoat folded over one arm. A gun was barely visible.

"Nadja," I whispered.

"Yes, something wrong, Sh.."

"But that man beside--"

"Sh, no talk."

Suddenly others sensed the trouble. In whispers the word spread. The singing continued but grew less. I could smell the tension in the air. Those Ukrainians yet unaware of the intruders continued singing. Our fears were quickly justified when an unseen signal incited the police into action. Men, now suddenly armed, shouted commands and rounded us up like cattle. Men were separated from women and we were prodded over the bridge and up to the Police Headquarters.

"Inside!" the men shouted. "Inside quickly!"

This building had an annex that was a jail. They must have watched and planned their whole police action from the top floor of this building that overlooked the island park.

I gripped Nadja's hand. She drew me closer and whispered, "Stay close, no let people between." Her voice sounded reassuring but we both knew the police could make quick and deadly decisions at the least provocation. We learned they were looking for "illegal" people, Gypsies and deserters. They were going to question everyone. It was impossible to run. We stood silently with others in a large room, hoping they would not notice us. People were singled out and taken away. From another room we heard screams and the thud of clubs smashing human bodies. As beaten persons were pushed back into the large room they wiped blood from their heads with their handkerchiefs. Truly a night of horror! What had started as a pleasant evening of singing and laughter broke into a thousand pieces of ugly sounds. Blood, blows, and screams congealed the atmosphere into solid fear.

Hour after hour we waited our turn to be questioned. I felt numb from the cold night air. The eastern sky was changing color and the morning light had not yet revealed the redness of the blood as we were summoned for questioning. Frightened and bone weary, Nadja and I showed our ID's to a stern policeman. He scanned through them and asked me what I was doing among all the Ukrainians. He felt it was very suspicious and he played with my ID, as if he wanted to keep it. I told him my mother had sent me to look for Nadja.

He looked at Nadja while talking to me. "What was she doing in this part of town, whom is she meeting with? We can keep both of you right here!"

"Oh, no no no," I stuttered. "She was only seeing some friends from her hometown. I just had to give her a message. Please let us go. It is just ill-timed that we are here at all."

After he talked with one of his colleagues, he said, "You are dismissed this time. I never want to see you both around here again!" and "You won't get off so easy next time." We left the building in a great hurry and ran much of the way home. Mama's worried face dissolved into tears and smiles all at once as she held us while we told her our story. Nadja did not meet her friends on the island again. They found other places to congregate.

* * *

"My father owns the building where they keep the pilots," said Margot Kleinschmidt, a classmate of mine.

"The prison for the English pilots?"

"Yes, and some Americans too. They fly for the English."

"Yes, I know. Where are they?" I asked.

"On the other side of Chemnitz. Do you want to meet them?"

"Sure, why not?"

"But you must promise never to tell anybody anything."

"My lips are sealed." I was certainly used to keeping secrets by now. As we rode the streetcar across the city my excitement grew about seeing the men who had dropped bombs on us.

"What do they look like? Do they look mean?" I asked.

"You'll see." Margot seemed to relish withholding the information I was so intent upon learning.

When we arrived her father said we could not go into the building. It was a building just like any other except the windows were crossed with bars. Oh, how curious I was to see these men who had dropped bombs on us. They were here now and their own bombs might be dropped on them. How strange life can become, I thought. I knew there were air raids on England and I wanted to ask them how they felt about the war.

"They work outside somewhere," said Margot, "but around five o'clock they all come marching back. They have the rest of the day off but they must stay inside."

"Maybe we could talk to them," I volunteered eagerly.

"The guards are friendly with the pilot prisoners. They even play cards with them. Not for money but for chocolate."

"Money is getting pretty worthless," I said.

"If Father sends me on an errand I get to go inside."

Sure enough, in a little while Margot's father asked her to get something for him. We slipped into the building. There were many rooms in the building but they had no doors. Each room had four to six beds in it.

"Hey, you kids!"

I looked up and saw a tall man. He was smiling. Perhaps he was interested in practicing his German. I walked toward him. He looked like any ordinary man, certainly not like a monster.

"*Guten tag.*" (Good day.) I liked saying this rather than "Heil Hitler." Using this greeting to another German in this town could have gotten me in trouble. He held out a Red Cross package and took some chocolate from it. It looked so good and I had not smelled chocolate for a long time. I held my hand out for it.

"*Oh, Schokolade, vielen dank.*" (oh chocolate, thank you very much.) I curtsied.

"Will you mail this letter for me?"

Thus began a secret friendship with the imprisoned pilots. Once they knew we would carry and mail their letters we were in business.

Sometimes Margot and I would be in the courtyard when they came marching in. We would hear them from a distance. I liked the clipped sharp step of their boots. They too had a disciplined armed force but their marching steps were somewhat different then the German Goosesteps. These men looked just like our soldiers. They did not even look mean. I could not believe they would be capable of doing all the things the Joseph Goebbels propaganda machine was telling us.

Once inside, the soldiers hurried to get their letters and chocolate. Margot and I both carried them faithfully to the post office and they shared their rations generously. Their letters were usually sent to the Red Cross in Switzerland. They probably wrote to get more packages and to say that they were alright. When they ran out of postage, they were trying to sell some of their canned goods to us, which Mama, of course, happily bought through us.

Across the street from the prison was a large china warehouse and store. It was a two-story building with the usual look of neglect that warehouses had. The store entrance was on the opposite side of the building and the street there was cleaner then this side in the back. The floor inside the warehouse was covered with straw from the packing crates. Even the street was covered with loose straw. We entered through a side entrance where the wind blew straw in all directions. Not many people were working there, some were even foreign and just one German supervisor. They were too busy to pay attention to us kids. When I saw all those thousands of different items of good china fresh from the porcelain factory in Meissen, I had this doomed feeling that only one bomb was capable of destroying it all. So we took some cups with us. Later, in March 1945 this warehouse was destroyed by bombs as was the entire inner city of Chemnitz.

* * *

Just before Christmas in the forties, we were told that Germany was now in war against the United States. Ortwin and Hartmut wanted to know why Germany had to get into more war. Mama got some world maps out and showed them where Germany was and all the other countries around Germany, including Russia. Then she pointed out the United States of America.

Hartmut looked at the maps for a long time then he said, "Mama, look, Russia is so big, the United States is big too. Germany is so small between those two big countries. Does Hitler know that? Somebody has got to tell him."

Scarcities of the finer foods made preparations for our coming Christmas meal difficult. Mama and Grandmother Thekla sold several pieces of their silver on the black market to buy ingredients for our

Christmas *stollen*. Mama saved ration coupons and we skimped on meals until we had all the necessary ingredients. The baking was a job for the baker. Only he knew how to put together the flour, yeast, spices and sugar. He also had the large baking oven neither we nor other people in the neighborhood had at home. Mama and I carried the measured ingredients to the bakery where everyone's package was put in a line to wait for the baker's skilled hand. We were given an approximate date and time to pick them up.

Carrying home the holiday *stollen* was a special Christmas custom in Saxony. When our loaves were ready, Mama and Nadja carried them home on large flat boards, showing them off to our neighbors all around. The fragrance of the vanilla-sugar made the whole street smell like Christmas. I just loved it. We did not know this would be our last *stollen* for many years to come.

* * *

The word came from Propaganda Minister Goebbels that all able people, young or old, must work in the defense industry. "The weapon industry must be kept running. Work days will now be 12 hours long." Same low pay of course.

More inflammatory speeches came. "We must stick together in our great German effort! Self-sacrifice and discipline will help us work for victory. Anything for the fatherland!"

People walked around like shadows. Some people broke down under the strain. Sometimes bad accidents happened in those factories. I heard people talking about them, but there was never anything about it written in the newspaper. Victims were sent to hospitals and we never heard about it anymore. In order to survive most people just hung in there and worked as best they could.

Our teachers in school taught us that the Russian people had a low mentality saying, "Their police pick up their people and send them to Siberia. They go like slaves and do not revolt."

Outside school we talked about what a terrible thing the government of Russia was doing to their people. We did not know the Jewish population in Germany was being reduced by millions too.

The word went around our neighborhood that Hitler was going to destroy the Polish intelligentsia. Father was among the first to be arrested. We were summoned to appear before a Civilian Military Committee. We knew people these days were not given a proper hearing.

When Mama and I arrived we were taken to the second floor of an office building and told to wait. I was called into the office but Mama was told she must stay outside. As soon as the door closed behind me, I heard loud commotion and voices outside. Later I learned Mama got worried and did not want to leave without me. She was frightened to death, not knowing what they wanted from me.

Inside my attention was focused on a police lady in civilian clothes asking me in a friendly voice if I wanted to go on a trip with her. I got nervous and asked for Mama. From then on the woman got stern and gave me orders. I was terribly frightened and intimidated. I had no idea what was happening and why.

When the police and I stepped out into the corridor Mama was gone. Not without a fight though, she later told me.

The police lady took my hand and we walked outside into the street, heading toward the railroad station. To my great surprise we went into the railroad police station. It looked like a huge office. People were being questioned, sitting next to desks where police typed papers. The woman took me into the back, opened a door, and pushed me in. Before I knew what was happening, the key turned and I was locked in.

This little cage was not even big enough to hold all our brooms at home. I could hardly stand and a very tiny bench took the rest of the space. It was at least one story high. I could look up to the glass ceiling. Down where I was half standing, half leaning, I could not even turn around. If this was the jail cell for adults it must be torture for a large person to be in here for any length of time. Only with great difficulty did I finally get both of my legs on top of the shelf which at first glance looked like a bench. Now I could stand straight. I had to endure being locked up like this for hours. It had been before noon when Mama and I arrived at that Military Committee office. I looked up at the ceiling and watched as the sun stood high and, finally after hours, disappeared. It got dark and still I heard people coming and going on the other side of the locked door. I had knocked several times during the day, asking for water, food, bathroom. It was all denied.

It was dark when another lady finally opened the door. She was dressed in civilian clothes. All my questions remained unanswered. She took me by the hand and we marched out into the railroad station hall. She did not need tickets, so we walked toward a train and into a compartment which was reserved for police and also for train personnel when they wanted to take a break.

Here, I finally was able to go to the bathroom and also got something to drink, but nothing to eat. The train personnel looked at me sympathetically but tried to avoid my eyes. Everyone was afraid and too intimidated to help others. They knew I was under arrest. I was glad I was able to sit, thinking all the time of Mama. How could I get a message to her?

The train we were on was packed with people all in uniform coming and going to the fronts and numerous military police were checking everybody's ID's. On every stop the train made, there were people hurrying back and forth with much noise and carrying beat up luggage. The train made its final stop. L e i p z i g: What in the world was I to do in Leipzig? Just as we left the train, busy people were all around us. The sirens were howling, and I already knew that Leipzig got more air raids than we did in Chemnitz. The railroad station here did not look as intact as the one in my home town.

We were running right into the railroad police station and into a cellar. To sit among all those police people scared me more than if they had left me upstairs alone. Of course they tried to ignore me. Since I was under arrest, they did not want to talk to me. I was subhuman now. The police woman asked directions to some place I did not know. After hearing a few explosions, the sirens sounded again and we were able to leave. Outside we took a streetcar. The police woman was holding my hand constantly. Maybe I should have tried to run, but in a police state there is no place to run to. Eventually they find everybody.

We arrived at a large building, the biggest women's jail in Saxony. Tired as I was we went through some offices. I remember they pushed me through a door and it slammed shut with a loud noise. "The door is out of iron," I thought in astonishment.

Immediately I gagged from a terrible smell I had never known before. I was handed from one person to another, up stairs and along a hallway of doors. One door was unlocked and I was pushed in. It took me a while to get accustomed to the dim light.

I saw the entire floor covered with old mattresses and bodies. An arm pointed for me to go further away from the door and get myself into a corner to sink down and I did. I must have fallen asleep right away as suddenly a terrible noise awakened me. It came from the outside. Women shrieked and others bellowed.

Some old enamel washbasins were half filled with water and many tried to wash themselves as well as they could. A toothless old woman sat next to me. She said she was a midwife and was caught giving an abortion to a girl who got pregnant by a foreigner. Now, she and the girl were going to a concentration camp called Mauthausen just as soon as a whole transport was put together.

I knew that those women were German, not foreign and not Jewish. But I still thought a camp was a summer camp and said so. I was informed right away, that those who went on that transport would die. It took me some days to realize what would happen to me. I had only one question in my mind, "Why? Please somebody, tell me why?"

There were also many young women, most of whom had begun friendships with French POW's. Nothing the German authorities hated more. They said our men are fighting at the front and our women make love to Frenchmen, they will pay with their life for it.

I remember the air raids. They locked us up in our cells and the guards went into their bunker. Upstairs we put mattresses on top of each other so we could reach the small windows which were secured with iron bars. During the day air raids we could see the airplanes coming in waves and dropping their bombs. They were very close too.

Why they never bombed those huge buildings we were in, I will never know. Maybe they thought they were empty office buildings or did they know it was a prison?

When we saw bombs exploding, we heard shouting "give it to them" throughout the prison cells. Everybody wanted to see what was happening. There were so many women in our cell I was never alone to feel sorry for myself. They freely told me why they got arrested and there was not one criminal among them. All had the same old story, loving a foreign POW and abortions. Everybody waited for the transport to be formed to take them away.

I don't remember anymore how I was able to eat that terrible food; at first I thought I would vomit. But once a person is hungry everything looks good. The noise in that large building made me very nervous. It seemed that everything was made out of iron and also voices were always shouting something. The kitchen must have been downstairs, everyone got a stainless steel bowl and everything went in it except the small piece of bread we received each morning. I loved to chew on it as long as possible to quiet my stomach.

When I cried there was always some woman who tried to console me. Some got very religious. They even welcomed death and prayed so loud that the wardens told them to stop, though they continued. Many had their time of crying; that scared me very much. Most of them were very young and pretty, but we were all destined to go to the same place.

Every time the door opened and I saw the guard I asked to write to Mama, but they did not even answer me. I got used to that strange stench and to keep my sanity, I prayed. "I am sure God knows where I am and he will help me." I was about 12 years old at the time. The youngest among about 20 women in our cell. There were many other large cells filling up slowly with more women as young as 16; the oldest must have been little over 70.

One day, the cells were unlocked and all of us were called out. The guards went into the cells looking for something. They made a big mess kicking water pitchers over, so we had to wipe them off.

One morning several of us were called outside, we were needed to go work on the outside. I was very happy to see sunlight and breathe fresh air again. At least forty of us were marched out of the building and into a courtyard where an old truck was waiting. We were told to get in. The sides and back of the truck were secured with canvas and string and two police men and two police women were among us.

We were forbidden to talk and we did not know where we were going but after a good thirty minutes the truck stopped. We were ordered all out and I saw a garden restaurant. The Nazis must have had a big party there the night before. It looked like a pig sty and we were ordered to clean it all up. Once everybody had a job to do, I was left. The police man who had assigned jobs looked at me in surprise. "and you?" he said. " What have you done to be in jail?"

"Nothing," I answered.

"That is what they all say. Now, out with the truth." But I told him, "I don't know but I'd sure like to know." Could he please tell my Mama where I am, so she can get me? He got angry and assigned me with a troop of women picking up paper.

I only remember this one outing, all the other time I was inside that terrible stinking building.

One day, I was called alone out of the cell. A guard was walking me down toward the exit and I was full of hope. She took me through courtyards, into another building, up steps and down steps, until we finally reached the right office. I was to sit outside with the guard. She did not speak a word.

I was too excited and did not ask anything. I did not want to spoil the good fortune to be out of the cell.

When we were summoned into a room with huge doors, I saw-- could it really be? "Father!"

We saw each other at the same time and tried to walk toward each other but we were both held back. He looked so tired and we were not allowed to speak but our eyes met and spoke more than words.

What's more, here came Mama through another door! After all I had been through, I was so happy to see her that we hugged each other and we both cried.

One of the men in civilian clothes said, "The child is the blood relative of him." Then he barked at my mother, "You must leave if you repeat that scene again." We sat quietly on the bench.

They began reading something saying "paragraph number...which under this law and according to that law..." Then they said Father's full name, "Basil Walter Skaskow and his daughter Irene will stay under arrest. If certain conditions are not met, the SS will pick them up immediately after this meeting."

They went on to say, "The girl's mother is an Aryan who will not be arrested" and to my Father "Irene will be sent to the Mauthausen camp!"

Mama must have known something about this camp because she was visibly shaken and in tears. She fell to her knees.

"Please take me instead, don't take my child into that camp! She does not understand! She does not understand!"

I was shocked to see Mama on her knees begging those awful men.

The police woman held me tightly by the arms and shoulders and forced me away from Mama. Mama screamed and Father lunged forward but was jerked back. Mama grasped the arms of the police woman.

I thought she was going to strike her. Then Mama pulled back with a sharp gasp.

"There is one solution," a big man growled.

Mama and I were sobbing and I was still held in a vice-like grip by the police woman. They spoke to Father.

"You are a translator of many languages, including Russian. Is that correct?"

"Yes," Father replied.

"If you will sign here that you will translate into German all the documents we confiscated in Kiev on the Russian front, you and your daughter may go home."

I knew Father had resisted them for a long time, but now that they were using me to get what they wanted, he might give in.

He looked at me with tears in his eyes.

"I'll sign. I don't want her to suffer because of me."

He looked tired and bruised. They could not get him to sign for his own sake and later we learned that they had kept him from sleep and had beaten him.

He looked at me, "I'll do this for you, Irene. I want you to live."

All three of us stood very close together in front of those who hated us so much. Mama and I left immediately. Father was released later that day. As we left the building the air raid sirens sent us hurrying into the nearest shelter. There in the circle of Mama's arms I felt secure and knew that no bomb would touch us that day. We both knew my life had been spared but every day ahead would be a fight to stay alive.

CHAPTER FOUR
EVACUATION

I visited Father almost every Sunday after I attended Sunday school in my home church. I would arrive at Father's home just in time to go with him and Aunt Johanna to their church services. It was a very friendly church up on Bergstrasse near where they lived. After church I would spend part of the day with them. Each time I boarded the streetcar to return home, Father would say wistfully, "I love you, my little Renichen." (Renichen was his pet name for Irene). "Hurry back and tell your Mama I said hello." I would give him a last hug goodbye, each time thinking "We don't know what will happen until next week." I knew he thought the same. I still remember his big warm hands holding my shoulders.

Life went on; business was conducted in any buildings still standing. So far, our school had escaped destruction and we went there every day carrying our *schulranzen* or schoolbags on our backs. The row of apartment buildings where the Cohens and the Goldbergs had lived were totally destroyed and there were many casualties.

It became increasingly difficult to get food for the hidden people. It was well past two years now and our rations continued to be reduced. Some people that had helped were no longer alive. With almost all the men gone, the women had to do real teamwork to keep things going.

I continued working in the butchery after school and the big package of food Uncle Albert gave me helped us and the hidden families.

One evening, Uncle Helmut and Aunt Martha came visiting for just a short time. I heard them saying, "The situation in Germany is getting more serious every day. People are disappearing all the time. If we protest we risk not only our own lives but also the lives of our family. The Jews are in the worst position but so is anybody who opposes the Nazis. We are no better off than the Russians under Stalin. All Germany is scared, I tell you. Scared to death." When I heard that, I got very scared too.

The Gestapo picked up Herr Wabra again. He had talked to several people about his labor camp experiences and was overheard by one of our neighborhood spies. That was all it took.

We heard Frau Wabra screaming when they took him away. Her shrieks sent chills through my body. It was hard to think that my Father and I could receive this same treatment. Frau Wabra told Mama, "He was drinking too much beer. He did not know what he was saying." She also knew he would never come back and so did we. When after weeks a telegram arrived telling of her son's death in a camp, she said resignedly, "I knew when it happened. I felt it in my bones." Frau Wabra died a short time later. She did not go into the bomb shelter and a bomb hit her apartment building. The dull feeling of death seemed to be everywhere. Almost every day I saw a policeman carrying a telegram to some family telling of the death of their father or son.

To lighten our feelings of despair sometimes, Mama would let us kids go to a matinee movie. For a few hours we could forget the bombs and destruction around us. There were still several movie theaters untouched by the bombs.

One day I went alone to see the movie "Lady in White." Just as the movie started an air raid was called.

"Go immediately to the big bunker!" came the order.

Mama had warned me never to go into those huge bunkers. This one was in the heart of Chemnitz, where large numbers of people congregated. It could hold at best 800 people. I saw all the people entering the bunker and I heard Mama's voice in my head: "It isn't safe." The air shafts that opened on top did look too vulnerable and I shuddered to think that a bomb could fall through them. I knew this part of town pretty well and looked for another shelter. I ran into an apartment building and down into their shelter. No one objected when I got in.

It all happened so fast--that deadly explosion. They must have dropped a "block buster." It sounded big and muffled and the earth shook. When we came out into the street we could see there were some direct hits and there was a strong smell of gunpowder still in the air. Several buildings and a part of the bunker were demolished.

Many people in the bunker were trapped and had very little air. I saw work teams already coming and digging. There were many very old men among the crew, yet they worked frantically to try to get them all out. Onlookers were chased away but I wanted to go home anyway. I had seen them at other locations digging for days and when there was no more life they sprayed white lime powder over the rubble, which kept down the odor of rotten flesh. This powdered lime was to become a familiar sight in the months to come.

People were not the same anymore. Some went to work like robots and lived like robots, never knowing if they would survive the next day or not.

***

"Evacuate the children! Save the future of Germany!" I was the first to go from our family.

"But Mama, you need me here to help." I protested.

"It's orders, Irene. They want to save you from the bombs." I was very unhappy as we packed my suitcase. Mama and the boys walked with me to the railroad station. Seeing other kids from our street readying to leave made the parting a little easier. That trip to southern Germany with the Red Cross nurses was pleasant. We sang songs to pass the time and it delayed our feelings of homesickness. We opened the sourdough bread sandwiches to see the usual spread of salted lard, but it was tasty.

"Just the way we eat at home. How about that," said one boy. About fifty girls, myself included, were unloaded in the small, very picturesque town of Feuchtwangen. We were checked in at the station and assigned to families.

My family lived on a medium sized farm. The father and son were in the Army, leaving the mother and daughter with a young Ukrainian man to do the farm work.

Everything was strange to me. The brick stove, built into the kitchen wall, provided open hearth cooking where vegetables and meat were cooked in large black pots hung above open flames. The bricks were blackened up to the ceiling. The other kitchen walls were all white. The outside walls of the home were about three feet thick and reminded me of the air raid bunkers in Chemnitz. Their home was furnished only with the bare necessities and so was my room.

The mother was an excellent baker and pulled large round loaves of fragrant herb bread from a black hole beside the fire. They hung hams in the chimney to smoke them. Our breakfast consisted of bread broken into steaming bowls of broth. I scrubbed my clothes in a wooden bucket and there never was enough hot water.

Even though I was Lutheran, I was expected to go to their Catholic church, which I grew to like just as much as our church. After church we ate lunch, then we prayed. I liked the matter-of-fact way they talked to God. They also prayed to a little Madonna and child that stood on a tiny shelf above the table. They prayed to the Madonna to speak to God and ask Him to send their father and brother home from the war. I prayed, "Dear God, send me back home. If you do, I will buy a Madonna one day and pray to her." And I did too.

Although here there were no sounds of the bombs, I was extremely unhappy and got sick because I couldn't sleep nights.

I was thinking of home all the time and could not concentrate in school, where I felt out of place and I was always tired. Although I had food, I stopped eating and must have looked terrible.

One day the farmer's wife took me to the authorities and said, "This girl is so homesick she won't eat any more. I will not be responsible if she gets sick. Let her return home." A few days later the farmer's wife packed my suitcase and took me to the railroad station. I knew I was needed at home and I cried with happiness. Arriving at the railroad station in Chemnitz, I picked up my suitcase and walked home. Every step brought me closer to the place I loved. I even greeted the ruins. I was home and that was all that mattered.

"Ortwin! Hartmut! I'm back!"

They saw me coming and rushed to tell Mama. "Irene is coming, Mama. See!" They never tried to send me away again.

In a short time word came that Ortwin and Hartmut were to be evacuated. Ortwin cried and Mama would not say she did not want her children sent away. She said, "The law must be obeyed."

We packed Ortwin's suitcase and helped him carry it to the railroad station. He looked so unhappy standing there with his big white tag saying who he was and where he was to go.

Hundreds of children were saying goodbye, many were crying. Later, Ortwin told us his story. He arrived in Annaberg about six o'clock in the evening. He was assigned to a middle aged couple with no small children but with sons in the war. They unpacked his suitcase and hung his clothes in the room that was to be his.

After supper they bathed him and, since he did not say much, they sent him to bed thinking he was exhausted from all the excitement. Ortwin obeyed all their suggestions without saying a word. When the couple retired Ortwin packed his suitcase and found his way out of the house. He walked out to the main road and looked for a road sign. When he saw one saying "Chemnitz" he knew where to go.

He walked all night carrying his heavy suitcase. The next morning when Mama went out for milk, there stood Ortwin, totally exhausted and dirty from his more than 30 kilometer (22 mile) walk back home. Mama laughed and cried at the same time.

"I guess if we have to die, we shall all die together," she said.

"There was a full moon, Mama. It was easy to read the signs. When the air raid came I jumped in a ditch. They sure flew low. I never saw airplanes fly so low, Mama. I sure was scared. Nobody stopped me, although many refugees and other people were on the roads. There are a lot of homeless people out there, Mama."

Ortwin was allowed to stay and went back to school. We were not the only children who came back from evacuation. A few others found their way home to their mothers too.

Then Hartmut's turn came.

"Don't send him, he will come back." Mama pleaded with the authorities.

"Orders are orders, he must go. This time we shall send him so far he will not be able to walk home like his brother." The man laughed. "Get him ready for evacuation."

"Maybe you will like it." Mama tried to cheer him. "If you get to a farm where they have good food, stay there until the war is over. They will take good care of you."

Hartmut wiped his eyes on his sleeve and looked so forlorn. "Mama, I don't want to go."

My second brother left with a train load of children for Sudetengau, in Czechoslovakia. The family he stayed with spoke both German and Czechoslovakian. He felt he was in a foreign country where people spoke another language but they did eat good food. It seemed that there were still many places where people were not starving in Europe.

But he sat every day on the Elbe River which was flowing through the town where he stayed. "I wanted to build a boat and paddle home, Mama!" he said. The people felt he would be happier with his family and gave him a ticket home. Our need to stay together was very strong and we all helped and depended upon one another.

Another letter came from Willi Springmann, telling us of the Russians shelling their bivouac. "We had to run and leave all our possessions behind. We have no food and we are very short on ammunition..."

A short time later we received a letter bordered in black from his parents announcing his death. Willi was their only son. We felt very sad about this young man's death. Death was everywhere. The world seemed cold and gray. Mama did not want us to ask about all the people and friends we had lost. Too many dead. Too many broken hearts. She told us rather that the war must be over soon.

We could now see for miles out of our windows. We knew it was just a matter of time until we would be hit. We were cornered by death and I began to feel resigned to this end. There was no place to go. Buildings numbered 19, 21, and 23, still stood on our street. Cardboard now replaced most of the glass in our windows. While it kept out the rain and wind, our rooms were dark.

Direct hits usually killed most of the people in the bomb shelter under the building. People were simply buried alive to either suffocate before help could arrive or were burned to death in the intense heat and fire of the blast.

Bombs destroyed the milk store across the street and more dear friends were lost. We now walked eight blocks for it and it was often only skim milk.

Many months providing for the hidden families was becoming a great strain on those of the few families left. No one had thought the war could last this long. We still had a good source of food from a family with relatives on a farm. Those people cooked for the hidden families until they too died in an air raid. The home of my two Sunday school teachers was bombed. They and their two children, the little "angels" of the neighborhood, were gone. They could not get out and the diggers gave up when there was no sign of life. With the Wolters gone, an empty lonely feeling filled me.

Fires lit the city at night, turning the sky pinkish red and cloudy. We sat in our bomb shelter and guessed where the English planes were throwing down the different colored flares to mark the places to be bombed. Those flares looked like Christmas trees falling from the sky. We feared to be inside the boundary markers set, where everything inside would be bombed to the ground. When we heard the motors of the planes we felt safe as any bombs disconnected above us would fall further away. But when we could not hear the motors above us and the bombs came whistling through the air, we knew our area was under attack. Fear stalked our shelter on those nights and we put our heads on our blankets and prayed hard for God's protection.

Mama was the brave one. "Try not to be afraid," she would say. "We will be spared. Keep calm, that is the most important thing we can do." She told us over and over again, "If we ever get hit and make it to the outside, run and we'll meet in our garden. Never run toward the city but run away from it!"

Broken water lines dried up our faucets. As the bomb destruction increased, water lines became irreparable. Power lines needed repair after almost every air raid.

Everyone shared the heavy chore of carrying water for household use. As more neighbors were killed, Esther and her mother dared to come out of the caves, dressed in dark clothes, and with shawls wrapped around their faces, to carry water. Survivors now had so many problems, less attention was given to spying on others. The men and boys could not carry water since it would have been suspicious that able men were still at home.

Before the war, the city constructed a large building that housed a huge swimming pool and a smaller one for school classes to use. Therefore, every child eight years and older knew how to swim. The building had health equipment in different departments, saunas, massage rooms, and on the second and third floors, rows and rows of little cabins with bathtubs. Thousands of people, including our family, went to this building for baths and shampoos as the city's water supply was choked down. Thus, we maintained some semblance of personal cleanliness. This beautiful building never got bombed and is still in use today.

My friend Brigitte and I occasionally went to the railroad station where much activity took place. Its two restaurants, numerous shops, and large waiting rooms were always full of people involved in the war. The Military Police often made raids in all those places and we could see people scrambling and running, trying to get out even through windows. It was great luck that we were still children as adults had a very difficult life then.

One evening a Red Cross train pulled into the station. They usually came later in the night. All the shades were drawn and no one was allowed to open the doors to the train. Curious to see what was on the train, we told a lie.

"Our mothers work for the Red Cross. We're supposed to meet them here."

This statement got us on the train. We gasped when we saw the wounded men. Bloody bandages were everywhere. We saw men with no legs, others with one or both arms missing. One man with no legs was crying, his face reflected unbearable pain.

Brigitte and I left the train after seeing the men in one car. That was too much for us. We stood looking at each other and cried as we clutched our sweaters tight around our bodies. Speechless from the shock of seeing this extreme suffering of so many young men, we walked home in silence. From that day the idea slowly developed that I might someday be a nurse and help the suffering.

The air raids continued like clockwork. One night we came out of our shelter to see an enormous fire. The sky toward the railroad station was orange-red and cloudy. We ran to the iron bridge and saw that a circus train had been bombed.

The fires in some places were so bright that we were able to see things in detail. Wild animals roared and screamed, fighting to get out of their cages. Some were running free, trying to escape the flames and smoke. We watched them turn the elephants loose. The fire fighters, mostly women and a few men, were trying to put out the fires with a very limited water supply, so all the animals were released. The animals roamed across the tracks, trampled down the fences that enclosed the rail line, and ran with much noise into the dark streets. The word spread like wildfire that lions and elephants were roaming loose. The next morning those poor creatures were found in the park, hiding in the only bit of nature they could find.

That night I saw the Cohen boys out of the caves. Everyone was so excited about the fires they were not recognized. I knew the hidden people came out occasionally at night to keep their sanity during their long confinement.

Herr Helbig's family was the next to be bombed. He was on the road driving his truck when his wife and baby son were killed. When he returned to his home it was a heap of rubble. He went berserk. His uncontrollable anger was taken out on everyone he saw in uniform. He was taken away and we never saw him again. They were such a lovely family, it was frightening how many whole families had already disappeared. With Herr Helbig gone, we lost a good source of food for our hidden people as he had hauled tons of potatoes and cabbages to help feed them. Most of our food sources seemed to be drying up.

One morning I pushed the cardboard back from the window and as I looked out on the desolation, the sadness of losing our friends and neighbors engulfed me. I sobbed uncontrollably. Mama took me gently by the shoulders and turned me around. She looked so worried.

"Irene, we need a change of scenery. Let's go out to the garden. There are some blankets there and we could stay overnight. Would you like that?"

I nodded but the tears and sobbing continued. Only when Nadja and I busied ourselves loading the hand wagon could I stop crying. We packed some food and took a hatchet to cut up some debris for fuel.

"Irene, get some bags to hold vegetables," Mama directed, "and don't forget your accordion. We haven't heard you play for a long time."

Off we went, Mama pushing Claus in the baby carriage that he had somewhat outgrown and Nadja pulling the hand wagon.

"Maybe we can get some big pieces of cardboard from that trucking firm next to the park," Ortwin said.

"Yes, we could use more to keep out the fall rain, and winter is coming." Mama was always hopeful.

It was a bright and sunny but cool day in October. We dug the potatoes and cut Brussels sprouts. Nadja and I found some big pieces of cardboard near the warehouse and tied them together for our return trip. Keeping busy helped me feel better. Mama cooked us a good stew with potatoes, Brussels sprouts, and some meatless bones. The spices made it tasty and the sprouts were very flavorful this time of year. We even had water since the water lines in this part of the outer city were undamaged. We cuddled together in our little hut and sang the songs Papa used to sing. I played the accordion.

The first air raid that came in the night dropped bombs in the distance. Toward morning, a second air raid came so close we decided we should get home to our shelter before another night came.

"The bombs Mama, they are everywhere."

"Irene, we have to be patient. This war will soon be over and things will be better. We will be free."

"Free," I said aloud. I thought about the word "free" and what it would mean. Free of fear when we talked to our neighbors. Free of fear of uniformed military police and the Gestapo--what a relief that would be. Now we also feared the bombs that brought so much destruction to property and lives. Freedom to sleep at night and walk in the daytime in the streets and not be killed.

When we came back home the blockwarden was very cross with us because we had not told him when we were going away. We explained where we had been and he had a fit, telling us that it is forbidden to spend the night in a garden colony since they have no bomb shelters. He forbade us to do this again and promised to keep an eye on us. We knew he would be only too happy to report us for something, since he did not like us.

Whispers. Just bare whispered rumors began. "We are losing the war" or "No matter what the propaganda machine says, we are losing the war."

I overheard two soldiers saying to each other. "Enjoy the war, the peace will be dreadful for us."

"Why do you say that?" I asked, greatly annoyed.

The soldier looked at me sadly and said, "Little girl, you don't know what is going on in this war. It is much worse than the First World War and the end always brings hunger and inflation."

Like bloodhounds, the dreadful military police walked everywhere, but mostly inside the railroad station. They stood with expressionless faces and sharp eyes--no movement escaped them. They were like the Gestapo with their harsh voices and domineering ways. Any soldier caught without his papers in order or AWOL was sent to the "Suicide Unit." Here he was trained to perform a suicide mission or other dangerous task; then ordered to undertake the mission, knowing that he would likely be killed.

One soldier said, "Whoever falls into their hands has never returned."

The Nazi system had become a strong net from which there was no escape. There were courageous men who wanted Hitler out of the way, like the Lord Mayor of Leipzig, Dr. Carl Goerdeler, an associate of Hitler, who tried to kill him. He, and those who made the attempt, were hung in public. Others tried to persuade Hitler to stop the war. A bomb planted to kill Hitler missed. When he survived one attempt after another upon his life and lived to punish those plotting against him, we felt it was our fate to have him rule until the bitter end.

The next air raid bombed our general store across the street. This was where we were required to shop with our ration stamps. Life would be much harder now.

The day the store was bombed, Papa came home on a 24-hour leave. Ortwin was so happy to see Papa he hardly left his side. He hung onto Papa's hand and asked constant questions.

For dinner Mama made us a feast of potato pancakes with some canned applesauce she had hidden in the bomb shelter. I remember Papa talked to Mama about many things I did not understand. I heard Mama sigh many times. Much of their conversation was so low I could not hear it. Papa nailed up more layers of cardboard over the windows and fixed things for Mama. At four o'clock the next morning Papa had to be at the railroad station to leave for the Russian front.

"Ortwin must say 'goodbye' to you at the station. He'll get sick if he doesn't see you off," Mama said. "The grief of losing friends is causing so much heartache for the children. Irene's having a hard time over the loss of the Wolter's."

When it was time to go, Mama woke Ortwin. Papa carried him, half sleeping, on his shoulder to the railroad station. I stayed home with Nadja and the children. It seemed colder when Papa left.

A few months later we received a letter saying Papa was ill with Russian typhus and was in the military hospital in Loschwitz, near Dresden. Mama visited Papa frequently. When he recovered and it was time for him to return to the front, she took all of us to spend a day with him in Dresden.

No art treasures could be seen in Dresden. They were being kept in a safe place underground until after the war. The city was full of life and people were not as tense as they were in Chemnitz. It was like a sanctuary away from the war, although police boats on the Elbe River ran up and down constantly, checking peoples' papers, because the city was full of refugees from everywhere. I saw no bombed buildings at that advanced time in the war.

We all had something to drink at the famous restaurant high on the hill where we had said goodbye to Willi Springermann. The waitress refused to serve Nadja in the dining room so she and I sat outside and ate our homemade sandwiches and drank the tea Mama also brought with us in a thermos. We liked it better outside where we could see the city and all the Elbe River bridges. Everything sparkled in the cold afternoon sun under a clear blue sky.

Too soon we were saying a tearful farewell to Papa. "Help Mama all you can, Nadja. She is going to have another child and I doubt that I'll be there to help her."

"Da, da, I help." Nadja put her arm around Mama's shoulders. Ortwin turned pale when we left Dresden and was very quiet for several days following Papa's departure.

We knew our ration cards could not provide us any extravagant foods for our Christmas of 1943. "It's one of the most important holidays of the year," Mama said. "It's going to be a happy day in memory of the birth of Jesus."

"Mama," Ortwin said wistfully, "We don't expect any gifts."

"No Christmas *stollen*, no apples, oranges or gingerbread," Mama added. "But we will be happy and thankful. Many people are sharing their homes with those who have been bombed out. Some do not have enough coal to heat their apartment, but we have saved enough coal from our allotment to heat our big kitchen nice and warm on Christmas day."

Coal was scarce and the winters in Germany were always harsh.

Inside our home we each wore two sweaters and heavy socks under our felt house shoes. Ice had formed on the outside of the cardboard windows. When we talked, we could see steam-breath coming out of our mouths and the cold was painful. We often warmed our hands around the flame of a candle. A warm kitchen for Christmas would really be the nicest gift of all.

The day before Christmas we carried the boxes down from the attic that held the pyramid Papa had made. Ortwin, Hartmut, and Grandpa Michael put it together. After all five tiers were standing in the middle of our large table, we added the little hand carved figures such as Jesus in the manger, the mother Mary, and Joseph. There were tiny shepherds with their sheep, characters from Bible stories, and pieces showing mountains and desert. We topped our pyramid with a large angel. The pyramid turned around, powered by a hidden clock mechanism Papa had attached to it. It was beautiful.

We talked about past Christmas holidays and the meaning of the different foods we ate. One tablespoon of gruel meant we would have enough money for the coming year. Potato salad meant we would never be hungry during the coming year. Sausages had to be eaten and sauerkraut was a must. The main dish usually was duck with dumplings. Those dumplings were almost as big as tennis balls. Mama used to make at least twenty and always put a silver one-mark piece in one dumpling. The one finding the coin was supposed to be rich one day. I never found one in my dumpling. My grandmother found it one time. She was never rich in money but surely rich in love.

On Christmas Eve, after we bathed in the city bath house and put on our best clothes, we walked to the church. The bells were ringing in the cold air and we hoped the air raid sirens would not spoil this peaceful event. The planes usually came about 8:30 p.m. We still had an hour and a half if they were on schedule. The Sermon the Pastor talked about was: "Christians are at war against Christians." I heard that Hitler had been raised as a Catholic and now he had proclaimed himself an atheist. He will rot in hell, I thought. Please God let peace come soon, I prayed.

The air raids did not come. All was quiet. People streamed into the church from all directions and the building became overcrowded. People stood in the aisles and on the bases of the great pillars. The lofts on either side held more than 100 chairs, and all were filled and still they crowded in. The church was not heated but the masses of people warmed the large building. The organ swelled its rich chords of Christmas music over the congregation. I wondered if the resonance of the organ tones and the voices from the choir could shatter the stained glass windows. It was impressive to see the relaxed faces of the people and the many tears and hopeful eyes, as they enjoyed the traditional music.

A large Christmas tree was decorated with white ornaments and white lights and the altar was festive with greens. That night we had two pastors speaking. "Peace on Earth" was what we all wanted to hear, but when would it come?

After the service we hurried home, talking about the past when Papa was with us. Mama scurried us to bed saying, "Santa will not bring gifts if he sees you up." We looked at each other and dared--

"Maybe we should keep the window open just a little bit to let Santa in," Hartmut suggested as he tried to tear on the cardboard. I felt it was not necessary,

Although Nadja's Christmas came in January since she was Russian Orthodox, she was just as excited as we were. She helped Mama with baking and caught the Christmas spirit. There used to be a class for baking without butters and other ingredients. Mama had become a master at substituting. When she had no eggs, she used milk. Instead of milk she used watered milk. If no milk was available she used water. When recipes called for honey she used that black syrup which tasted like wood. Saccharin was in big demand those days, although people were not sure if it was a cancer causing substance. Instead of baking powder Mama would substitute wine or vinegar or baking soda. Whatever was available. Even our Christmas mood was somehow a substitute for the peace we all longed for.

It was still dark when Mama called to us on Christmas morning. Her call was not for an air raid but for our traditional Christmas presents. We were all astounded. Eagerly I opened mine, a package of bobby pins made of metal. This was a precious gift since I thought all metal was being used for the war. Those things had not been in the stores for years. My brothers got mittens, and Grandpa Michael made each of the boys a wallet and Claus a wooden toy. We each received little straw stars from Nadja. I shall never forget Nadja's face as she unwrapped her package and took out a yellow satin blouse with black trimmings. It was from Grandma's closet. Her eyes were bright and her broad smile told us of her happiness.

It was still dark outside as we admired our pyramid with real candles on it. The music box played Christmas songs and we sat around soaking up the heat in our warm home. We were the luckiest people in town, we thought.

"Get out your accordion, Irene. Let's sing some Christmas songs." Mama said softly. While the pyramid slowly turned, loaded with lit candles, our room was lit with a spiritual warmth and our voices blended in soft Christmas melodies.

"Look, the daylight is coming through," said Grandmother.

"It is morning, the birthday of Jesus Christ our Savior."

It was a precious moment. As the daylight filtered in around the cracks in our cardboard-covered windows, I could see tears in Mama's eyes. I knew she missed Papa. He had always led us in singing.

Ortwin snuggled close to her and whispered, "We all miss Papa.

Grandpa stood up and started to jig. "Irene, play me a dancing song."

I swung into a cheerful polka and he grabbed Grandma and they stepped a lively dance while Ortwin and Hartmut kept time with their hands. This started the games. Our favorite was "throwing the shoe." We each took turns standing with our backs to the door. We would take three steps forward and throw a house shoe backward over our heads. The position of the thrown shoes, of course, had special meanings.

In April of 1944, I was confirmed in church. At the age of fourteen I was looked on as an adult. Now people said "Fraulein

Irene," (Miss Irene) not just "Irene." Of course family and friends, they continued saying "*Du*". In general people address each other with Missus or Mister. That is Frau or Herr so and so. In most conversation they use the formal "*Sie*" instead of the informal "*Du*."

It was now emphasized that I must have more responsibilities and this meant more school work. Mama wanted me to become a registered nurse. Considering how few professions were available for women in those days, it was a reasonable choice. We learned that the surgical Hospital Administration at Zschopauer Strasse was interested in training girls as young as myself. So I began pre-nursing classes.

Although regulations were that a student as young as myself should not work at night, the circumstances of war made it necessary. On many weekends I had one and sometimes two evening assignments as a first-aid nurse in the opera or Schauspiel House Theater. Movies, variety shows and all kind of operas and plays were all on a full schedule of performances during the war to keep up the spirits of the people. Performances stopped only when their show places were destroyed. I wore a Red Cross uniform and kept a bag like a first-aid kit with me. I even got a special seat in each theater, ready to apply first-aid if needed.

My night duty at the hospital was on the children's ward. It was my job to get child patients into the air raid shelter when an alert was sounded. The air raid shelters under the large hospital buildings made me very uneasy because of the big hot water pipes overhead. Months later, when the hospital was bombed, I was not on duty. Only part of the building complex was destroyed, but still, many people lost their lives and many others were left with complicated wounds which added to their illness.

Although pre-nursing classes took up most of my time, I was able to spend a few hours each week with my father, Basil. That is, until he was assigned to bring wounded soldiers home by Red Cross trucks from the Russian front. The war situation at the Russian front was already so bad that the trains with the wounded soldiers did not come through anymore.

I cried as Aunt Johanna and I walked with him to the railway station to say goodbye. It was raining, and even the skies seemed to be weeping about all the sadness and destruction around us. I would miss my father's special attention to me.

"Come back Father! I need you."

His train sped away into the night and the war.

CHAPTER FIVE
THE FINAL YEAR
1944 - 1945

Rumors of the D-Day invasion reached us immediately when it happened. My whole family was so anxious for the war to end, we expected the Allied troops would come into Chemnitz and liberate us within a few weeks. Still, Chemnitz and other places around us were bombed even more often and our anxiety grew daily. We kept hoping Papa would return and we constantly asked soldiers coming from the east if they had seen him.

We would hear, "I saw your Papa here or there," but no one really knew for sure. Other families were as anxious as we were to see their men come home from the war. Thousands of families were separated during those days. If they survived after their homes were destroyed, people put up signs near the heaps of rubble, telling where they had moved.

After my pre-nursing classes I usually went to the children's ward to work. There I saw large amounts of leftover food, especially cereal and soup. I brought a pot and pitcher with tight fitting lids to the hospital and filled them with the surplus food, and when I was on lunch or standby duty, I carried it home and Nadja took it to the hidden people. If I ran, I was able to make it home and back in 40 minutes.

Uncle Albert was also one of our best resources of food. He provided vegetable salad, made from all kinds of vegetables that were in season, and potatoes in mayonnaise. We carried buckets of this home and to our friends.

One day before noon an air raid alert came just as I reached home. When the all-clear sounded, Mama said, "We'd better go and see Uncle Albert. From the looks of the smoke over there I think the butchery may have been hit."

Dear God, I hope it isn't so, I thought. As we walked toward the butchery, Tanja came running toward us. She was crying. We followed her back to the butchery: now a mountain of rubble.

Uncle Albert was digging where the front of the shop had been. Aunt Margarete was laughing hysterically and repeating over and over, "We'll build it up again!" We'll build it up again!"

Aunt Margarete's laughter worried Tanja. It was plain to see that Aunt Margaret was in shock over the loss of their home and their livelihood. We all dug into the rubble but found few things of value. I found some tiles from their store walls and a stainless steel kettle, now very black and dented.

The block warden came by and warned us not to look for things. "There might be unexploded bombs in there. There may be time bombs that will explode hours from now. It happens all the time. Don't risk it."

In spite of the danger, Aunt Margarete started to walk over the rubble and they had to restrain her. Aunt Margarete's brother and wife came to help and soon persuaded them to give up the idea of digging.

Now, I was glad that Mama had sold most of our valuables on the black market. We at least had something to eat for it. Nothing was left after a direct hit.

"Let's go to our shop, Irene," Mama said. "Come with us, Nadja. Ortwin stay here and help Uncle Albert."

As we hurried up the street destroyed buildings became a foreboding sign of what to expect.

"No, it can't be!" Mama looked stunned looking at our shop.

All the windows were broken and one side of the shop was blown open. The roof sagged badly where the wall was blown out. Disregarding the warnings about the danger of sorting through rubble, we searched for usable items. We found most of Papa's small hand tools and some broken cartons containing dusty but undamaged merchandise. The rest was useless. Broken glass had pierced so many things it was dangerous to look further.

Mama stood by the salvaged materials while Nadja and I hauled several hand wagons full of merchandise to the shed behind our apartment building.

Aunt Margarete's brother took his sister, Uncle Albert and Tanja to live with them. Within a few days the officials took Tanja by force, saying she could come back after the war was over but now she must work in the ammunition factory. Tanja was never heard from again.

Soon after the loss of our shop, another much worse tragedy came. Thirteen year old Herbert Kobler and his widowed mother took a deserter from the army into their home. Frau Kobler must have been in love with him and did all she could to hide him, thinking the war will be over soon anyway. Her son, Herbert, complained constantly about not having enough to eat. His grumbling was aggravated further by getting mistreated and neglected by his mother. Because of this unpleasant situation, she asked that her AWOL soldier be hidden in the caves with the Jewish families. This was allowed under the condition that she provide his food.

Frau Kobler sold everything valuable she had on the black market to buy food for them. The money and food were soon gone and Herbert's complaining began again. His whining about being hungry fell on the ears of curious informers. Their suspicions about what was going on at the Koblers led to questions.

"You have the same rations as all of us. We are hungry too!"

"I haven't had anything for two days!"

"Why doesn't your mother give you some food?"

"She has nothing for me, only for him."

"For whom?"

"Oh, she has a friend and he eats our food."

"A friend. Where is he?"

"Oh, he comes here sometimes."

"But he isn't here now, where is he? Where does he work?"

Herbert's answers led to more persistent questions as to the whereabouts of a man they had not known about.

When Herbert talked, he told about all the hidden Jewish families. Who they were and where they were hiding was revealed by this vengeful 13 year old boy. Our cautiously guarded secret, the work and sacrifices of neighborhood friends for almost two long years, was spilled to the police.

The anger and frustration this act generated among us who had helped our friends, equaled that of the police who threatened to burn the entire block to the ground. Herbert needed police protection from us, there was no doubt about it.

Big reports went out on what we had done and there was nothing we could do about it. NOTHING! We were fearful now for our own safety.

An army truck rumbled into the street and stopped in front of the building where our friends were hidden. There had been SS guards from the moment of the betrayal. All of us who had helped our Jewish friends, and many others, surrounded the truck. We cried, we cursed! We threatened, but to no avail.

Then they brought them out, my best friend Esther, her brother David and their parents. All huddled together as shouting soldiers tried to ignore our screams. I ran forward and tried to touch Esther but was thrown back by an SS man. Our eyes met briefly. I'll never forget her grief stricken glance.

The Cohens and their three sons were next. Knowing they would die, the boys spit on the uniforms of the SS men. Sharp jabs from gun butts, delivered by the soldiers, shoved them into the truck.

Last came the AWOL soldier. Frau Kobler threw herself to the ground and begged to be taken with him. She was distraught with the awful shame of her son's act. They dragged her up and pushed her into the truck.

"She's on the list anyway," shouted an officer. "She was harboring an enemy of the State!"

"Leave the area at once! You are next on the list!" threatened the soldiers as they banged the truck door shut and roared away down the street.

I wanted to walk to the caves but was warned not to. Everyone that was seen there were arrested immediately. Everything was barricaded and the Winkler's had gone days ago, someone told me.

We waited to be punished. There was no place to go, no place to hide. The air raids were still intense and we debated whether we would prefer to be killed by a bomb or by the SS for helping our friends.

A few weeks later we heard that Herbert Kobler was found dead. He had moved in with his grandmother. When he did not return from school one day, she reported it to the police. In their search they found him lying in the rubble, killed by a heavy blow on his head. Few people cared that this jealous boy, who brought death and sorrow to so many, was killed.

Mama was soon to give birth. Early one morning she asked me to go for our milk. "If there is an air raid this morning, we will have no milk."

"I don't want to go, Mama."

"You must!"

Still I dragged my feet. Everyone seemed nervous and upset.

Mama was furious. She grabbed the broom. "Irene, get going, right now!" She swatted me with the broom. I ran but for some reason I came back. At that moment the sirens started to howl and we scurried to the shelter.

The first bomb came so close it shook the building. The impact of the second bomb twisted the chimney. The clean-out disc fell off and black soot spurted out, swelling into a black cloud that engulfed us. I had experienced this soot cloud before. Children were screaming. Mama covered Claus with a blanket. We coughed and spit and got very black from soot.

After the all clear signal, we climbed out to survey the damage. Two five story apartment buildings across the street were leveled. We could see right through the space to others destroyed beyond. The explosion was so fast the families could not get through their loose-brick section into their shelter. All were killed. I kept thinking about the Haberkorns and their five daughters.

"I talked to some of those girls yesterday Mama, today they are all gone!"

"Irene," somebody said. "You don't have to go for milk anymore, they got hit bad. No one is alive there either."

Mama looked at me and we realized I could have walked to the milk store but not home again. The air raid warning would have signaled me to stay there and I would have been killed. Mama put her arms around me and we cried. We knew my life had been spared again.

When it was time for Christine to be born it was a nice warm day in July of 1944. Nadja and Frau Mirse, a midwife, helped Mama while I took care of my brothers outside. There was not a woman in the neighborhood who had ever delivered a baby in the hospital like in our modern time now. Mama did as good as expected under the circumstances and we had our first sister. It is amazing all the things that can occur between air raids.

With no more business in our shop, Mama had to declare to the City Hall that our shop was destroyed. She was notified that Nadja must report for another work assignment like Tanja.

Mama took the new baby and Claus, who was still small, and went to the authorities. "With these two small children and two more at home, I need Nadja's help."

"Irene is fifteen, she can help you!"

"Irene is in school and she works in the hospital. She cannot help me at home. I need Nadja until the baby is older." There might have been more said, but, Mama gave the man who authorized foreign labor in households a lot of the merchandise which we had salvaged. He probably sold these items on the black market, since there was not much to buy anymore. Mama came home with the happy news that Nadja could stay.

We knew the Americans had landed on the French coast weeks ago and that they had crossed the German border. We heard that Germany was going to be divided into four pieces. We could not understand why the Americans did not advance more quickly and finish the war. We also hoped that the Elbe River would be the new allied border line in divided Germany. This would have given the Russians plenty of territory and for us, we then would live in one of the allied zones. But it turned out much worse.

Bombs continued to diminish our city to rubble. The planes came around nine in the morning, after eight in the evening, and again around two o'clock in the morning. Several kinds of bombs fell on us. One we called the *sprengbombe* came down and exploded when it hit any surface. The *branobombe* started fires as soon as it hit a surface; it burned even when we poured water over it, we figured there were chemicals inside. Firebombs with those chemicals in them were the most feared. It burned people alive.

Although repair crews worked during every daylight hour to restore our electricity, we were without power much of the time. Hospitals used emergency power. As power lines were destroyed, hand wound sirens with weak signals replaced the loud clear call of electric ones. This weak signal left us more vulnerable to air raids.

Christmas of 1944 came and went with scarcely any observance other than attending church. Survival was our major concern and carrying water was a strenuous chore. To keep from freezing we stamped our feet and slid our hands under our arms. Those who talked soon became silent when they realized keeping the mouth closed helped keep in body heat.

People with leaky buckets tried to repair them by placing two small metal disks, one outside and one inside, over the hole and tightening them with a short bolt screw and nut. Even then little trickles of water came dripping out, prompting observers to hurry them along to save the precious water.

When bombs destroyed the place where we got water, we went to an open well on the west side of the city four miles away. It was an underground spring, inside a courtyard, partially surrounded by an apartment building. A large plank was placed across an open hole and men stood in four-hour shifts, drawing bucket after bucket to fill containers held out to them. We used to travel this four-mile distance by streetcar. But now we walked and the buckets were heavy. The line of people, usually two or three abreast, stretched through the courtyard then outside and down the street.

Across the street from where we waited for water, the narrow Chemnitz River flowed in a small trickle through a wide, almost flat river bed. Polluted with chemical wastes, this half frozen stream was no use to us for drinking. Dive bombers flew along this river and shot anything that moved. Pilots seemed to use the river as a guide to their targets.

One cold grey morning a distant humming quickly grew into a thunderous vibration. None of the sirens were working. There must have been a hundred or more women and children and some old men standing in line for water. The dive bombers dipped low and strafed us like a scythe cutting grass. A string of bullets hit the street and ricocheted into the line of people huddled against the wall. Men and women slumped lifeless to the ground, others staggered and fell. Some ran to hide in the rubble but were shot because they were spotted while running.

As quickly as they came, they left and I wondered if they knew what they had done. We carried the dead bodies into a half destroyed building and loaded six of the wounded onto a two-wheeled cart with a flat bed. Some of the wounded were able to walk with the help of others. Carrying our buckets, we dared not leave them behind. We pushed the wounded to the hospital, which was a good two miles away.

Once an air raid was over we could always count on a few hours of unmolested time. Nadja and I hurried back to the spring to fill our buckets. As we rejoined the line I saw that there were no more dead bodies on the street. In one of the washhouses (which every apartment building used to have) the bodies had been laid until they could be picked up by the authorities. I looked at their faces. Their expressions of pain and fear were gone. They looked relaxed and at peace, as if they were saying, "We made it. We don't have to worry about food, water, air raids or killings anymore. We are at peace."

I thought about all my narrow escapes from death. I looked upward into the cold gray sky, past the torn walls of the buildings. "It must be God's will that I live," I said aloud. I was no longer afraid of death.

We became used to seeing dead bodies and our hearts were heavy from sorrow. Besides our dangerous but necessary trips for water, we began to feel very hungry. The gnawing pain of hunger went to bed with us and often kept us from sleeping. Sometimes Mama made hot chicory to quiet our stomachs until sleep could come. We hungered for a decent meal we had not had for months. As in all places, as hunger increased household pets disappeared. Luckily, we ourselves had none; we would have hated to eat a beloved pet.

Almost in defiance of the air raids some of our buildings still stood tall. We were sure the pilots could see our city hall, the *Rathaus*, a tall building with a spire. Perhaps the spire led them to think it was a church. The city bathhouse survived to provide its customers bathing facilities.

We slept in the morning, as increased air raids forced us to spend more hours in our bomb shelter at night. Since the hospital got bombed, I was again able to stay home. The city was not organized anymore and people were pretty much now on their own.

Cold gray concrete floors down in the shelter and bone-chilling air gave us restless nights. Each family's lantern provided a dim pool of light revealing figures huddled together, waiting, trying to survive one more air raid. Our blankets never quite kept out the cold damp winter air.

One night, down one of those cold corridors, Frau Muchen gave birth to a baby boy during a bomb attack. I could hear her crying out in her pain. Those helping her were rude and rough. Their profanity and contempt made her delivery seem vulgar and obscene.

"Stop crying, you bitch," yelled an old man. "You didn't cry when you conceived him!"

When I saw them remove a big bowl of bloody tissue, I hid my face against Mama.

"Oh, Mama, how horrible those people are. I never want a baby! Not like this!"

"Try not to listen, child. It shouldn't be ugly like this."

I was grateful for Mama's gentle arms and her understanding words.

I kissed Christine and was glad she was not able to understand the words around her. I heard one old man singing softly some song like "Cry when a soul is born, rejoice when a soul dies." Mama and I knew those people smelled death everywhere and could not cope with a new life; that was why they used profanity. I was glad when that long night came to an end.

A few weeks later fresh snow covered the ground. Although it mantled much of the rubble, it also silhouetted our crippled city's wounds. No amount of snow could blot out the agony of a dying city.

One night in February of 1945, the beautiful city of Dresden, that I loved so much, was destroyed by bombs. The entire historic inner city was blanketed by one of the heaviest air raids of the war. Not a single building or historical complex could withstand this immense fire storm. Not only the city, but even the Elbe River was on fire.

The city was overcrowded with visitors and refugees from all over Germany. Wounded were housed there since the city was thought to be safe. Most air raids had been over Berlin and other larger cities up north. We in Germany thought Dresden would not be destroyed because of its world famous art treasures; this was wishful thinking. The death toll was enormous.

Just before we went into our bomb shelter we heard the news on Papa's radio. We were stunned and great fear gripped everybody as they had heard the news also on their radios. Many wept openly. I thought we had no more tears but this affected us deeply. Everything seemed bleak and useless. Esther and the hidden families were gone, many neighbors had been killed, and destruction was everywhere. I felt the cold and shivered. Even Hitler's SS was short on manpower now. But they would kill us if they won the war. They had told us so already when the hidden people were picked up.

Snow still covered the ground in March. The cardboard over the windows could not keep out the cold and there was no coal to keep us warm. The door still hung loosely on its hinges. Ours was one of the very few remaining buildings.

"Tonight our home will be hit, I can just feel it," said Mama. "Get your knapsacks ready Irene. See that the boys have everything in theirs."

"Yes, Mama."

I laid out one change of underwear for each, an extra amount of sweaters and towels, and wrapped soap and eating utensils together. I tried to stuff as much as possible in those knapsacks, being careful though not to make them too heavy to carry. Nadja also packed one for herself and checked everything. We had only one pair of shoes each and they were in bad shape. Since shoe ration cards had not been issued for the past three years. Besides Christine and her baby needs, Mama tucked into Christine's baby carriage a metal pitcher with a lid, some milk, sewing notions, emergency items and important papers.

Ortwin looked at Christine, not yet a year old and said, "Christine, you're in a real snug fit. You should be warm tonight."

"Get your blankets ready, we'll go down at the first sound of a motor or any explosions." Mama was apprehensive. We sat in the dark, not even lighting a candle. Our supply was gone.

Right on schedule at 8:30 p.m. we heard the hand wound sirens. We rushed into the cellar. The bombs had such a cold whistling sound as they fell.

One hour later we went upstairs again. "Don't get undressed, we'll be hit tonight." Mama warned. We felt doomed.

I walked around the windowless apartment. I could see the street through the holes in our walls. Again we went to bed with our clothes on. This time I put my accordion at the foot of my bed. At 3 a.m. the sirens roused us again. We rushed down the long steps into the cellar. I helped Mama with the baby carriage, clutching my accordion with one hand. Christine was asleep and did not know of our anxiety. Lucky her. Nadja supervised the boys and carried the blankets and other items.

The first explosion left a strong smell of gunpowder in the air. Just as Nadja lit the lantern and we settled into our places we heard the deafening blast. The building shuddered then seemed to settle. Our home was bombed! Mama had been right.

People were hushed, even the children. Another blast shook the ground under us. We crouched down in our blankets frozen with fear. The fierce burning and noise of explosions overhead roared ominously. A fine dust spread through the shelter and people coughed. Blast followed blast as bombs exploded above us. The building was a five-story brick house; I always regarded it as one of the strongest in the neighborhood. But now, it died too.

I looked at the fear-filled faces of our neighbors. Thank heaven we were dressed. Some of them were still in their night clothes, their street clothes hung over their arms.

Christine choked and started to cry. "It's going to get very hot in here," Mama said as she stood up and went to the water barrel kept for this kind of emergency. She brought back two buckets of water. The other people did the same.

"I'm going to pour this on your blankets." She doused us. We gasped as the cold water drenched us. We wrapped the wet blankets around us and waited, as did our neighbors. Nervously, we watched the arched ceiling above us. The steel ribs reinforcing the concrete were still holding. I had never seen a basement ceiling the same as ours. We could hear heavy pieces of wall and furniture come crashing through the floors of the burning building.

"Our home is burning, Mama. If the floor caves in we'll all die!" I screamed.

Our fright distorted reality. An old man ran up the stairs and opened the door. A mass of heat and flames licked down on us. Screams of fear filled the air.

"You old fool!" screamed some woman. "You can't get out that way!"

Panic had taken over. As people began shouting and milling about I looked at the barricaded windows, now brightly lit by the raging fire overhead. The windows were so small, only a child could get through. We instinctively knew we would all get out or we would all die together. It was getting very warm.

Mama's calm reassurance kept us from the panic now mounting to a high pitch among our neighbors. The boys were very quiet. I hugged my accordion close and kept my eyes on Mama. She was as frightened as anyone but her eyes revealed the same instinctive calculation an animal experiences when trying to protect her young.

We saw two women, each with a pickax beginning to knock the bricks out of the unmortared section of the wall to the adjoining shelter.

We sat in our section and prayed, "Please God, don't forsake us, show us a way out of this inferno..."

Everyone started for the opening at once. Men shouted, "Don't push! Don't push! No one will get through if you panic. You must go one by one!" But people did not listen.

"Wait," Mama cautioned. "Let the others go first. Wait!"

"Mama! It's so hot!" cried Ortwin.

"Hush," she said. "God will not forsake us."

Hartmut and little Claus clung to Mama and cried. Nadja took Claus and tried to comfort him. Paralyzed with fear, I watched the people rush to get through a hole only large enough for one thin person at a time. They pushed and yelled, deaf to shouts of "Wait" and "Don't push!"

Mama knew Christine's baby carriage could never survive that crush of people. As we waited for the others to go through the opening we saw that the weight of people pushing one another with their bundles loosened more bricks and the hole was now large enough for the carriage to pass through. I wondered if God would really keep us safe this time. We were entirely in His hands again. Frau Muchen, almost first with her newborn baby, had pushed through the crowd screaming and just hysterical. The baby was bundled up in a huge bulky feather pillow.

"It's hard to breathe," gasped Ortwin. "It's so hot!"

"Breathe through your wet blankets!" Mama ordered.

It was easier to breathe the damp air through our blankets that were beginning to steam.

"Mama! Please," I begged. "We must go now."

"Yes, now listen, come! Walk carefully and don't fall. Watch out for loose bricks on the other side of the hole."

We were the last family that moved through the hole in the wall.

"Irene, hold the end of the carriage. Ortwin, help her. We need to carry it when we get outside."

The hole was now wide enough to get the baby carriage through with some lifting. The next shelter was empty. All the people had already run out into the street through a huge hole leading out. Clutching our steaming blankets around us, we climbed over the rubble and up into the blazing street where people were shouting and running in all directions, looking for lost family members.

"Mama!" I screamed. "We must run where it's safe--but where is it safe?"

The entire street was as light as day from the fire. Every burned building had caught fire again. Even the rubble was burning. Off and on I remember light snow falling. We followed Mama as she pulled the baby carriage. We couldn't think; we just followed Mama in the scaring heat and confusion.

"We've got to get away from the heat and fire." Fiery sparks flew through the air, making breathing difficult.

"Da, Da!" Nadja yelled back. "Keep the blankets over your heads!"

Nadja hung on to Claus and Hartmut's hands. Clutching our bundles, Ortwin and I helped with the baby carriage as we picked our way through the burning debris. Many people had wet blankets just like ours. Before we could hinder it, a man with a big feather bed wrapped around him threw it on the baby carriage and covered it completely. Mama pulled it off. I screamed when I saw Mama fighting with this man. I let go of Ortwin and helped her push him away.

We threw that feather bed down on the ground. He stooped down and picked up his feather bed and shouted at us. I saw his panic-stricken face coming toward us again. This time Mama and Nadja together stopped him before he could reach the carriage. As he turned around leaving, he shouted some sharp words at us.

In the meantime many people had passed us, seeking higher ground where it was dark and where there was no fire.

Christine was now crying again. Maybe she sensed the danger when the feather bed had been thrown upon her.

We ran as fast as a family with small children could move. Little Claus, only about five, struggled to keep up. Nadja half dragged and then carried him much of the way. Flames were gutting buildings on both sides of the street, walls were collapsing. The heat was making soft spots in the asphalt.

Our fear made us more surefooted as we hurried away from the burning buildings. The explosions, coming from bursting gas pipes, made us hurry even faster. When we reached streets paved with cobblestones, we found they were slippery from the melted snow.

Everyone was running. Children stumbled as they were pulled along by panic-stricken mothers. Christine's crying continued as we bounced her carriage over the stones. As far as I could see the city was a flaming inferno. Mama turned in another direction. We followed.

Mama said, "We'll go up this hill, maybe the Humboldt School is still standing."

The light from the burning city made our shadows large and grotesque as we hurried away from the fire and smoke. The school was still there. Mama stopped in front of it and said, as though talking to the building we were about to enter, "We have lost everything: our store, Papa is not with us, our home and all our personal things are gone. Everything is lost but we are ALIVE! Thank God for that!"

The schoolhouse was already filled with hundreds of people and more kept coming. Everyone was streaked with smoke and melted snow. Some people had been injured and for the time being were just brought into the school out of the street. We found a space in a classroom filled with people just like us. We dropped our blankets and knapsacks on the floor. That was when we heard that Frau Muchen had suffocated her new baby in the large pillow when she pushed through the crowd in panic to escape our burning building. Her cries of agony were heartrending.

"Ortwin! Where is Ortwin?" Mama ran from the room calling his name. She returned a few minutes later without him.

"We've lost Ortwin!" She sat down and took Christine in her arms to quiet her frantic crying.

"Irene, you and Nadja will have to care for the children. I'm going back. I know Ortwin got out of the burning building."

"Don't go," warned people around us. "Walls are collapsing, gas lines are exploding everywhere! You'll be killed!"

Mama would not listen. "I must get my boy," she sobbed as she hung our blankets on desks to dry. "I have to go back."

Leaving the five of us huddled together she hurried out the door. Through the broken windows we could see the whole city ignited by flames. Once I saw Mama, wrapped in a wet blanket, briefly silhouetted against the flames as she hurried in the direction of our home.

"Please, God, bring her back to us," I prayed. What would we do without her? She was our strength; our lives depended upon her. I looked down on Hartmut, Claus and Christine. They were trying to sleep even with all the loud noise around us. Shuffling feet, crying children, excited loud voices, and the moans of wounded people revealed our chaotic situation. Those with wounds hoped that in the morning they could reach, with the help of others, some Red Cross station if one still existed.

I sat down, leaned against Nadja, and closed my eyes, trying to shut the confusion out of my mind. Nadja held Christine and we prayed Mama would come back to us.

Just as the sun rose to compete with the fiery flames of the city, Mama returned with Ortwin. Confused by the noise and fire he had run to the inner city. After looking and calling for him everywhere Mama found him huddled in the ruins of our store. She seemed to know he might be there. From that day on I had a deeper appreciation for Mama and the heavy burden she carried.

"Lie down everyone and try to rest," Mama ordered. She collapsed on the floor with us but Ortwin could not sleep. He stared straight ahead, unaware of the rest of us. Mama took him in her arms and gave him some of her famous valerian extract drops and after a while he fell asleep.

Christine started to cry. Mama got a bottle of milk out of the carriage and held Christine while she nursed. After quieting Christine, Mama lay down but was unable to sleep. Over the last several hours more people had come into the schoolhouse for the last several hours. The injured were taken into another room but brought back with only minor first aid treatment. There was no Red Cross to care for anyone.

As far as we could see, few buildings had escaped the bombs in the inner city. Although apartment buildings around the schoolhouse were still standing, there were no tenants to be seen. They all had their doors shut. Mama said she saw the church still standing, but the pastor's home was totally gone. The shelter next to the church was destroyed and no one had lived through the blast. Smoke still blackened the sky as flames belched upward. Occasionally we heard explosions indicating bursting gas lines or maybe time bombs.

We feared the bombers would come again and the schoolhouse would provide no shelter from another attack. We were lucky to be alive.

"We cannot go back. There is nothing there. We cannot stay here, there is no one to help us," Mama said.

I looked at Mama's tired face. "Let's go into the country, Mama."

She and Nadja nodded in agreement. With knapsacks strapped on our backs and blankets over our arms, we left the school, pushing Christine in the baby carriage. When people saw us move out they began to follow, not even asking questions. About 30 families walked behind us, most of them mothers with small children, a few grandparents, and some soldiers with ripped and dirty uniforms. Some were even slightly injured and some limped.

We walked out of the city, hoping the bombs would not fall again soon. At the edge of the city we walked along a street next to the Zeisigwald woods. A group our size could be easily spotted by dive bombers and if another air raid came our way, the woods would provide quick cover. The street was fairly level for about three miles, but then we walked uphill and into the woods. This was a tough climb for small children so we stopped briefly to rest.

Everyone was uneasy. We knew the bombers could return at any time. We had seen many very large bombs lying in the street and nearby trees unexploded. The March snow was deeper outside the city and our feet were very cold. Some of the children did not have enough warm clothing, their shoes had already been eaten up by the slush on the roads. In those war time days, the quality of shoes was unbelievably poor. No one complained, except the children who cried. Their short legs stumbled often as they tried to keep up with the adults holding their hands.

After three more miles we came to the Zeisigwaldschenke restaurant in the forest. In peacetime it had been open to tourists and hikers. Even though it was closed we were sure people were inside. We knocked, but no one answered. We heard footsteps inside and a door slammed. Crying children and knocking on doors and windows brought no response. We sat huddled around the steps of the restaurant for more than an hour. Realizing there was no solution here, Mama stood up and said, "Let's go to Euba."

Children started to cry again. The men in our group stood around in a daze, offering neither help nor ideas. Mama felt a sudden anger toward them. "You men, pick up some of these children without shoes and carry them!"

They picked the smallest children with no shoes and followed us. Nadja, carrying Claus, and Mama, pulling the baby carriage, were walking ahead. The rest of us followed. At last we were moving toward a possible source of food and shelter. At the edge of the woods we walked into open fields with about three inches of snow. It was now daylight and no snow was falling as we trudged wearily on. The soles of my shoes were separating from the upper part, making it difficult to walk. I guess everybody lost a great deal that day.

People in the village saw us coming. We must have looked like a bunch of invalids. When we reached the main street of the village, some were so exhausted they sank to the ground, unable to go on. There was one compassionate man, I assumed he must have been the mayor of this little town, who ordered the farmers to bring several bails of straw and spread it in a thick layer on the schoolhouse floor while we waited in the village pub for something to eat. A big kettle of soup was soon set on the table. Hungry, we lined up to get a portion.

The first person served took one swallow, gagged and spit it on the floor, crying "Salt! It's just salty water, ugh!"

No one else would take any. Children started to cry for food, not understanding the heavily salted liquid could not be consumed.

Those who had brought the salty water had left the room quickly.

"They resent people from the city even now," Mama said under her breath.

After awhile the man in charge came from the school house where they had delivered the straw for us. We told what happened and he got very upset. Angered by this unkind act, he shouted, "I want a big pot of chicory made for these people. You there, go and bring several loaves of bread. Bring a dozen loaves and quick!"

His voice had a ring of authority. They had resentment in their eyes but the people moved. That piece of bread and cup of chicory was our only and most welcome meal that day. While we slept on the straw-covered floor, plans were made for us by the village authorities.

After giving our names and former addresses we were assigned living quarters. Ours was a three-room apartment in the second story above a large horse barn on the state owned farm. There was always one government farm in almost every village. The barn containing our apartment was at the entrance of the village.

Euba was a typical Saxony village. Sturdy brick houses with dark blue slate roofs lined the street for about a mile and a half. Homes, nestled by gardens and fruit trees, were backed by barns and animal courtyards. Thick brick walls comprised the first story of the barn; the second story was of sturdy wood construction. Our two rooms were large and we had all the water we needed from a water faucet in the live in kitchen. Our wood-burning stove provided heat for cooking and hot water for bathing. We found an old zinc tub to use for a bathtub. In the evening we sat around a table that the boys had to repair (it needed the fourth leg), and played homemade games while Mama and Nadja repaired ripped clothes. We felt content to have a roof over our heads again. God had blessed us and we thanked Him for our new home.

However, we had mice, mice by the dozens! They came into our apartment at night as soon as we turned the lights out. Why wouldn't there be mice? We lived in a barn above piles of straw, root cellars and horses with strong odors. No wonder the caretaker of the horses was glad to move into the main house, left vacant when the farm manager went to war.

Mama kept our food covered tightly. Still the mice came, crawling over everything all night long. They snooped their way over our floors and slithered up into the cupboards. Mice crawled over our beds as we slept. We kept pieces of wood alongside our beds to drive them away and became accustomed to hearing thumping of wood on the floor at night. I awoke one night screaming when one ran into my hair and became tangled. Nadja caught and killed it.

We scrubbed and cleaned but could not eliminate the strong odor of the horses. Mama begged the village administration to give us different quarters.

"I have too many children to fight those mice!"

"Families who lived there before did not complain. You have no right to complain, there are many bombed out people and refugees here who would be more than happy to get your quarters," shouted the administrator. "There is nothing else available."

"We have to accept and fight those dirty mice the best way we can," Mama said. "Lets keep the light on at night. Maybe that will help." Of course we still had to cover the windows with black paper, which was available at the farm office.

Five French prisoners of war lived below us in quarters near the horses. They helped with the farm work.

During the months that followed we learned how little we were wanted in Euba. Those villagers expressing resentment about our leaving Chemnitz did not know that we were just the beginning of a flood of refugees yet to come. There were some friendly folks who helped us establish some kind of a home. Their friendly words made our life bearable.

Mama's child allowance never came, the German mothers lost that when everything was in turmoil. The Army did not send Papa's salary and we had to make do with what we had brought with us. Just about everything was hard to find now.

We all worried about Grandma and Grandpa and wondered if the fire had spread to their home. When the snow was almost gone, Mama asked Ortwin and Hartmut and me to go into Chemnitz to see our grandparents.

"If their home hasn't burned and they are alive they must be very hungry. Bring them back if you can. Ask Grandpa for some nails so you can fasten our address to a post. Papa must know where to find us."

"But look at my shoes Mama," I protested. "The soles have come off and I'll be bare footed."

She went to a box and returned with two strips of heavy fabric. With this she wrapped and tied the soles to each shoe.

With a small bag of potatoes, some onions, and a bag full of rutabagas, we started on our journey. Since the ground was still frozen we walked through the fields to shorten our trip. As we approached the woods we came to trenches the soldiers had dug in the fields.

"They must be moving the front line back toward us," I said.

"The Russians must be pushing through."

"Look!" Ortwin shouted, "There is a *blindgaenger* (bomb). It hasn't exploded. There is another one!"

"Don't touch it!" I warned. "It might explode."

We trudged on toward Chemnitz, carefully avoiding other unexploded bombs lying in the fields. We stayed close to each other, watching the ground for other deadly surprises.

"I feel as if we are between the lines, Ortwin! See those trenches. That means the Russians are coming from the other side."

"We'd better hurry." he yelled as we broke into a run.

"Wait!" I called, "Listen!" We were breathing so hard it took a moment to hear them. Great rumbling noises could be heard in the distance.

"That's gunfire, big guns!" we said.

"I can hear planes," Ortwin called out. "Run for your life!"

Suddenly the planes were almost overhead, big bombers, and very low. I could read the numbers and symbols on them. We could not make it to the woods in time.

"Bombs!" Hartmut yelled. "They're going to hit us!"

There was no hole to jump into. We fell to the ground, pressing our bodies against the earth. A deafening blast shook the ground as fountains of soil exploded around us. The smell of gunpowder was strong. Then it was all over, the planes were gone. "Ortwin, are you alright? Where is Hartmut?"

"I'm okay," they both said in one voice.

We stood up and brushed the dirt off ourselves. Two huge holes in the earth showed how close we had been to death. I was shaking all over.

"Ortwin, you look white!"

"You do too," he said. "Look at Hartmut."

"That was close. Should we go on or turn back?" I felt weak and doubted whether we should go any farther.

"Those bombs are leftovers from an air raid they just did," Hartmut said. "And now they have dropped them into the woods before going back to England. We'd better go on and see how Grandma and Grandpa are doing." Hartmut was the courageous one.

The rutabagas had rolled out of my bag so we gathered them quickly and were on our way. As we hurried through the woods the thunderous rumble of guns grew louder. The ground was covered with pine needles and litter. The litter was paper leaflets. I picked one up and smoothed it out:

GIVE UP! SURRENDER!

We laughed and decided those messages were for soldiers hiding in the woods. We had been ready to surrender a long time ago.

The rest of our journey was uneventful. The church was still standing and across the street, a half block of buildings were in fairly good shape. Grandma Thekla lived in one of them. She was overjoyed to see us but worried about our long trip. Grandpa helped us take off our coats. His eyes were bright with excitement. He inspected our shoes.

"I'll fix them for you." He took them and left the room.

"Grandma, we have water in our new home and we don't have to carry it." I continued. "Our home is warm, too."

"We're glad you made the trip safely, child. We have artillery shells now in addition to bombs. The artillery shells come with no warning." Grandma's voice was tense. She looked so worn and famished. "Those shells bring instant death and horrible mutilation. There are no sirens now, nothing to warn us of air raids."

She discouraged us about going back to our old home but we wanted to post a sign so Papa could find us.

"We have some furniture that we can get along without but you will need a wagon to haul it," Grandma said.

"We'll borrow a wagon and come back." Then I added, "Mama wants you both to come home with us. You will be much safer in Euba."

"The war will be over soon. It's only a matter of weeks now." Grandma said. "We are better off here in our own home."

"But Mama worries about you two," I persisted.

"Your Mama has enough to worry about without us." Grandma sounded final. "We are very glad for the food, especially the onions." She right away put a pot of potatoes on her kerosine burner as there was no other power in the city.

Grandpa fixed my shoes with a strong cord. "This will last you for a while," he said, handing me the shoes. Now I could walk without flipping my foot backward to keep the loose sole from bending under my foot.

We found one of the high walls still standing at our former home. Each floor had broken off and fallen. All the buildings around were destroyed to rubble.

"Look!" I shouted. "There are two large paintings still hanging on the wall of our living room." They were blackened by smoke and hanging crooked, but they had defied the war by remaining intact.

People were looking around in the ruins in spite of passersby's warning about unexploded bombs. Paper signs with messages telling of new locations of families were posted here and there. We added our sign to let Papa know where we had gone.

"We'd better go home n--" Hartmut's words were drowned out by the fiery explosion of an artillery shell a half block away. Another explosion followed, closer this time. The rush of air felt like a great weight on my body. The loud metallic noise of artillery fire was much different than the explosions of bombs. We ran for our lives, without thought of anything but escaping. It was already dark when we arrived home.

"The artillery shells leave huge holes in buildings, Mama," I explained. "They come without any warning. It is not safe to go in there anymore and yet I know we need the furniture Grandma can spare."

"If we get that furniture, we'd better go before things get worse," Ortwin said. "Nadja, would you go with us?"

"Oh ja, I help," she smiled willingly.

Ortwin left to borrow a large wagon from the Klainsteuber family. Early the next morning we were on our way. As soon as we started we realized that with the wagon we made a larger target for dive bombers. We took turns pulling and pushing the wagon, our eyes constantly on the sky watching for planes. About half way to Chemnitz we heard the dive bombers. We jumped into a ditch and let go of the wagon. It rolled down a little hill and the bombers shot at the moving cart. Luckily they missed.

Near our destination we began to see the effects of the shells from the big guns. Large gaping holes, some covered with cardboard, opened into the rooms of those buildings that were not yet destroyed by bombs. Few people were around and those we saw looked like living shadows with dark hollow eyes. As they rushed by us, Ortwin said, "They look like robots."

Artillery shells came swishing over our head. Then came a terrible blast. The shells were so near they seemed as if they were meant for us. After a dark cloud of smoke cleared the explosion, we realized the people who had been sitting in a room only moments before had been destroyed.

I began to perspire. I could see the terror I felt reflected in the eyes of my brothers. Pulling the wagon we ran as fast as we could. Once we reached Grandpa's house there was little time for visiting. Grandpa tied a small closet, a sofa, a chest of drawers, and some chairs onto the wagon. The wagon was fairly large, but now looked small under the heavy load. Nadja and I pulled and the boys pushed. Downhill was easy, since all we did was steer. We did fine along the road by the streetcar tracks but any upwards incline strained our arms and legs to the point of intense pain.

An old man wearing a white arm band called, "Move it along fast. They're about to close the main roads. They're going to block them with streetcars."

Ortwin looked at me and said, "They think they can stop the tanks from coming through."

"No talking," Nadja urged. "Hurry, hurry!"

We struggled to keep our load balanced and moved with total disregard for either planes or artillery shells. No problems developed until we pulled our ungainly load next to the woods. A wheel came off! That old wagon had seen better days. The people who had loaned it to us doubted that we could pull much of a load on it. Darkness came and our efforts seemed futile. Others on the road kept moving past us. Some would stop and lie down in the woods to rest. With bundles of belongings hung over their backs or some with nothing at all, soldiers in ragged uniforms, women, children, and teenagers without parents, all looked exhausted. When we asked where they came from, they said from far east. Even their dialect sounded different than ours. They wanted to be done with the war and their destination was West Germany. Although Germany had yet to be divided, the population sensed already what was going to happen.

"Ortwin, Hartmut, help! Furniture off," Nadja commanded. "Get wheel on."

Nadja was strong and with our combined efforts we unloaded everything. Nadja put the wheel on and fixed it with the help of two soldiers, as best as they could. We were glad for the cover of darkness when the planes again flew overhead.

Reloading the wagon was not easy but seeing the wheel in place gave us new strength. When we reached the last open field we wanted to stop and rest.

"No sleep," Nadja prodded. "Work first, then sleep. Come on! Come on!"

We obeyed, pushing our heavy load foot by foot toward Euba.

When we saw the dark outline of the big barn where we lived, we gave one last spurt of energy to deliver our load. Mama came down and asked two of the POW's to help carry the heavier pieces upstairs. While we didn't have many clothes to hang in the closet, the chairs and sofa gave us new comfort. The chest could have held all our extra things in one drawer.

School attendance was required in Euba. The boys went to elementary school in the village and I attended secondary school in Niederwiesa, a two mile walk from home. Everything seemed so temporary. We expected the war to end any day. Mama got word that Nadja must leave us. With Christine in one arm and holding Claus by the hand she went again to the authorities and after some heated arguments was granted another stay. Nadja now was required to work at the farm where we lived.

Mama hoped Papa would return soon. She prayed about him often. We received no news about Uncle Helmut and Aunt Martha, but we knew their electrical shop had been destroyed.

The days became warmer and the farmers started their spring work with some hesitation. The POWs worked in the fields along with the women, including Nadja. She became a close friend with one of the POWs named Poul.

When the air raid alerts sounded we took shelter in the root cellar under the barn. Here they stored vegetables and apples. During those long waits we ate some of the farm's vegetables.

We stuffed our blouses full of all kinds of vegetables that we saw laying in large piles. The taste of fruit was most welcome. At all other times the food storage areas were locked. Our diet consisted of rutabagas and potatoes. Nadja was allowed to bring Christine a half liter of milk each evening. This was more milk than we got in Chemnitz.

Ration cards were still given out but the amounts allowed were very small. Each person could buy one pound of bread, one tablespoon of preserves and some barley in each ten-day period. No meat, no other kind of food. Ration cards had many items printed on them that were not available in the stores. We often stood in line for many hours to get a pound of grits only to have them run out before our turn came. Survival remained the first priority for everyone.

We were a family of seven and knew we were better off living on a farm in a small village than in Chemnitz. People in the city did not even get that small amount as what we did. They were getting nothing and starved.

Typhoid was reported. Those people who came out of the city at nights to steal potatoes that had been buried in the ground and covered up with many layers of straw (which was a favored way to keep them over the winter) were beaten up mercilessly.

Nadja was paid in food for working on the farm. There was no money. Food was of course what everybody liked. Once after school in Niederwiesa, I went into a bakery, showed my coupons, and asked to buy a pound of bread. All the shelves were empty and there was no smell of baking. The baker stared at me as if he thought I had made a bad joke.

"I'll throw you out!" he shouted angrily. "We have no bread. Out! Out!"

I left the bakery realizing how frustrated and angry people had become. Our future looked very uncertain to me but Mama had complete faith that Papa would come back soon and the war would end any day.

Now that everyone knew that we were losing the war, Nazi officials in Niederwiesa and Chemnitz donned civilian clothing, thinking this would erase their Nazi identity. It did not. Many Nazis fled to the west, hoping the Americans would treat them better than the Russians. We kept wondering why the Americans did not move forward more quickly. The Russians were advancing and everything seemed confused.

The intensity of the war increased and refugees by the thousands came by foot and on horses, from the east to west. They came from Upper Silesia, Prussia, Sudetengau and the border country of

Czechoslovakia. They came from Estonia, Latvia, and Lithuania. Long wagon trains were seen for hours every day as they passed by. Thousands of German families and foreign refugees who had fought with the Germans, were now transported in box cars coming from Yugoslavia, Czechoslovakia, and Poland, and freight trains were full of people fleeing to the west. The remaining people that governed Germany wanted to distribute themselves equally in eastern and western Germany. Those assigned to eastern Germany packed up and moved toward the west with the others. No one wanted to stay where the Russians would come.

"You'd better run too," they warned Mama.

Her answer was always, "We must wait for Papa. He will never find us if we leave this area."

We were so naive about the political situation. We did not know the extent of the hideous crimes committed against the Jewish race and others.

Among the refugees was a family from Silesia who asked to sleep in the barn beneath our quarters as one of them was ill. The entire family was exhausted and their horses needed rest. Mama let them use our stove to cook soup and make tea. I helped them spread fresh straw on the barn floor for a bed. For this they gave us a pound of smoked bacon as they had a barrel of it on their wagon. What a delicious treat that was.

One day when walking home from school, I saw a man running from the field carrying a bloody horse head. After I recovered from the shock, I realized a horse had been shot by low flying planes. Meat! I ran home as fast as I could.

"Ortwin, Hartmut, MEAT! Mama, they shot a horse and everybody can butcher on it!"

We grabbed buckets, a pillowcase and knives and off we ran to the fields. A dozen people were there before us. As we crowded around the dead horse, struggling to get a chunk of meat, I realized the horse was still warm. The dive bombers came again but we were so intent on getting meat that we did not hear the planes until they were upon us. They fired a few very close rounds, then gave up and left.

In triumph, we carried home our meat. Every bone of that horse was taken and it helped vary our diet of potatoes and rutabagas.

By late April all farm work during daylight hours was abandoned due to artillery shells and the relentless dive bombers. Work was done at night in the darkness and I remember Nadja saying the moon came out very romantically. Poul was working nights too. The dive bombers did not shoot into refugee lines unless they suspected soldiers were among them.

The little village of Euba was overrun by thousands of people fleeing west. At times they were detoured to Floeha, where schoolhouses gave them shelter for the night. There they also got something hot to eat but it was closely guarded so that people from the city would not get food. I always thought that was very cruel. Meanwhile, refugees hid their own supplies in their wagons. They ate the food so desperately needed by those starving in the city. I saw sacks of flour and barrels that smelled like cured meat, but those refugees made their way unmolested to the west. They told us stories of babies who had died on the way because of the cold and because there was no time to stop and rest. When overtaken by Russian fighting troops they were shot at and had to run away.

The rumor went out that any German carrying a weapon would be killed immediately. Fleeing soldiers, now numbering in the hundreds each day, threw their weapons in a large pond near the farm and kept heading west. They hoped to become prisoners of the Americans or even to be free right away. The soldiers came alone or in small groups, crossing the fields at night. Some slipped quietly into the barn below us to sleep a few hours and exchange a few whispered words. When dawn broke they were gone as silently as they had come. The soldiers uniforms were battle worn and ripped, their faces darkened and scarred. Some had dirty bandages around their heads, around their arms or feet.

"Mama, their eyes--they look so terrified. They must have seen horrible times at the front. They must be very hungry."

"Yes, Irene. Let's take that big kettle we use in the washhouse for boiling clothes and make some chicory for them."

The washhouse was across the street in a building that belonged to the farm. We made chicory and even though it had to be diluted to little more than dark water, it was hot and they thanked us warmly for it.

"If we help them, maybe someone will be kind to Papa." Mama's faith in Papa's return was unshaken.

Although Mama frequently heard the urgent words of, "Run away, Frau! Don't wait until the Russians come!" she was never convinced by either the fleeing refugees or the soldiers that we should join the westward trek. Village authorities warned all the people in Euba that if east German citizens go to the west, they will all be sent back. The west only accepts people from the territory that Germany had to give up to border countries.

Each night we hoped Papa would be among the soldiers who came so silently through the fields.

Euba was now between the front lines. While the dive bombers could not shoot through the thick double brick walls of the barn, they did shoot through windows and hit the opposite wall while we were eating. Our dishes jumped and rattled but no one was hurt. We looked at each other in disbelief. I ran into the hall, crouched down on the floor and screamed. Ortwin came and tightly held my shoulders. We were both shaking.

On another day, I was outside when it seemed the dive bombers came from all directions. I sat with my fists clenched, screaming. Poul picked me up and carried me upstairs. Mama gave me a sedative made from an herb that grew in the woods, her Valeriana leaves. It also can now be bought in stores as tincture Valeriana, a mild Herb. It soothed my nerves and the cramps in my body stopped.

The frequency of the air attacks began to affect me but not so with Mama and Nadja. They had nerves of steel and remained outwardly calm. Mama encouraged us to endure each day as it came. She was our rock during the worst time of our lives. She repeated often, "The war will be over any day now."

We began seeing strangers in the village who spoke perfect German and asked many questions. They were easy to identify by their polished brown boots, well-fitted civilian clothes and well-nourished appearance. Judging by the kinds of questions they asked, they must have been intelligence officers. We had been told by Nazi propaganda that such people would kill, steal and rape but they did not. We saw them sitting outside the only village pub which was now closed. During this time it was dangerous even to walk in the middle of the main street, but there they sat and we teenagers, as curious as we were, made contact with them.

They spoke perfect German and even made some jokes. When they offered us chewing gum they also asked questions. We knew that they were searching for information. But there was nothing to tell. When asked if we knew any soldiers our answers were always, "No, all the soldiers have gone to the west." We did show them the pond into which all the guns had been thrown.

A refugee family with eight daughters, fleeing from Latvia, stopped in Euba and was assigned living quarters. Later I realized they were a group of people bound together temporarily to be able to leave Latvia. Those Latvians were fun-loving people. They invited the intelligence officers to their quarters and I was asked to come and play my accordion during the evening. On other times in the evenings, the Latvian girls sat on their porch and sang German folk songs while I played. Neighbors came and joined in or just listened. People seemed starved to hear some music and sing together. We did not have a radio anymore that would play.

When I mingled with these people, I realized how shabby my clothes had become compared to the pretty dresses worn by the refugee girls. Of course they were able to bring things with them. We had lost everything in the fire. There was absolutely no clothing of any kind for sale in the remaining stores.

The mayor decided to take the only existing, broken down truck Euba had and try to drive to a uniform factory in Chemnitz. This was the only hope that we had to get something warm to wear. All of the bombed out people were beginning to suffer from not having any clothes. He asked a few of us from Chemnitz along, since we were familiar with the location of the factory.

On our way into the city we were the target of the dive bombers. To escape being shot, the driver swerved in a wild zigzag pattern while we hung tightly to the sides of the open bed truck to keep from being thrown out. Just as we got to the factory someone yelled, "Raus! Stukas! (Duck! Skydivers!) They were upon us again, shooting at everything. Lying near the wall on the ground, I saw one plane come so low I could see the gunner. I didn't think he would make it up again but they were highly skilled pilots.

The factory was abandoned of any form of authority. Other people were already there squabbling over the clothes. We were actually fighting over those hated SS uniforms. Quickly we loaded bales of clothing into the truck. The mayor and his driver helped fend off other grasping people who cursed us as we carried large boxes to the truck. We were able to get all kinds of apparel: pants, shirts, coats, boots, gloves, underwear, and caps, the ones that cover the entire head. Oh, how I needed some new shoes. Perhaps some boots would fit me.

We heard the big guns again, and very near. I feared the big guns more than the bombs. The swishing sound and the air pressure when they came overhead made everybody extremely nervous.

As soon as our truck started to move out we were attacked again. We ran alongside the truck for a while, then dropped back to escape the flying bullets. The driver got shot but was still able to drive. Ortwin stumbled on the rubble and fell. The truck stopped and waited for us. The mayor slid the wounded driver aside and took the wheel.

We picked Ortwin up and jumped onto the truck. His knees were bleeding profusely. Other people with their hand-wagons and other primitive vehicles were all around us and every time a plane dived for us they quickly crawled underneath their wagons.

"You'll have to wait for help until we get home," yelled the mayor as he drove rapidly out of Chemnitz. Once the truck reached the countryside, we had to hold on tightly as the mayor zigzagged to avoid another dive plane. We bounced about among the bales of clothing, holding on for our lives.

People in Euba welcomed us eagerly. Everyone needed clothing, especially the bombed out families. They clustered around the truck hoping for something to wear.

I was given more than one whole outfit, black coats, and felt-boots, enough clothing for everyone in our family. Mama, Nadja and I now wore men's long john underwear, but they kept us warm. Mama said she would cut something small and sew it for Claus. The felt boots I received were heavy and quite large for my feet. From that time on, I wore the black uniform with no military markings, shirts and everything else. It was nice to have clean clothes again, even though it was ill-fitting.

Rumors increased that the war would be over in a few days. We watched the village bulletin board daily for new announcements.

Finally we learned that the Americans were at the city limits of Chemnitz.

Then we learned that the Allies had signed an agreement in Yalta and the Americans would not occupy Saxony. Saxony would belong to the Russians.

The Americans had come and gone overnight. The intelligence officers left with them.

I wanted immediate "democracy." I already knew quite a bit about it and knowing we would belong to the Russians left me with a sense of uncertainty about our future.

I felt that Stalin would be no better than Hitler.

World War II was over, but my family's battle to survive was just begun.

Book II

Behind the Iron Curtain My Years Hidden As a Boy

Book II

Behind the Iron Curtain

My Years Hiding As a Boy

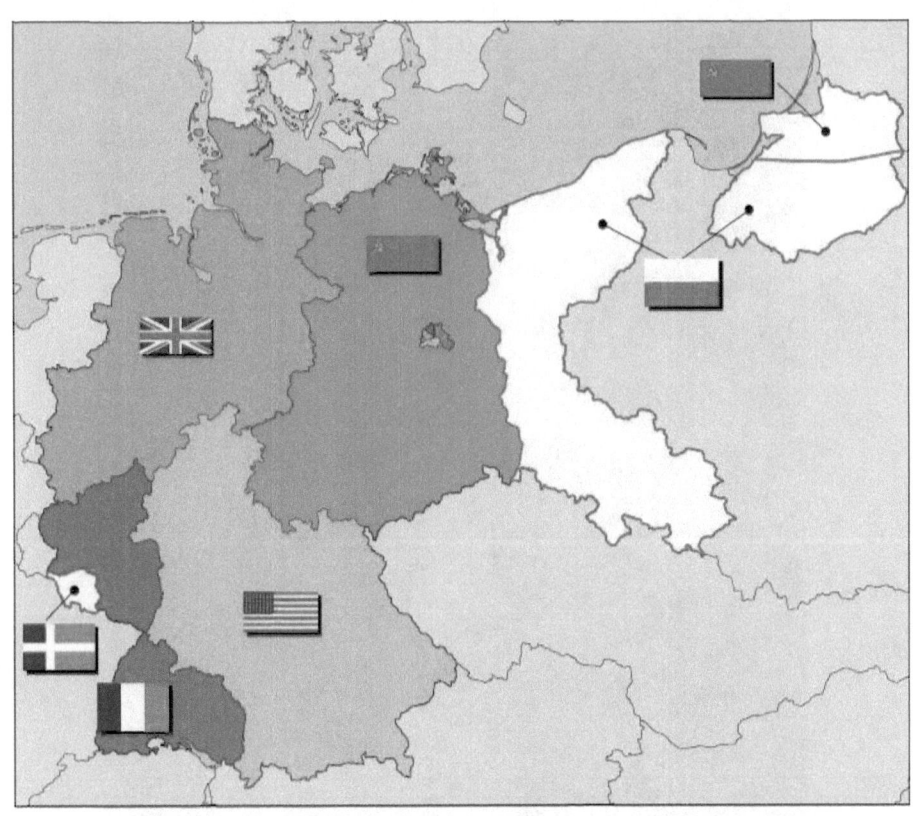

Germany after WWII, divided into occupation zones and having to surrender territory to Poland and the Soviet Union

Irene at age 6 holding a *zuckertuete*, a colorful cardboard cone filled with candies, cookies and school supplies, a gift for the first day of school.

Opera House in Chemnitz

Intersection at Johannisplatz, Chemnitz

Trolley cars in Johannisplatz, Chemnitz

Downtown Chemnitz from the air.

Broueckenstrasse Market in Chemnitz

Stair stepped Schocken's building in Chemnitz

Jewish family forced to wear stars

A 1930's Dreirad

Dresden before the war and after

AFTERMATH
1945 - 1947

The war was over! On May 6, 1945, I joined other youths in the village to celebrate. We laughed and talked about being able to walk around without watching for dive bombers. I sat in the middle of the street and shouted, "Nothing can happen to me now. The war is over!" We heard that many high ranking Nazis, including Hitler and the Goebbels family, had killed themselves. We knew they got what they deserved.

The five French POWs were taken away in a truck. Nadja wanted to go to France with Paul but was not allowed to do so. Paul told her he would come back for her. I did not realize how much they cared for one another until I saw them standing in a long embrace. Paul walked toward the truck only when ordered to do so by an officer. Nadja stood with tears streaming down her face, helpless and sad.

"Come back! Come back!" she cried as they drove away waving their tricolored flag. We could still hear their singing even after they were out of sight. We never saw them again.

As peace was declared, Russian tanks rolled through Euba. We were warned on the village blackboard to stay inside for fear of being shot. During the night the Russians came. Hour after hour we listened to the squeaky rumbling of massive tanks vibrating our building. We stayed in bed, too afraid to even peer out of the darkened windows. We knew Germany was to be divided into four parts. The Americans got the south; the English the northwest; the French a part of the west;

and the Russians the east. We knew the city of Berlin was also divided into four parts.

Since we were so hungry, we said among ourselves, "Russia is closer. They can bring in supplies much faster than the Americans. The Russian zone will do alright." We had been told for years that Russian farmers had fertile land and worked as hard as the German farmers. Once Papa had come back from the Russian front, he said, "Their farmland has beautiful black soil. When the war is over it will be the breadbasket of Europe." No one told us then that the Russians were starving. They were not able to feed themselves. They did not send us food, rather they took what little we had. People were confused and we knew more hard times were ahead.

When Stalin heard that so many people in Germany wanted democracy instead of communism he said, "What, they don't want to be communists?" He laughed. "We'll starve them and they will come crawling to us!"

Statements like this and other rumors began to make the rounds. No one knew what was ahead for Germany's defeated people. The feeling of uncertainty about our future was most evident in the constant stream of refugees still fleeing westward. It was called *Fluechtlingstreck* (Covered Wagon Trek). We could see them in the distance, the steady slow procession of people from early morning until late at night. The refugees often walked beside their horses, seeming to talk to them as both man and beast strained to keep going.

We were told by the refugees coming through that we could take a document, which listed all our lost belongings and our destroyed store, to West Germany where we would be compensated. East

Germany would not make any restitutions and people had to be quiet about what they had lost in the war.

Borders between the zones were established and guards were assigned to patrol them. A Russian commandant patrolled our streets. With a large dog trotting beside him, he strutted around our village acting like a king. The commandant then acquired a motorcycle and ripped the air with its accelerating motor. He also imposed an 8 p.m. curfew.

We requested and received from the State Farm a very small garden plot. It was late May and we looked forward to some fresh garden vegetables. We also planted a small patch of tobacco which we hoped to sell. The farm administrator gave us rutabagas, sugar beets and potatoes from their storage in exchange for working in the fields. We cooked and stirred diced sugar beets for hours to make a tangy black syrup (molasses). Nadja worked on the farm for her *deputat* (food-for-work-wage). She would often slip something by for little Christine. Records were kept of the hours Ortwin and I worked. We were to be paid at harvest time.

All the *deputat* portions were measured according to the size of the family and were very tight.

Early each morning Nadja and Mama picked leaves from the stinging nettles that grew along the edges of the fields. When picked early, these slender leaves were fresh and tender. If picked late in the day, they were tough. Mama made nettle soup that tasted like spinach but quieted our stomachs for a while. There were many days we had nothing at all to eat.

The farmers hired guards to keep people from stealing food from their farms. Armed with horsewhips and clubs, men hired by the farmers rode bicycles around the fields or lay half concealed in the bushes guarding the fields 24 hours a day. They seemed to know we were picking leaves from the nettles and did not stop us, but they watched us constantly. I remember a big sign at the corner of a farm, saying: "Thieves will be prosecuted."

People in the city suffered most. Only a few came to get something from the fields. If they were successful they ran for their lives back into the city. The field guards were masters with the whip.

Although we continued to receive ration cards, our stores had nothing to sell. Euba's general store sometimes sold grits and people ran to get in line, but it was never enough for everybody. We could however usually get vinegar and salt. Empty store shelves were filled with advertisements of things available before the war. The few stores in Chemnitz, not destroyed by bombs, were empty and the owners simply closed their doors.

There were some who had food enough, mainly the farmers and the Russians who came to govern us. The Russians assigned to our village stayed in a villa up in the woods. A large red star on their roof was lit by spotlights during the night. They had their own parties, drinking vodka in large amounts, and playing their music as loud as possible. Since the Russians also had their food rationed, they were always looking around the village for something extra to eat. While doing this they found out where women lived, then returned at night, abducted them and took them to their villa.

"Frau, komm" (Woman, come) and *"Wo ist Frau?"* (Where is woman) were calls repeated over and over by Russians prowling our village streets until small children took up the sayings, not knowing the serious intent of our occupying intruders.

One night, after curfew, Nadja and I slipped through the darkness up to the Russian villa. We were very hungry and thought this might be a place to get some food. We stayed in the shadows of a picket fence and some bushes where the searchlights would not fall on us. Our hunger was greater than our fear of what the consequences would be if we were caught.

Several soldiers were cooking in a large pot out in the open. We could smell the meat. "Borscht" Nadja whispered. When they dumped a lot of vegetables into the pot my stomach cramped with hunger. They were singing and talking loudly as they drank their vodka and sang "Kathusha" and "Nabasitzia Djewuschka" over and over and over.

Finally they talked about finding women. After eating huge bowls of borscht, four men left to go into the village.

"After they eat, they sleep," Nadja whispered.

We waited. Some of the men went inside and apparently went to sleep. We waited and all was quiet.

To our astonishment three of the four soldiers came back with women. They were the wives and daughters of the farmers, not the starving refugee women. These were the women who gave us that salt soup when we first came to Euba. These women had refused to give us even one potato when we were hungry and without a home. Usually these women hid in their barns but the soldiers apparently knew this and had persuaded them with their guns.

"Let us go!" shouted a stoutly built woman. "You will be punished for this."

A soldier bellowed back at her in Russian. She said nothing more. One woman was slapped when she bit a soldier as he tried to put his arms around her. The three women huddled together and the guns kept them constrained.

"They wait for commandant," Nadja whispered. We waited. The commandant did not come. The soldiers divided the women and gestured to them that they would let them go after awhile. The man they called "Stachina" forced one of the woman into the house.

When they offered the two remaining women food, the women spit on it. If they had been one of the hungry people, they would have eaten it. The men drank and danced and laughed. They were like children. One by one each Russian grabbed one of the women and forced her into the house. When they protested they were slapped into a whimpering silence. I could feel no pity for them when they screamed and cried out. I could not forget that these were the women who had denied very small children even one bite of food when we came from Chemnitz.

"It soon be over. Wait more, they sleep," Nadja's voice was low. "We'll take food."

We heard the men fighting over one of the women. It must have been another hour before we were sure the men were sound asleep.

"Now!" Nadja whispered as she climbed out of the bushes and over the fence into the garden. I followed. Slowly, quietly, we crept toward the house. The kettle outside still had some warm borscht in it.

We poured it into a pitcher we had brought, then crept into their kitchen. We took some big pieces of commisbread. I saw a box I could carry and took it, not daring to risk the noise of opening it.

A man cursed and we knew a soldier was awake. We held our breath in fear, then it was quiet and we heard snoring. He must have been dreaming.

We knew the women were awake. One of them tried to cry out but her cry was muffled, probably by a Russian's hand. We doubted that the women could get away. Perhaps they thought we were their husbands coming quietly to rescue them. Carefully we picked our way out of the kitchen, through the moonlit yard and into the safety of darkness.

"Thank heaven their commandant did not return," I whispered. "I can breathe much easier out here in the dark."

"Yap," Nadja said taking my arm. "Hurry home."

When we arrived home with our food, everybody got out of bed. We sat down and ate bread and borscht. It was the first meal we had eaten in two days except for one rutabaga. The box I had taken was full of Knorr's Instant Soup mix.

"My guess is they stole it from the factory warehouse just outside of Dresden," Ortwin said.

This was the first of a few more dangerous trips to their villa. Our trips were not always successful but when our hunger was great we were able to take some food from their kitchen. We always took reasonable amounts to avoid suspicion.

The Russian soldiers' constant search for women was greatly feared by the women in Euba. When the women learned they could not be protected within their homes they left their children and slipped away to sleep in the trenches dug by German soldiers. The trenches were deep and fairly dry. Some trenches had small wooden sheds with straw floors which provided cold but fairly comfortable places to hide. German men were afraid to protect their women from these assaults since they were not allowed to have weapons.

Refugees assigned to settle in Euba and in surrounding towns were offended by the Russians who grabbed their daughters and wives. They soon packed up and moved on to the Western zone.

German families gave many things to the Russian soldiers in hopes that they would not be molested. When they returned to Russia they took many of these things with them. We learned of one Russian colonel who took an entire boxcar of furniture, but it was all confiscated by the Russian government.

Russia had few of the then-modern things we used in Germany and the Russians wanted everything. Stalin did not like his soldiers coming back to Russia talking about the nice things they had seen in Germany. Watches and jewelry became "hot" items with the Russian soldiers. They suspected every German was hiding a watch somewhere. Grandpa Michael told us of a Russian taking an alarm clock to a jeweler and demanding that he make him two wristwatches from the parts of the alarm clock.

One day Ortwin came home riding a new bicycle.

"Mama," he bent over in laughter. "A Russian traded me his new bike for my old one. He thought my old bike would be easier to ride. He didn't know it was his lack of skill that kept him from riding his new bike."

Ortwin was elated since his old bike was pieced together from parts of bikes found in the rubble.

July and August brought a welcome harvest from our garden. Fresh cooked beet greens, onions, and tomatoes were followed by kohirabi and tiny new potatoes. These foods were delicious additions to our table. Summer passed and the fall of 1945 brought an order we found hard to accept. All Ukrainians were to be gathered up and returned to Russia. This would include Nadja. Some Ukrainians became frightened about their future and ran to West Germany. We learned later that they were put in camps for displaced persons. A few lucky ones made it to Canada but the majority of them were sent back to Russia, because of the Yalta agreement between Russia and the Allies.

For a few weeks we hid Nadja in an abandoned hut in the woods. One morning when I went up to take her some food, she was gone. Grief stricken, we thought we would never see her again.

A few weeks later Nadja returned, driving up to our barn with a horse and wagon.

Surprised and pleased, I ran to her shouting, "Mama! Ortwin! Here is Nadja, she's come home!"

Joyous to see her, we had many questions. "Where did you come from? Why the horse and wagon? We'll never let you go again!"

"I promise take horse and wagon back. We stay in villa, near Planitz Strasse. Many Ukrainian women there. We go back to Russia." Our joy was brief. We learned she could not stay with us. She had promised to return and they knew where she was.

"I'm going to come and see you Nadja," I promised. Her smile beamed with her love for us.

When she left she warned, "You come. Wait outside. They no see you. Like we go Russian Villa." She pointed toward the place we had taken food from the Russians.

With this arrangement I made several trips to see Nadja. A large garden with many shrubs and chestnut trees surrounded the villa. I found it easy to hang around outside, hiding until Nadja would see me and signal for me to come closer. On one visit I found Nadja's eyes red and swollen from crying. All the women were to be sent to Siberia rather than to their previous homes in Poltawa. "Stalin has given orders...." I dissolved into a flood of tears on her shoulder. Losing this dear friend was not going to be easy. My sadness was so great I was unable to give her the comfort she needed.

During other trips to see her, she was allowed to leave the villa for brief periods. We usually walked about and talked. Late one evening, while waiting to see Nadja, I watched some Russians drag a cow they had stolen and killed into a small clearing to butcher it. Nadja signaled for me to wait. While they were carrying some of the meat inside, Nadja and I rushed to the freshly butchered carcass. I carried a whole liver and she gave me another heavy piece of meat. Nadja carried other pieces. Hidden by darkness we ran across the fields, carrying our stolen prize all the way to Euba.

Mama was happy to see the meat but shocked to see our bloody clothes. She embraced Nadja. "We will miss you, Nadja. I'm going to awaken the boys so they can see you, but not before you take off those bloody clothes. You girls would never have gotten all that meat here in the daylight. Look at yourselves. Oh."

Nadja stayed with us that night so Mama could wash and dry her clothes. Nadja's clothes were very ragged. Early the next morning, at Mama's suggestion, we took a piece of our pirated meat and set out for Niederwiesa. We planned to trade the meat for a dress for Nadja. On the main street of Niederwiesa we knocked on the doors of homes where people had not been bombed and asked if they were willing to trade a dress for meat. We soon found a family with a daughter Nadja's size. Nadja could choose among three dresses. She decided on a colorful pretty summer dress and both parties were jubilant over the exchange. That morning Nadja and I parted to go our separate ways with the warmest feelings of friendship. One day I returned to the villa and found the building empty. A Russian soldier was sweeping the steps in front. I approached and said, "Where Frauleins?"

"Frauleins all go home to Russia." He smiled at me. I backed up as if struck. His blunt statement felt like a blow. His expression turned serious as he watched me. I turned and walked away. Tears blurred my vision and I stumbled against the gate. After a few moments I started my slow, heavy-hearted journey home.

I felt so sad as I climbed the stairs to tell Mama the agonizing news. We all mourned Nadja's absence and like so many of our other friends, we never heard of her again. After Nadja was taken away, we were moved into a two-room apartment on the second floor of a small white building which belonged to the farm. We shared a bathroom with another family. Our garden plot was located behind this house, and best of all, we moved away from the mice.

Ortwin and I worked in the fields after school hours and received a cup and a half of milk each day for Christine. Other than our garden produce, potatoes, sugar beets and rutabagas in small quantities, continued to be our diet. Now and then we managed to get an egg. Before time to go to school, Ortwin would lie down outside the chicken coop and watch the hens through a small hole. If an egg was laid, he pushed himself through the opening and took it. He would break it and drink it raw. When he found two eggs he brought one to Mama. When we helped harvest the corn to make winter feed for the swine I husked an ear of corn and ate it raw. It was fresh and sweet. I liked it.

"Pig! Pig!" shouted the farm workers. I turned to see them pointing at me and laughing. "Irene eats food for pigs!"

I called them "dumb cows" because they did not know what they were missing. I liked the sweet taste of fresh corn and took some ears home with me. Mama would have none of it, saying, "It's pig feed, Irene." She dismissed the idea promptly.

Nevertheless, all during the harvest I ate fresh raw corn and I had no ill effects from it.

With Nadja gone, I never dared to take food again from the Russian villa. I most certainly would be caught had I gone up there alone or with my brothers. We just had to think of another way to feed ourselves. One day Mama said, "Irene, with your slight build you look more like a boy than a girl in those black SS trousers and your felt boots."

I laughed. "Maybe I should get a man's haircut."

"Not a man's cut, but with a shorter cut and that cap pulled down, you'd look more like a 14-year-old boy than a 16-year-old girl."

"I'd feel a lot safer from the Russian soldiers if they thought I was a boy."

Thus I assumed the disguise of a boy. Mama cut my hair shorter and I kept part of it hanging over my forehead. The poorly fitted black pants and shirt, along with the oversized boots, made it possible for me to look many a Russian in the eye and be mistaken for a boy. I often made it a point to have a runny nose to further my disguise. This pretense as a boy was to serve me well for a few years.

One night a Russian patrol on horseback came into the area where we lived. One of them knocked on the door. We opened the door and saw a big soldier smiling at us. He grabbed Mama. I thought my heart would stop beating. We knew immediately what would happen to Mama. We screamed as loud as we could. Mama screamed too. Ortwin and Hartmut kicked him. With all the people living in that building, we thought someone would come to our aid, but they shut their doors tight and kept quiet.

By now five soldiers were standing in the open doorway. We raised so much commotion that their horses tied to the picket fence outside became frightened and bolted, pulling up a portion of the fence. Their horses ran wildly down the street.

Our unwelcomed intruders left, now more concerned with their runaway horses than with their sexual gratification. We could hear them swearing as they ran after their horses. We hoped they would never come back.

Our neighbors in the building were unhappy that the fence was broken and not at all concerned that a neighbor was in danger of being raped. From that night on, until we were discovered, Mama and I joined other women to sleep in the trenches.

A Russian troop maneuver early one dawn revealed our hiding place. We were routed out, cursed at, and sent home. Following this incident, soldiers were kept under more strict control. Even so, some soldiers continued to rape the women. On those nights when everything was quiet and we heard no "Frau komm, Frau komm," we would say, "Tonight the good ones are on patrol."

One day Mama sent me to Niederwiesa to get a few pounds of oat kernels ground. When I arrived, I went to the home of my friend Ursel Kilian and asked her to show me where the mill was located. Ursel had lived in the town all her life and I was hoping that she would accompany me to the mill. Ursel told me of the danger of being outside. "Russian soldiers stop and force women into trucks. They take them to their barracks and make them scrub floors all day and rape them. At the end of the day they are given a bowl of grits and the lucky ones can walk home. Others are made to stay. They'll pick up anyone available off the streets. Some even go willingly to get a bowl of grits."

"It's one way to get a little food," I said. "We all know our stomachs hurt most of the time. I must get the oats ground. We really need the food."

Ursel and her mother decided to go with me. We walked rapidly and made it to the mill with no problem. We had to wait in line to get the kernels milled. It was late afternoon when we started home and knew it would be after curfew before we could reach Frau Kilian's home.

At dusk a group of five Russians, patrolling on bicycles, passed us and turned around to begin following us. We walked faster. They advanced and wheeled around us in a threatening circle from which we could not escape.

There was no doubt as to their intentions. They suddenly wheeled closer, dismounted and grabbed us by the shoulders. Would I be mistaken for a boy? Evidently so. I was to be taken care of first. A hard blow to my face sent me reeling dizzily backward. A sickening kick in my stomach knocked me down. Four of the men grabbed Ursel and her mother, forcing them to the ground. I tried to slip along the wall of the building, thinking the growing darkness would hide my escape. A big hand on my neck shoved me against the bricks. I was warned not to move if I wanted to live. Another blow in my face and stomach left me in great pain and unable to move. I could only lie there and witness the sordid scene of rape.

They pushed the women's dresses up to their necks and tore their underclothes. The noise of the women's screams and male cursing must have been heard for some distance by many people, yet no one came to help. The lights went out in nearby windows and I knew people must have been watching from their darkened houses, afraid to intervene since the Russians were armed with guns.

The men laughed, knowing no one would come to help us escape their fiendish act. The men took turns climbing on the women while the others pushed their fists into their mouths, pinning them to the ground. Each soldier shifted from Ursel to her mother without even pulling his pants up.

When they finished their grunting and cursing they left, laughing about their monstrous acts of repeated rape. The air reeked with the odor of alcohol and garlic. The profanity and coarse laughter that blasted the air moments ago echoed in my mind. Ursel and her mother lay on the ground in agony. They looked like bundles of wet clothing. Ursel's mouth was bleeding and each groaned with pain as they sat up.

The curfew was already in effect and their home was about four blocks away. This distance proved to be a painful walk for all of us. Just as we turned into another street a second Russian patrol came on bicycles. Fearful, we started to run. I stumbled and fell, which brought the Russians quickly in front of us.

After explaining our situation, the Russians walked the remaining distance with us to protect us from more violence. We just had the misfortune to encounter a bad patrol before them. I still had my bag of oats as they had not taken it from me.

I slept at Ursel's home because of the late hour and because I was in much pain from the blows to my face, stomach and other parts of my body. The next morning I was horrified to see our swollen and bruised faces. When they told me this kind of attack had happened to them before, I hid my face in my hands and cried.

"Don't feel bad, Irene, we'll go to the hospital today."

When I arrived home, Mama wept as she washed my black eyes and swollen face. We were grateful my male disguise had saved me from being raped.

"I'm so sorry for Ursel and Frau Kilian. I am to blame for what happened. I'll never let you go there again."

Fall passed and winter came. If we had not looked at the calendar we would not have known it was Christmas 1945. We had a few sacks of potatoes and very little else to keep us going, but the people in the city did not even have that. They were starving badly. Typhoid fever reached the epidemic stage even though everyone in the city was vaccinated.

I began scouting further from home in the hope of finding more food. With few rations available and money worthless, it took large sums to buy food in the black market. One pound of butter cost 200 Reichsmark, equivalent to fifty 1946 U.S. dollars.

It was the same year, when the communist party put out a resolution of the people, demanding that all the big firms, plants, businesses and farms be given to "the people." Once that was done, all the capital of the city was confiscated and now was owned by the state. The repayment to Russia started. Those plants that had worked for the economy and later for the war, now worked for Russia. The German people were told that it all belonged to "the people." But if a person would take as much as one pencil from their working place, they were branded as an enemy of the people, the Communist party, and peace, and they lost a good position if they had one. I knew farmers who lost their farms with every animal on it. It did not belong to them anymore yet they were now allowed to work as farmhands on their own farm. The same thing happened with hotels and many other businesses. Many people, who had built up their businesses for generations, did not want to give them up. Those people perished, and no one knew where they were taken.

I spent more time with my friend, Krista Neubert, the daughter of one of the foremen from the state farm. Krista was my age, the same height, and her blue eyes contrasted with my brown ones. She wore her light hair in two long braids. Krista's pretty white teeth and clear complexion led me to believe her country life with fresh air and more food had given her an advantage over those of us from the city. She came from a large family: eight brothers and sisters.

One cold winter morning Krista and I walked into Chemnitz. I carried my accordion but my fingers were too cold to play. Most of the activity was, as usual, at the railroad station, so we went there to see what was happening. People were sitting around on top of bundles and luggage, waiting for trains. The large restaurant was packed with people. Tables were spread with white tablecloths but no food or drinks; the serving counter was closed. A few soldiers were playing cards. The only sound seemed to be the shuffle and snap of cards as they were played. It was plain to see that people wore any kind of clothing they could get. Parts of military uniforms were worn with mismatched civilian apparel. A common sight was the gray military boots with worn out uniforms. A melancholy mood was everywhere.

"Let's sing and I'll play, Krista."

We started. Heads turned and people smiled. This was the encouragement we needed. We sang some of the old German folk songs: "A Penny and a Dollar," and "When All Fountains Are Running" and others.

Coins were tossed toward us as we played and sang more. A young man picked up the coins and put them in his hat, gathering more as they were tossed.

After a long while we stopped to rest. We spread the money on the white tablecloth before us. I can still see it today. Happily we counted it and divided it between us.

"Krista, we could use this money to ride the trains out to places where food is more plentiful."

An idea was born and we decided to try it. With permission from our mothers, who gave it only reluctantly, we traveled out toward Dresden, and from there to Cottbus and into farmlands. We came home with kernels of wheat and occasionally some lard.

We travelled to Riesa and Meissen. Our singing and playing in railroad stations brought more coins. We used those coins for travel and necessities.

When night came we slept in waiting rooms of railroad stations, hunched against the wall, or on a bench if one was empty. Sleeping in railroad stations had become a common way for everyone to travel, since no hotel rooms were available in bombed cities.

Police occasionally disturbed us when they came to check our IDs and tickets. Some German police overlooked our playing and singing, since it was clearly evident people seemed happier when they heard us. More often though, they forbade us to play in no uncertain terms, whether we had a ticket to travel or not. Anyone without a ticket had to leave the station and might even be arrested.

We were told, "You better watch out for the Russian patrol. They won't allow any singing and playing in railroad stations," and they warned us that we could get arrested just for that.

Some young kids around the stations kept watch for us. When the Russian patrol approached they whistled a warning and we stopped and disappeared into the crowd.

The Russians usually checked identification papers at random. Sometimes they ordered us to open our bags to inspect the contents. They were always on the lookout for escaping Nazi officials or Ukrainians trying to get into West Germany. They arrested enough people that it made all of us afraid whenever they came through the door.

Since few women went out during evening hours or at night because of the danger of rape, my boy disguise gave me some protection and much greater freedom to move about. With Krista in the role as my sister she was not bothered by the Russians. We became skilled at bartering as we roamed the countryside and the railroad stations looking for food. We traded some of the Meissen porcelain figurines that Grandma had given us for food. Of course the Meissen figurines were valuable antiques, but hunger hurts. We bartered everything away.

At the more prosperous farmlands around Magdeburg we could get a piece of bacon or a tiny bottle of oil for a figurine. For a silver spoon I could sometimes get a small piece of butter or a small sack of flour. We traveled to places where refugees had not come in such large numbers. Mama worried when I was gone but she was thankful for the food I brought home. Krista and I carefully divided our bartered items and broadened the area of our search.

One day while singing and playing in the waiting room at the Riesa railroad station, the Russian patrol came so quickly we could not escape. Shouting in Russian that we had committed a crime, they arrested us.

"We have been looking for you two a long time," said one of the patrol. "You have broken the law. No entertainment is allowed in railroad stations."

They yanked my accordion from me, forcing us outside and into a truck. It was evening when they took us into the military police headquarters. Searchlights were all over the building and a red star on the roof looked like a Christmas tree top. Their music was so loud we did not hear what they said, they just motioned us where to go. We were taken into a large room where an officer shouted orders in Russian we could not understand. The men who had arrested us were shouting and cursing. I could not see my accordion. One of them looked at us and shouted something. He paused as though waiting for an answer.

"Do you have my accordion?" I asked.

Apparently he did not understand me. I pantomimed what I meant and my question was answered in clumsy German. "I don't understand."

"You broke the law and you will be punished," was what they repeated over and over. They took us out in the hall where we waited for about an hour with a soldier guarding us.

Suddenly a door burst open and two men shoved us back into the office where we had been. They took our ID cards, the contents of my pockets, and Krista's handbag. After looking at our things they dumped them in a box. They made fun of me for all the girl stuff I had in my pockets, but I did not reveal myself and would not dare, since I always used my brother Ortwin's ID.

With nothing left but our clothing and I with my large felt boots, we were forced up a flight of stairs, through the building and downstairs again. They opened a door and pushed us down another flight of stairs into a hall below ground level. An iron door was unlocked revealing a dark room. After coming from the lighted rooms upstairs, the room looked totally black. They pushed us in and I stumbled and fell down a step I could not see. The door banged shut and someone helped me stand up. My hands were wet and we were standing in ankle deep water.

As my eyes adjusted to the darkness I could see we were in a room about 8 by 10 feet and it was full of people all standing close to one another. The cold water looked very dirty and the odor of urine grew stronger as my senses became more aware of our prison room. I shuddered to think I had touched the water and dried my hands on my clothes.

In the dim light I saw a well-dressed couple next to us. The man looked like a black marketer, because he did not look hungry. Krista grabbed my hand and whispered loudly, "They've put us in here until they kill us or send us to Siberia!"

"Don't be frightened," a calm voice said.

His soothing voice sounded inappropriate in this strange prison. Other people, mostly men, stood quietly, sometimes speaking in low voices. I touched the wall. It was slippery and wet. Hours passed.

"How long can we stand this?" Krista asked. "My knees ache and my feet are numb."

I didn't answer. We held each other and cried quietly. Others sobbed and moaned.

"How long? How long?" I groaned. "I can't feel my legs anymore."

Hours later the couple still talked to each other ever so quietly. I was amazed at everyone's calmness. We counted the hours by the chimes of a church clock we could hear ever so faintly through our prison walls.

Many hours later we heard footsteps. Someone turned a key in the lock. The door opened and a man called out our names. I could not walk. I tried and fell against a man. They lifted us out but my legs still would not move. I dared not rub them for fear I'd fall back into that stinking hole. The Russian guards lifted us and dragged us up the steps and down a hall. They talked in Russian, which we did not understand. When they let go of us we fell. By flexing the muscles in my legs the feeling gradually came back. We helped each other to a standing position.

We were taken through the same passage as the evening before and to the same office. A different officer was there now. With much gesturing he said, "You will be put away for good if you are caught in a railroad station again."

He said much more that we could not understand. When I saw our things I knew we were going to be released. I could not see my accordion and asked the officer for it. He questioned the patrolman. By their gestures I could see they told him they had not seen it.

"You didn't even have an accordion, you little liar," he bellowed. "If you don't shut up and get out of here we'll arrest you again and never let you go!"

We left quickly, anxious to be free of that awful prison. As we hurried to catch the train, the cold wind penetrated our wet footwear. My boots weighed a ton. After hours of waiting we finally boarded the train to Chemnitz, but not without using our elbows to push our way on since hundreds of other people wanted to get on the train as well. Though we stood all the way home, the train felt very comfortable after the sleepless night standing in water.

BARTERING

As we arrived in Chemnitz, I said to Krista, "We're in pretty bad shape to go home." I looked down at my old wet boots. "They aren't much to look at anymore."

We were hungry. Our trip was a total loss and I had seen my accordion for the last time.

"I have some friends on Zschopauer Street. I said. ALet's go see if we can clean up there and rest before we start walking home."

Krista nodded her approval and we sloshed along in our wet footwear toward the Hillebrandt home. On the way I told Krista about this amazing family with 12 children.

"They have a coal business. It has been in their family for generations. When the coal comes in, the whole family helps to shovel it into heavy black sacks, and in the good old days, deliver it to the customers. Since the war, people are lucky if they can pick just a halve sack up themselves. Right now, times are hard for the Hillebrand's too. That family always used to look black and grimy from their work but Mama used to say, 'that is black gold.' My parents knew them since before the war. They are really nice people.

"When I was smaller, I went there and they thought I belonged to them. When I hugged their Mama she said, 'Sit down baby and eat your soup.' Everybody was 'baby' to her. I sometimes wonder if she remembers all their names. They all help take care of one another because Frau Hillebrandt works with her husband. They have six bedrooms and feed anyone who is there at mealtime."

When we arrived, everyone started talking as though they had seen me the day before. Herr Hillebrandt said, "Go wash up you dirty little sparrow." His glance included Krista.

Their house was always kind of dark. Most of their windows faced a brick wall that seemed to take away all the daylight. Nevertheless, it was a place to live in this bombed out city.

I pulled Krista down the hall and we found the bathroom. After lighting a briquette in a little hot water stove we waited for the water to heat. After bathing we washed all our clothes with curd homemade soap and hung them to dry. In borrowed house robes, we joined the family in grinding a sack of wheat kernels in a hand turned coffee mill. Since I offered to help, they accepted me as one of their own.

We stayed overnight to let our clothes dry. Next morning, after a bowl of grounded wheat cooked in water and topped with cinnamon and saccharin, we left and walked all the way to Euba.

With no accordion there was no way to make money and we had no articles to trade for food in the black market. A few days later, Mama, carrying a large bag of rutabagas for that family, made a visit to Zschopauer Strasse to ask Herr Hillebrandt, to make a trip to the Musik and Toy Towns Klingenthal and Zwothal to find a new accordion for me. Krista and I joined her. Sure enough, he wanted to go with us. His oldest daughter Rosie, his friend Gustav Neumann, Krista, myself and Mr. Hillebrandt made up our group. We caught a train to Klingenthal, where we changed to a smaller train which took us to Zwothal. This train traveled slowly because it passed many pedestrian crossings and the engineer continually clanged its warning bell, "Bim, bim, birn, bim," which gave the train it's name of "Bimmelbahn."

From the windows of the Bimmelbahn we could see the spectacular mountains and lush green pine forests along the Erzgebirge. In Zwothal we walked to the factories where they made accordions and other small instruments and wooden articles. "We are not making instruments for the German population, only for Russian needs," was the disheartening information we received.

Seeing my fallen expression, one of the workers in another factory thrust an accordion at me saying, "The Russians have a different musical scale. Here, try it. You cannot play it." I looked at an accordion smaller than the one taken from me and certainly not as attractive. I reached for the instrument and found it difficult to play. The notes didn't sound right. I thought of the Russian who would have to learn the scale on my accordion and wondered if he had thrown it away or really learned to play it.

Herr Hillebrandt had heard me play my old accordion. He looked at me, scratched the back of his head and asked, "You want it? Think you can learn to play this one?"

"I'll learn, no matter what." I promised.

"Okay. You got it. He turned to the factory representative and said. "Sell it to me. The Russians took her accordion."

He peeled some money off a roll he carried and with a wink at the factory people I now owned a new accordion. I put it in its brand new case and said a silent prayer of thanks to God. It was not as shiny as the first one but it was a nice instrument and brand new.

We stopped at all the little factories where tiny hand-carved and painted figurines were made. They were so beautiful and painted with much bright color, making it feel as if we were visiting Santa Claus's workshop. We needed these items for trade on the black market.

Russians who traded on the black market liked these figurines too. One shopkeeper refused to sell us anything and said, "These are all for the Russians and we have to account for everything." We knew these wooden carvings and parts for larger items were made in the homes of village people who had been carvers for generations. We explained our need for small items so that we could trade them for food.

"Some of these items were brought in today and we could let you buy some of them. The carvers will be glad for some extra business."

Once again persuasion had worked and we were able to buy some wooden carved items. On the train going home I gave Herr Hillebrandt other addresses where he might get food in exchange for the carvings he bought. After all, he had a very large family to feed.

After many days of practice I was ready to play my new accordion. Since Krista and I did not always have money to buy train tickets, we traveled in empty boxcars on freight trains as many other Germans traveled. People who were looking for lost relatives mostly traveled by boxcar.

Sympathetic railroad employees allowed people to ride in the empty boxcars. Upon catching someone riding the freight train illegally, the kinder employee would ask the rider to get off at the next stop. Railroad authorities took no responsibility for the safety of free riders and not all railroad workers showed sympathy.

Russian patrols were greatly feared by everyone. They were everywhere, swaggering about with machine guns strapped to their bodies. The government occasionally used the boxcars to transport large amounts of refugees. When this happened, there was usually a full transport, organized and handled by authorities. Refugees were still coming out like that from Silesia, East Prussia, Poland and Sudetenland, Czechoslovakia.

It was in this kind of situation that Krista and I first learned to catch free rides, using the uncomfortable boxcars. We soon learned how to appeal to the sympathetic ear of the railroad worker. When caught, we were "just a couple of kids, lost," or "trying to find my Papa." Using these sob-stories, we talked our way past the police and railway employees. We figured out how to stand along the railroad tracks in hopes of learning where the train was going while not appearing to want a ride. Because of undetermined time schedules, we never boarded until the train started to move. Then we would run and jump into a boxcar.

One morning Krista and I caught a freight train going north to Leipzig. From Leipzig we changed to another freight train going on to Halle, about twenty miles further north. Halle lay in ruins.

Once thousands of people lived in this city. Many had moved away and a large number of people had perished. We did not see much of the population that day. The chemical plants and food industries built along the Saale River were totally destroyed and most of the rail-yards lay in tangled wreckage. I felt the wasteful defeat our country was suffering all because of Hitler.

"Koethen is almost straight north," Krista said. "Should we try it?"

"Let's go." I said. We shouldered our knapsacks and boarded the next train heading north. Koethen was damaged by bombs but not like the city of Halle. We made our way out to a farm area and bartered our tiny figurines for oat kernels, a small sack of flour, some barley, and a 4 oz. bottle of beechnut oil. Beechnut oil was made from the

Beechtree fruit, a tiny little nut-like fruit, that we called *"bucheckers."* In late fall, they told us to "pick your own *bucheckers* if you want oil." So we spent many hours picking up these little kernels to have enough for just a tiny bottle of oil.

Our load was heavy for two skinny kids and we stopped many times to rest as we returned to the railroad station. We soon caught a freight train back to Halle. We jumped off in Halle only to find the station filled with people. Another train had just rolled in but it was so full that people were hanging on the steps of the railroad cars and outside the doors. There were soldiers in tattered uniforms sitting on top of the train. I wondered if Papa would come home this way.

We learned that Russia was demanding restitution from Germany. The one who loses a war always must pay to the winners. However, Russia wanted more than what Germany had ever been worth. We saw railroad tracks removed by German POWs to be shipped to Russia, along with just about anything else that was of value. From a clothing factory, every single sewing machine was sent to Russia. By losing so much railroad track, we now had such a crippled train system that it was no wonder people were so excited about the arrival of two trains at once.

We stood at the place where people boarded trains. Even as we watched, we knew we would not be able to get on this train with our bags of food. It was just too crowded. We plunked down to rest and waited in front of two low basement windows.

"Look Krista, we can see down into the kitchen of the restaurant. I wonder for whom they are cooking?" Hungrily we sniffed the kitchen smells. The cook saw us and smiled. We waved back then and turned to watch for the next train.

A tap on the window caused us to turn back around and see the cook gesturing for us to come in. "You kids out there. Come into the kitchen and I'll give you a bowl of soup."

He didn't have to repeat this offer. We quickly gathered up our bags and found the stairway down to the kitchen.

The aroma of food brought tears to my eyes. I'll never forget how good that warm soup felt in my stomach.

"You kids look kind of undernourished. Here, have a piece of bread."

Grateful for his kindness, we devoured the soup and bread. That meal was one of the best I had ever eaten. The cook asked us where we came from and told me to take my hat off. When I didn't, he took it off for me, His eyes opened wide.

"What kind of a boy are you?" For an instant he was not sure if I was a boy or a girl.

Slapping me on the back he said, "Break your neck and a leg," which is an old German saying for wishing someone luck. I think he decided not to give my disguise away. A sudden commotion outside caught our attention. The cook and other people in the kitchen ran to the high basement windows to see what was happening. We heard people running. Krista and I scrambled up on a chair next to the cook to look outside. A train had just pulled in. People were sitting on the rooftops and hanging on doors and windows. Only a few people got off and at least a hundred tried to get on. People were trying to board the train from both sides of the tracks. They were pushing one another and shouting.

Then to our surprise we saw two nuns in their black robes screaming and running away from the train and over the tracks toward the main station. Several Russian soldiers were in full pursuit and were apparently very intoxicated. The nuns were trying to reach the station building where they thought they would find safety.

No one dared to stop the Russians in their drunken state. People were forced to watch as they knocked the nuns to the ground and raped them. Bottles of vodka stuck out of the pockets of the Russians' overcoats. Those who saw it clenched their jaws in anger, then hung their heads in despair.

"I'll kill them!" cried the cook, grabbing a large butcher knife and starting for the door. Quickly his two helpers restrained him and said, "We lost the war. We have to put up with these acts of violence."

"Not to nuns!" The cook sat down and put his head in his hands and cursed. We finished our meal and thanked the cook. "You kids be careful getting that food home to your folks," he warned.

Touching my shoulder, the cook whispered, "Survive, little buddy. It's better for now, to be a boy."

I put my hat on and we left. "We've got to get on that train for Leipzig in order to get home." We worked our way across the tracks, then pushed and squeezed ourselves into one of the cars.

"I'm glad we have train tickets to get home this time," Krista said as we squeezed into an aisle and sat on our bags of food. There was a heavy scent of soap in the air. Several people were probably carrying large amounts of it. This would make it hard for us since the police would be more likely to inspect our bags and take our food. The authorities called us hamsterers (hoarders). Police had forbidden people to barter for food. Farmers, busy with the harvest and other farm chores, grew impatient with hungry people coming to their doors. They became overloaded with silver, crystal, oriental rugs and fur coats. In one village, the state farms had hung out a sign saying, "No bartering. We have everything we need, except an oriental rug in the cow barn."

Arriving in Leipzig, we learned that the next train to Chemnitz would leave early the next morning. We slept on the floor of the station's waiting room to catch the early train for Chemnitz and then on to Niederwiesa.

Krista sniffed the air. "This car smells of coffee." We tucked our bags of food down as tight as possible and I put my accordion on top.

Loud talking at the other end of the car alerted us to Russian patrols with two German police officers acting as interpreters. As they began checking IDs and tickets, hands moved rapidly to conceal belongings and to have IDs ready.

The Russians held their noses high in the air looking at the overhead luggage. As they neared us, we could tell they smelled the coffee.

"Who is the one with the coffee?" an officer demanded.

"This woman has the coffee," said a man pointing to the woman next to him.

"I have only a little more than a pound," she protested.

They took it from her. No amount of begging or crying helped.

They moved on through the car, deaf to her pleading. Fellow travelers expressed anger and disgust at the informer. The woman scolded and cursed him.

When the patrol left the car, the man said to her, "Calm down lady, I have a whole knapsack full of the stuff. I diverted them to you so I could keep mine." He reached into his bag and gave the lady the amount she had just lost. People smiled and held on tight to their bags.

In Chemnitz we changed trains to Niederwiesa and were soon carrying our heavy bags of food home to Euba.

On another day Krista and I caught a freight train north, planning to go to Riesa. My accordion was strapped to my back and a sack of tobacco from our garden was fastened in front. Somehow we ended up going in the wrong direction. For hours we did not know where we were.

When we realized our mistake, we didn't dare jump off the moving train. A train man found us when he came to check the boxcars. "What are a couple of kids like you doing on the train?"

"We are looking for our folks," I ventured.

"Where are we?" Krista asked.

"This train is going east. You are east of Finsterwalde, going toward the border of Poland."

"We were trying to get to Riesa," I said.

"You are on the wrong train for sure. I'll see what I can do at the next stop." With that he left us.

We weren't sure if he would help us or turn us in to the police. After a while we decided to believe him and stayed on the train. He returned just as the train slowed for the next station and pointed to another freighter.

"See if you can get on that one, but don't get caught. Run!" We jumped off the slower moving train, ran across the tracks to a freight train going in the opposite direction, and scrambled into a boxcar. Greatly relieved, we relaxed. I played my accordion and other free-riders, hiding in the boxcar, sang along with us. The war had scattered people all around and a big migration was in progress. The train had to be side-tracked so often for other trains that we slept the night in the boxcar.

Early the next morning we saw the sign "Riesa" and got ready to jump off. Most of the others stayed on and we waved to them as they rolled on toward Dresden. The first thing we looked for in the station was the washroom. We needed to clean ourselves up and tidy our clothes as best as we could.

"Riesa has a black market, we just have to find it," I said as we walked toward the main street.

We had heard the Russians would trade food for good tobacco. Their government allowance of tobacco was a coarse stinking stuff. Russian Machorka is one of the coarsest Russian tobaccos there is and is not made out of tobacco leaves, but out of the stems. Those stems are cut very small almost like sawdust, which is how it tasted too. Then the Russian soldiers rolled the stuff into a small piece of newspaper in order to be smoked. Surely, they would like our tobacco better.

As we approached a coffeehouse, we saw the large sign advertising movies across the street. It was midmorning and we were hungry. Few restaurants had food to serve and when they did the customer had to bring some of the ingredients. For example, three potatoes bought you a bowl of potato soup, etc. Most people did not even have a burner to boil their potatoes. So, the arrangement to bring produce to the restaurant in exchange for meals was ideal. However, patrons also had to pay a nominal charge for the service. A few customers were already inside and the owner was busy behind the counter.

"Do you have food?" I asked. "We have tobacco." I took some from my sack and his expression told me he was interested.

"You kids sit down, I'll fix you both a breakfast."

He served us a cup of chicory, a bowl of hot cereal and a slice of bread with plum preserves.

"A breakfast fit for a king," I said. We figured he must have a connection with some farm for his food supplies.

"Do you know the Russian guards? Do you think they would trade food for tobacco?" Krista asked.

"The Russian guards are across the street. They have that dance hall connected to the movie house and it's full of German POWs. They're waiting to be shipped to Russia. The guards won't come over here until after lunch. Wait here if you wish."

We decided to wait. We considered going down to the Elbe River to see what was left of the steel mills. We had been told the bomb damage was extensive and many of the 37,000 people who had lived there had been killed or moved to other places.

Shortly after noon we heard the guards coming. I was scared but tried to hide it. They were laughing and talking. Seeing Krista, they approached us, but I eluded their attention in my boy's disguise. I felt uneasy that they might try something with Krista and hoped that presence of the bartender would protect us. They were friendly and spoke a few German words. Krista had a quick answer for everything, causing them to laugh. Then I got down to business acting as her "brother." I put some tobacco between my fingers and held it out to them. I put enough tobacco on the table to roll two cigarettes. Our cigarette papers, bought on the black market in Chemnitz, were the finest. The Russians usually rolled their coarse tobacco in newspaper which makes it stink. They looked at me and then at Krista as they inspected the tobacco.

"Smells good, Karoscho. Where more?" He eyed my knapsack.

"We don't have it with us but we can get it." We used our hands to make ourselves understood.

"We want food. No money, food only."

They talked among themselves then left, indicating they would return. Sure enough, they came back and we exchanged our tobacco for commisbread, a small sack of flour, and 8 ounces of bacon. We were pleased. The bacon alone would have cost the whole bag of tobacco on the black market in Chemnitz.

"Krista, we must go now." I said nervously.

"Stay and go to the movies with us," invited the coffeehouse owner. "Several of us are going."

It was very tempting as I had not seen a movie for a very long time. So, with our food locked safely in the icebox, we went to the movies. The movie house was full of young German POWS. Their uniforms looked clean compared to the shabby tunic tops over britches and boots worn by the Russian guards.

While we waited for the film to start, one of the Russian guards took off his boot. He unwound a large cloth from his foot, then rewrapped his foot and pulled his boot back on again.

Amazed, I nudged Krista, "He has no socks, only rags wound around his feet."

"Do you suppose all of them are without real socks?" Krista whispered.

"I don't know but I suspect so."

We sat with the owners of the coffee house while the Russian guards sat in front and behind of us. We continued waiting for the movie to start, but nothing happened. Nothing but silence; minutes ticked by still no picture.

Krista whispered, "Play and we'll sing to them." She pushed me up and I got my accordion out of the case. We walked into the aisle and we began to sing. We started with the popular songs, then played:

Yes you men oh you men

you are all heartbreakers

we know your hearts are a dark hole.

The entire male audience replied as with one strong masculine voice:

But the women are not any better

still, lovely, oh so lovely

they are nevertheless.

Their voices rang with a thunderous rhythmic sound. We led them in another song, "A Penny and a Dollar."

A penny and a dollar

they were both mine, yes mine.

The penny bought me water

the dollar bought me wine, yes wine

The penny bought me water, but the dollar

bought me wine. Hydee hy do hy da,

by de hy do hy da, hy dee, hy do, hy da...

This powerful melody and their rich voices swept the air with a heart-stirring sound, vibrating the whole movie house. Fearful that we might start something, the Russian signaled frantically for the lights to be turned out and the movie to start. The movie started and everyone became silent again.

After the movie ended we got our food from the icebox, paid a strip of bacon for our breakfast, and went to the railroad station where we bought train tickets home. As usual, we walked home from the station under the cover of darkness. Food was of great value and we were safer carrying it during darkness. The police always confiscated everything when they caught "hoarders."

Krista and I divided our food and she walked quietly off into the night. I threw little stones at our window to signal Mama. She peered outside, then came down to unlock the door.

Each time I returned the boys would lift their sleepy heads and ask for food. It was hard to sleep soundly when we were so hungry. While Mama cooked us a meal, I heated water in the washhouse downstairs, using a few sticks of wood. I took a bath in the zinc tub in the middle of the night. Upstairs again, we talked a long time about my trip. The boys were always anxious to hear about my adventures.

"I don't know where you get your courage, girl."

"From you, Mama. You are my rock. You are able to keep us all together while others are dying of starvation."

"You are keeping us alive, Irene."

After a meal of commisbread, bacon and chicory we all slept without hunger pains that night.

Ration cards became almost worthless but still they were given out. At the store it was the same old story. "We are out of everything, but save your ration cards. Perhaps we will have something for sale next week." But they never did.

We continued our early morning task of picking nettle leaves which grew in abundance. While everyone slept, Mama was out picking stinging nettles, a weed difficult to get rid of that grew until heavy frost in November. Mama would serve each of us a bowl of spinach-like soup with one potato swimming in it. This was often all the food we had in one day. Word got around that a pig was being butchered and every person would get rationed 2 ounces. This meant our family would get 12 ounces. We stood in line four abreast for hours waiting for our portion. The butchers sliced the meat paper thin when our turn to buy came around and we got only four strips.

Winter arrived long and dreary. Grandmother, now 76 years old, often walked eleven miles through the snow to get food from us. Many times she walked back home with only a few potatoes and sugar beets in her net bag. She came one day in February, when Grandpa had walked in another direction to look for food. Mama gave her some of the food brought home from my black market trading.

She was extremely tired from her trip when she came home from us. Grandmother put some potatoes to boil on their gas stove, then fell asleep. The potatoes boiled over and extinguished the flame. The gas poured out and my Grandmother never awakened. Our sorrow was magnified since we wished that one of us had walked home with her. Grandpa loved her dearly and died ten days later. He just gave up living.

We inherited a few of Grandmother's things: her Meissen china, some blankets, featherbeds and a chandelier with teardrop crystals. One of Papas's sisters came also and took a lot of furniture away. Mama received a notification from the Chemnitzer Registration Office (*Einwohnermeldeamt*) that we could move into Grandmother's apartment which needed much repair. However, there was a new restriction that people must help in building up the city from the rubble in order to get worthless ration cards. Since working in the ruins paid such a meager wage and would buy even more meager food, Mama decided we should stay in the village. Food was easier to find there.

Krista and I continued our search for food. One day we went north to Leipzig. We planned to go on to Dessau but we were caught in a police raid. The raid took place in a partially destroyed railroad station. They crowded about a hundred of us into the police station located inside the train building.

Children were arrested since they were considered as cunning as adults in the black market trade and every bit as hungry. Sometimes a child could run away, but not today. The police saw my bag and I knew they suspected I was carrying forbidden items. Our knapsack held only a few items which we had planned to use for trading, I did however have a pile of sanitary napkins which I needed. Suddenly I remembered my bar of American Life Buoy soap. I had bought it on the black market in Chemnitz and I considered it a hot item. Now it was a dangerous piece of evidence for which I could expect a good several years in jail. I slipped the soap out of my bag and held it up my sleeve while looking for a place to discard it. As the police pushed us along in the line, I saw a crevice in the cracked wall. I threw it deep in the opening. If no one saw it I would retrieve it later.

At the police station, we were summoned to a desk where our names were recorded. They lined us up, men and boys on one side of the room, girls and women on the other. I stayed on the girl's side even though I was disguised as a boy. I was called to the officer's desk first. "What's in your bag?" he demanded.

I hugged it and replied, "Not much."

He stood up. "Come here!" he ordered. He grabbed my bag and dumped the contents on the desk, all my sanitary napkins...

People began to laugh. He was embarrassed.

"What are you, a boy, doing with such things?"

He checked my name and realized I was a girl. Frustrated and angry, he ripped off my cap. He seemed speechless. Finally he blustered, "Put your stuff together!"

He tore up the paper with my name on it and threw it in the wastebasket. People hid their smiles but worried for themselves because on such raids there were always arrests made.

"Out you go, and don't you ever let me see you again," he bellowed as his face turned beet red.

I left quickly. While waiting for Krista I looked for my soap. It was gone. I looked at the people around me and was pretty sure who had taken it just by the expression on his face. I dared not say anything, since that bar of soap was risky to possess if searched. I hoped the new owner would have difficulty when they searched him. We left Leipzig on a freight car going north. After that experience I was not fond of the city of Leipzig.

Rumors still came to us that Papa might be alive, but when I traveled to where he had been seen, I could not find him. I always combined my search for Papa with my search for food. It was a convenient excuse when queried by authorities, especially when I was a long distance from home.

We heard Papa might be in West Germany. If he had been at our old home and saw nothing but rubble he might have moved on, thinking we were all dead. The notice we had left to tell anyone our new address, must surely have been long since washed out by the rain.

"Mama, do you think Papa could be in West Germany?"

"If he thought we all died in the air raid, there would be nothing to keep him here, so he might have moved on with the others, to West Germany." She got out an old map and we studied it, trying to figure out where the trains traveled near the border.

"It would be dangerous, child, but perhaps he is there."

When I saw the hope in Mama's face, I felt compelled to extend my search into West Germany.

Krista's parents would not allow her to go. This time I was on my own. Since people could be shot on sight in the border area, I would have to be very careful. Mama and I decided it would be best not to tell anyone except Ortwin about this trip.

It was too risky to even tell Hartmut and Claus.

I did not take as much with me as I had on other excursions; no accordion and no items for bartering. I wore the only clothes I had: the black SS pants, shirt, coat and the oversized boots.

With a short haircut and my motorcycle cap I looked like a boy. In my knapsack I packed a spoon, a change of underclothing, a comb and a small piece of homemade soap in a towel. With Ortwin's ID card buttoned securely in my breast pocket, I was ready to take on the world.

"Just in case you get hungry take these." Mama held out two raw carrots. I put them in my knapsack, wondering where she had got them from.

"God go with you." As I left, tears were in her eyes but I knew her hope of finding Papa was constant.

BORDER CROSSING

Early in March of 1947 I set out to find my way across the border from East into West Germany. It was a cold wintery day. Snow still covered the ground and an icy wind was blowing. I had a few Marks in my pocket intended for train tickets in case I could not find a ride in a boxcar. From my hometown Chemnitz I was able to catch a train to the next town Glauchau. No freight train was to be found that went from there to the next town of Zwickau that day, so I bought a ticket and rode the passenger train. As I arrived in Zwickau I found that I had to change trains if I wanted to travel farther south.

This railroad station was very busy, although smaller than the one in Chemnitz. Here, people rode the train to go to work at the uranium mines, and they occupied every available seat in the waiting area. I was now in a restricted area. IDs were checked constantly by Russian and German soldiers; I felt it better to avoid them. I had only my brother's ID and no explanation for why I was traveling through a restricted area. I did not want to get arrested as a spy. They would not believe any other explanation.

It was a uranium mining district from here on, way up to the silver Erzgebirge, mountains with historical value. Once there was active mining for silver and other minerals. People who lived in those beautiful pine tree covered mountains were artistic woodcarvers. The famous Nutcracker was created here and many other charming delightful wooden figurines.

Now the Russian-German WISMUT Corporation mined uranium. Workers were working without protection from radiation; eventually they would all be sick or worse. Still, people fought to get those jobs, for the pay was good and WISMUT ration cards were honored in food stores. Food was more important than money. This railroad station was very busy, although smaller than the one in Chemnitz. But here, people rode the train to go to work into the uranium mines and they walked around in their large miner's boots and garb.

The MP's stopped mostly travelers who did not look like miners, so I knew I better spend my time waiting for the next train somewhere else. As I walked down the main street my eye caught sight of a neighborhood pub. It was closed, but people were inside, cleaning and preparing for the evening business. I must have looked like so many of the homeless pitiful children who had come from the Silesia, and East and West Prussia (now Poland) territory in search of their parents or any family members.

They had pity on me, and knowing that I must have been hungry, gave me a cup of hot water that smelled like bouillon to which I added my two raw carrots Mama had given me for my trip. I heard one of the cleaning women saying, "This little boy sure looks like he has come a long way." "Poland?" suggested the other. I thanked them with a smile and stayed quiet in my corner where they seated me until I had to go back to the railroad station.

The next train took me to Plauen. A once very charming small town, parts of it were in ruins from the war. Again I bought a ticket on a passenger train since I had a definite destination. Two men in western clothing were waiting on the platform, and I suspected by their speech that they were Czechoslovakians and that they must have been on the other side of the border before. A trail of ragged people, men and women, followed the two men, who tried desperately to lose them. Instead, more people hung on their trail. Of course, instinctively we sensed that those two men knew the way across the border and that was where we wanted to go but we didn't know the way.

As we followed them we had to catch a train quickly, no matter how overcrowded, and by not leaving the embankment we were able to change trains many times. We struggled on and off trains and those two men were always shouting "stand back." But I knew I had to follow them or never make it over the border. It was an exhausting maneuver until only the boldest and strongest were still with us.

After all that zigzag riding we came back to Plauen and here we regrouped. Now the two Czechoslovakian men decided it was easier to take the rest of us over the border rather than running around and drawing attention from the border patrol. They were everywhere. Plauen was a dreary place. The railroad station had been almost completely destroyed. A wooden shack took its place and was full of people. The stench of putrid air pushed me back ten paces.

I'd rather freeze out here then wait inside, I thought. But when I saw them putting their heads together I had to hear what was going on; I didn't want to be left behind. Just when I decided to go in, a Russian and German patrol drove up in an old, open truck. Somebody inside gave a signal and I heard many of the people scramble out of the back entrance.

I sensed we must be close to the border but I didn't know exactly where to turn. At this time and place, it was better not to have a map on one's person. If caught by the patrol it could be deadly.

Ragged people of all ages were standing around the embankment waiting for a train to take them somewhere. It was getting dark now and our group was still together. After catching another train which traveled away from Plauen, we had by nightfall worked ourselves closer to the border. Even though it was cold, I got warm from running, hiding, jumping, and just keeping up with the two leaders.

We finally reached the last train station, and beyond it was no man's land, several miles of land between borders where nobody except for patrols were allowed to be. So we had to start walking. The leaders counted 22 people. Among us there were German soldiers who ran away from the Russians and wanted to be a POW with the Americans rather than with the Bolsheviks. Some had come all the way by foot from the Balkan States and Prussia, and had stayed just a small step ahead of the Red Army. The Red Army, of course, would have made them POW's and Siberia would be their destiny. They knew Stalin had no mercy. Some women were among us but no children.

Everyone carried something, but most of us traveled light and we all were very hungry. We had apparently gone as far southwest as possible by train. Now we marched through small villages. It was dark and people had closed their curtains. No light escaped to the outside; it was a total blackout, as if the war was still on. We walked exhausted and soundless until we reached the little town of Lobenstein.

One person among us whispered, "The only light seen here is from Russian Patrol Stations."

"Quiet!" whispered one of the Czechoslovakians sharply. "No talking or else." He made an intimidating gesture.

The roads were still snow-covered and icy and although a cold wind pushed us forward, I was hot and my feet felt like a ton with those greatly oversized large felt boots I wore. These were the kind of boots that we had found at the uniform factory just before the war ended, and the only footwear I owned since we lost everything in the war. Almost at the end of the main street in Lobenstein we came to an iron gate. Beyond the gate we saw the contours of a medium building in complete darkness.

"Hurry it up," whispered a male voice as we passed through the gate and continued silently toward the building. As we reached the entrance someone gave the signal to halt.

"Once we are in, it is vital that you don't talk to anyone. Eat the food they give you and keep quiet. We are sure that there are informers around."

As we nodded in agreement, the door was pushed open and the smell of food reached us. It was a heavenly smell.

Only a small group of 6 at a time were able to go into a sort of vestibule which was pitch dark. Then, as the outside door was closed, another door was opened which lead into a spacious dining room. The sudden light and the warm air was a welcome sight. The warmth made my face and hands tingle. It was a village pub and the smoke-filled room revealed all sorts of shabby people; many local, but most of them strangers. There were several tables that seated four to six people I found a chair and put my bags beside it.

Over the kitchen window I saw a sign which read, "Noodle soup 35 Pfennige." While some people went to get something to drink, I went to get a plate of soup. Although there were no spoons, I fished one out of my bag. I had not seen such a rich noodle soup for a very long time; it even had meat in it. While I ate I became drowsy and I could hardly keep my eyes open. One of the soldiers in a torn uniform sat at my table, he kept saying, "Eat up, boy. Eat up." He meant me. I still wore my fabric Lindberg-type cap, which had moved down over my forehead and was almost covering my eyes. There was no reason for me to take it off, at least as long as I didn't want to be discovered as a girl. I thought, "If I could only close my eyes and sleep. Nothing else matters anymore. Just let me sleep, please..."

Just then I was pushed in the ribs and I picked up my bags along with the others. It was time to go. I saw some people arguing. Some woman had talked to a stranger and now the leaders of our group did not want to have anything to do with her. They wanted her to stay behind. We were told to move out into the dark room and then out into the street. The cold air woke me up some. As our group gathered silently our eyes adjusted to the dark. The leaders had come out along with the woman.

As we got in a single-file line our silhouettes were like black shadows in the snow. It was then that I heard a sound that reminded me of someone chopping wood. No one said so, but I knew that woman who had not obeyed orders was not with us anymore. That quickly made me wide awake. We moved faster and our breathing was labored as we stepped carefully, constantly reminded that sound travels a long distance in the cold winter air. Silently and swiftly we moved along. The food had strengthened us and we increased our pace. I began to doubt my strength to keep up.

We were told that anyone dropping out would give the others away. I knew they had knives under their jackets and might kill anyone that got in their way. I shuddered when I thought of the woman at the pub. The situation was harsh; one person's weakness must not endanger the others. Our two leaders were determined to make it with or without us. We did not know them and we did not know each other. After millions had died in the war, the death of one more person wouldn't make a bit of difference.

We walked on level ground for a while and I found it easier. The path turned uphill again but we still moved at such a fast pace that I gasped for breath. I wished now that I had stayed behind. I fell. I got up, and then fell again. I saw the distance between the last person and myself grow bigger, yet I knew I must keep going.

The soldier with a small bundle over his shoulder looked back and saw me struggling. Without a word, he grabbed my hand and pulled me a few meters uphill. But it must have been a strain on him too, as he let go and I again began falling behind. Those oversized boots I was wearing seemed like heavy weights on my feet. For a while I crawled on all fours; the perspiration froze on my hair and face.

"Come on!" the man motioned. I lurched forward until I was able to regain my stride. Finally, we made it to the top.

The leaders stopped for a few seconds to get orientated. This brief rest made me feel that I could keep up. The beautiful night scenery was all around us: the woods, pitch dark ahead of us, and the fields, glistening silver white in the moonlight. Somewhere dogs were barking in the distance. We could only guess what lay ahead of us as we fearfully entered the dark woods.

Our leaders whispered, "Don't talk. Sound travels. Don't step on any wood. It will snap and give us away."

My heart was pounding so loud that I felt everyone around me could hear it. As we walked for several hundred meters through a forest aisle, we were lead downhill and I heard running water. We fought our way through a thick brushy area until we saw a small river below us. The snow was deeper there. It must have snowed again the day before. The water was running so rapidly only the edges were snow covered. The stream was a good eight feet wide and too far to jump to the other side.

"Take off your boots. Shoulder them and cross!" was the whispered command. It had to be done in a hurry, the first ones were already in the water. One woman put her bare foot in the icy water and gave a shriek. The men with her hissed angrily. The soldier and I were just behind the Czechoslovakians. They saw how frail and tired I was.

"Look," one of them whispered in my ear. "Over this mountain in front of us, there is freedom. Let's go and don't stay behind!" I cried silently, knowing not to show weakness. I prayed silently. As I prayed, I felt my energy return. The icy water was not the worst of it. It was all the sharp stones on the bottom that made it hard to walk through. I knew if I didn't make it, they would kill me here on the border. It happened every day and Mama and my brothers would wait in vain for my return. I had to get through that stream and up the hill again. The water reached up to my calves and I stepped carefully so as not to fall. As I wobbled up the slippery bank on the other side, my feet were numb. I looked down in the snow to see if my feet were still there. Silently, we pulled on our socks and boots and, when ready, started to walk slowly and close together, a dark human wall swaying back and forth as we carefully climbed up the steep hill. My knees hurt as I lifted my heavy boots. The feeling was coming back into my feet.

Suddenly one of the women broke away from the group and ran recklessly downhill. She crashed into some bushes, snapping branches and knocking rocks loose. I thought the strain must have been too great for her or perhaps she lost something valuable when we waded through the stream. In that instant if it had been possible I knew the men would have killed her.

They cursed under their breath and urged us to run. "Faster! Faster!" Our dark figures could easily be seen in the snow.

By now border guards had heard us. We looked down as they ran along the river bank, shouting at us. "*Stoyi Stoy*!" (stop! stop!) and "*Sto to koy?*" (What is going on?) They were shooting up into the air.

The first guard running toward us from the underbrush had his machine gun aimed straight at us. We raised our arms high and stood still. My heart roared and my pulse pounded in my head.

They too, were excited, not knowing whether we carried guns or how many we were. A guard's gun went off, snapping a limb from a tree. I saw the holes in the snow where the bullets landed. More Russian soldiers came and they swarmed all around us, thrusting their guns against our backs.

"*Dawey! Dawey! Dawey!*" (Hurry! Hurry! Hurry!) We were marched about a half mile along the river to a narrow bridge which we had to cross single file. There was a wooden blockhouse, which served as a check point for the border guards. We were pushed into the house and our eyes squinted in the bright lights. Russian soldiers were all over the place. Some who were lying around sat up and put on their boots. I stared at their feet, and they folded rags around them before they put their boots on. They had no socks.

The two Czechoslovakians motioned for us to keep quiet. They would do the talking. We finally were allowed to take our arms down and to find something to sit on. Our two leaders went to the guard in charge and talked loudly in a Slavic language. I could tell it was not be perfect Russian but it was obviously a heated argument. The shouting got real loud but only our group paid attention to it. The rest of the Russians were telling us to put our bags down and wait.

The raggedy German soldier finally thought he understood enough. Our two leaders tried to convince the Russians that we were trying to get from West Germany to East Germany. What a plot! Our Czechoslovakians were indeed clever fellows.

A Russian who spoke better German came in. He joined the heated debate and then said to the rest of us, "This is not possible. You must have permission. You cannot go over the border to visit relatives in the Russian Zone without it."

"Why, is it not Germany too?"

"You must go the legal way. Now you have broken the law. You all must wait until morning for the officer-in-charge. Then we will see." He said something to another guard and walked out of the room.

Morning was still several hours away and the warmth of the room made me drowsy. I looked around. We were in a large room with a potbelly stove right in the center. Around the stove were a few tables with handmade wooden benches. Along the walls double bunk beds were lined up. This is where the soldiers slept when they were off-duty. I was sure this building must have some more rooms in the back which I could not see. Most people from our group sat at the tables, while others sat right on the floor leaning against the bunk beds.

I took my heavy boots off and rubbed my cold feet. I saw others doing the same. Some people hung wet clothes around the potbelly stove. Our leaders took them down saying, "Do you want them to think we crossed the river?"

I sat on a bench and cradled my head in my arms at the table. I tried to sleep, but stirred occasionally as the men walked around in heavy boots. They seemed to be talking all the time.

Some of the soldiers tried to talk to the women, motioning for them to go outside. Some younger ones even flirted. I guess to some women, men are men no matter what. I was glad to be looked at as a boy. I felt warm and safe. I dozed uneasily for several hours.

The guards changed at dawn. Everyone awoke and stood as the new officer-in-charge came in and looked around. He walked to a table covered with papers and read the report.

"I'll get a truck and transport all of them into town for interrogation," he said. We were frightened when we heard the translation.

I was worried they would ask for IDs, and I knew they would. I only had a paper with my brother's name on it. They would search us and then I would be in real trouble.

The two Czechoslovakians approached the officer and protested. He must have called them every name in the book, I heard some cursing and everyone who lived in the Russian Zone understood what they meant. Back and forth they argued until the Russian officer became very angry. He wanted every man in a German uniform on one side of the room and the civilians and women on the other side.

Those raggedy German soldiers were transported to the next town and we had no idea what became of them. As for us, we quickly gathered our things and started to leave.

"*Dawey! Dawey! Dawey!*" he yelled. (Hurry! Hurry! Hurry!)

Once out of the blockhouse, we were to go back where we came from.

After the hours of rest we'd had we felt stronger. We crossed the bridge in a hurry and started to climb the hill. It looked to be about half a mile to the top. The ground was still snow-covered but the morning's winter sun was trying to thaw the snow, making it very slippery. There were still heavy batches of ice.

About one-third of the way up, we heard shouting again, "*Dawey! Dawey! Dawey!*"

Then we heard shots. Maybe they regretted letting us go. We climbed faster, fearful of being killed. My chest ached and my legs hurt as I increased my speed. Bullets were hitting the rocks and ground all around us. My knapsack felt like a ton. Then I heard a "bang." One of the bullets had hit something inside my knapsack. Whatever it was, it saved my life. We saw people at the top of the hill and they were shouting.

Were we running into another police trap?

"Dear God, I can't take anymore of this!" I screamed.

"They're the Red Cross people on the western side!" one of our leaders called back.

Now the people above us were waving their arms. They must have heard the shots and come out to see what was happening. They didn't want to be shot at, but from up there they could cheer us on enough to give us strength.

I slipped on a piece of ice and slid back several yards before stopping on a hard rock. I crawled, digging my hands into the partially frozen soil to keep from sliding backward on the steep incline. My big boots made it hard to get a solid footing. I was getting tired. I had only one thought as the bullets flew passed me, I must make it to the top.

With bleeding hands and snow-soaked clothes, I finally reached the top. Crying and laughing I collapsed on the ground. I was not the first nor the last of our group to cross the border. Yet I was more thankful than any for having succeeded in this treacherous journey to West Germany.

People from the Red Cross helped us to our feet. We walked to their station about a half mile away. I learned later that this station was erected to help those who might attempt to cross the border. The station was a short distance from the town of Bad Steben in West Germany.

After we were able to shower, I debated whether to give my real name or to continue in my boy disguise. I changed to my other clean set of underwear and wrapped a blanket around me to go to the washroom and launder my clothes.

As I came to the door, I saw a girl struggling with a man. She was trying to resist his attempts to molest her. A feeling of anger and disgust filled my body.

"It is the same everywhere," I said to myself. Men are the same everywhere. A girl traveling alone is not safe in the West either.

I stepped back and made a noise to let them know I was coming, then entered the room. The man did not stop his advances, thinking I was a boy. The girl continued to struggle. I dropped several wash bowls on the stone floor, making a loud noise and making them stop. The man laughed, he was not in the least embarrassed; the girl fled. I gathered up the bowls and started to wash the mud and dirt off my boots and clothes.

Still wrapped in a blanket I stood in line for a bowl of soup. We were told that none of us could stay there more than three days, preferably less. We needed to make room for others who might follow. But they told us to take a good rest before we journeyed on. I sank into my bunk bed and fell asleep.

CHALLENGE OF THE BORDER
1947 - 1949

I slept all day at the Red Cross station, woke up to eat some dinner, then went back to bed and slept through the night. Dressed in dry clothes, I again stood in line for food. For the first time I could talk to others in our group. No one knew for sure who had been shot while we crossed; we were all nameless figures. The Red Cross only took care of the survivors and did not tell us what they had seen from above the hill. I was glad to be safe and asked no questions.

One of the Czechoslovakians explained that, the Russians had fired at random and that they had been very angry. He laughed. They probably found out from some of the guys they held behind that we actually did come from the East, and not from the West as we had told them. That was why they did not hesitate to shoot at us. "They were raving mad," laughed one of our leaders.

Grateful to have escaped injury, I bowed my head and thanked God for my safety. After my morning meal I explained to the Red Cross officials that Papa had been seen in an army hospital in Nuernberg (Nuremberg). I was given a train ticket to Nuremberg and was told I could stay one more day in the shelter. Amazingly, new people arrived every night from the other side.

I wrote a letter to Mama telling her I was across the border and safe. In order to protect Mama, I avoided using my own name should the letter be confiscated. Red Cross people mailed it and informed me that the mail would get through to East Germany.

I walked into the town of Bad Steben. Small shops were open for business and merchandise was in the shop windows. People walking in the streets looked well nourished and content. What a difference. I was still in the same country, the same language. But it seemed life in the two Germanies was as different as day and night.

The snow was melting in the sunshine. People stared at me as if I was just a pitiful creature. Timidly, I walked into the first shop, a bakery, where the smell of fresh bread was overwhelming.

For a while I just wanted to stand there and take it all in. When all the people in the place turned and looked at me, I was embarrassed and could not get a word out. I knew how to barter, but I had never learned how to beg.

The baker behind the counter did not hesitate and he pulled down an entire loaf of fresh baked bread from the shelf. "Here boy, you look hungry, have you just come from over there?"

I nodded my head when a lump in my throat prevented me from speaking. When I felt the bread in my hand I automatically pushed it inside my coat, curtsied, mumbled a "thank you," then suddenly remembered that boys didn't curtsy. His expression changed in astonishment. Everyone in the store laughed out loud as I ran out of the store as fast as I could.

Clutching my loaf of bread, I ran down the sidewalk. At first I feared investigation but, then, I realized where I was and guessed that it must have been all just a joke to them. Surely, if they really thought that I was not a boy they understood why and didn't care.

Nobody followed me and I had a whole loaf of bread, all to myself. The fresh bread was still warm. Tears came to my eyes and I felt out of place not having to hide from suspicious eyes. The fragrance of the fresh bread was too much. I stopped and leaned against the wall and broke off a piece. It tasted heavenly. It was partly rye, not heavy commisbread like we ate in East Germany.

A soldier stopped and looked at me saying, "Don't eat bread alone boy. Go into that butchery." He pointed, "They will give you meat. Just ask."

Meat! What a luxury. No one would give away meat, I thought. But he urged me on.

Finally I said, "I will try it."

I went into the butchery. I had not seen a butchery so well stocked for years. All those sausages. It was a sight--I stood there taking in the abundance of the meat display.

The man behind the counter said, "Here young soldier, have some of our daily special." Someone handed me a six-inch piece of tongue wurst. I stared and mumbled "Thanks" and remembered not to curtsy.

The butcher said, "Hey comrade, how is it on the other side?"

I replied, "People are still very hungry. Life is hard."

"Nothing has changed," he said nodding.

I stood there and ate the bread and tongue wurst.

"Here, have a glass of milk."

"Milk," I gasped. As I looked at the white liquid I thought of little Christine. Had she gotten any milk since I left? Mama always said, "You kids won't live long, you are war children. You just don't have the proper nourishment." If I could give Christine this milk I would do it instantly. Suddenly, having plenty and not being able to share it with my family made me feel uneasy. In my mind I could see them hungry at the very moment I was eating.

Back at the Red Cross Station, I inquired about staying in West Germany. I was told that people born in East Germany must stay in East Germany. They are not refugees like the people from Silesia, Prussia, Sudetengau and other Far East places. East Germans would not be permitted to permanently stay in West Germany. It was not until 1948 or 49 that residents of East Germany would also be accepted as political refugees. Still, I was sure many came and lied about their identity. I was only allowed to visit.

A Red Cross nurse said, "If we accepted East Germans, they would all come over here. No one would be left in Saxony and Thuringen. The Russians would completely take over the country just as they did with Latvia, Lithuania, and Estonia.

I did not know what was happening in those other countries she mentioned. I only knew that saying "no" meant much hardship to so many people. No one here could imagine what it was like under the Soviet rule. Here everything was so free and normal already after that gruesome war.

I asked the local police the same questions and was given the same answers. "You may look for your father but you cannot have a permanent permit to live in West Germany."

I knew I must return to Saxony. I wrote another letter to Mama, explaining everything I had heard and seen. The Red Cross mailed my letter and gave me shelter until the next morning.

It was very early, as I took the first train to Nuremberg. People with friendly faces were saying "Good morning." No one on the trains looked as starved as the people in East Germany looked. The train was not overcrowded and I heard people talking gracefully about the Marshall Plan. Everyone thought it was a good thing for the beaten country. I vaguely remembered hearing something about this in East Germany and their propaganda talked against it. What horrible people those Communists were, pretending not to need help when everyone was starving.

The bombed out railroad station in Nuremberg was partially boarded up and reconstruction was underway. There were many people of different nationalities and American patrols (MPs) were walking around. Shops in the station were not open yet but the restaurant posted a menu in the window and stated when meals would be served. With little money and no ration cards, I was holding on to the rest of the food I had received the previous day.

I boarded a streetcar going to Zirndorf, a suburb of Nuremberg. A hospital containing German prisoners of war was located there. All afternoon I went from ward to ward looking for Papa. Upon learning of a ward where soldiers from the Russian front were being treated, I hurried to see if Papa was there. He was not--it was now early evening and near curfew time. I approached a nurse and said, "I have no place to stay." She wrote an address on a slip of paper and warned me to get there before the curfew hour.

As I left the hospital I came to a restaurant. I walked in and saw people eating big dinners, just like before the war. I was hungry and I guess I stared. A man took me by the shoulder and pushed me out. I was not dressed well enough to be in there anyway.

As I walked along wondering where I would rest for the night, I passed a place with a high brick wall around it. Curious, I walked around the wall and came to an open gate. Inside I saw a large courtyard where men were brushing and washing beautiful horses. This must be the American cavalry, I thought. I took a closer look.

The men were talking to their horses and whistling cheerful tunes as they groomed them. No one paid any attention to me. I liked my boy disguise that allowed me freedom to do many things almost unnoticed.

Across the courtyard was a three-story building that appeared to be quarters for the American men. A man's face appeared at an open upstairs window and he began calling out. One of the men with the horses nodded and gestured for me to look up. I looked around just to be sure he was talking to me. I looked up at a very friendly face which I couldn't understand except for one word, "chocolate."

"Oh yes, thank you." I answered in the few English words I knew.

The face disappeared and I returned to watching the men groom their horses. Feeling tired, I sat on the ground to rest. Soon the man with the friendly face came through a door carrying an armful of all kinds of sweet stuff. In the twilight of the evening, his shadow appeared to be eight feet tall and three feet wide. He looked so big! Enormous! Startled at his size, I jumped up and let out a yell. The man gaped at me in astonishment. As I turned around and ran out of there as fast as I could I heard loud laughter. But I had never talked to an American before nor even been close to one. He was really strange, much taller and different from the Russians and Germans or even the French and English POWs. Yet, his arms had been full of chocolate candies.

I hurried since I still had a few blocks to go to find the address the nurse had given me. Curfew was very soon. The address was on the fifth floor in an apartment building. A woman almost as old as my grandmother opened the door. I explained my situation and my search for Papa to this woman, since she seemed friendly. She said, "Yes, you may stay with me." Later I learned she was a widow. I felt secure with my new friend, Frau Berger, and thanked God that night for my safety. I slept soundly on a big feather-tick under a feather comforter.

The next morning Frau Berger needed to get firewood and I offered to help. After eating a breakfast of rye bread, chicory coffee and jam, we set out to get a load of wood. We filled her four wheeled hand wagon, and she pushed and I pulled until we got it back to her building. Carrying the wood to the fifth floor was quite a chore. However, she had promised me some food and lodging.

When we had our vegetable stew dinner she asked, "Are you aware of the curfew, boy?" I nodded.

She continued, "The curfew starts as soon as it gets dark. The military police drive around in jeeps looking for all kinds of people. Entrances to buildings are locked just before curfew, so don't run into a doorway thinking you can hide in there. The MPs and German police work together. People without proper IDs are sent back to the East. This could be real trouble for you. They'll pick up anybody and take them to jail."

With Ortwin's ID I could not afford to be caught. I searched through hospitals all day with no luck. However, one day I went further into Zirndorf and found a camp for German POWs. American guards marched the POWs out in the morning and back in the late afternoon. I decided to wait until they returned.

With many hours to wait, I walked around and talked to any likely person about where to locate missing persons. There were many POW camps, refugee camps, and even more military hospitals. The Red Cross was busy with people who had lost citizenship from their home country. There were even camps for orphans who became lost while looking for their parents. Refugee camps were filled with families from the Eastern territories and housing was scarce. It would take a long time to bring order to things.

When I returned to the camp, the POWs were just entering the compound. As they passed, I slipped into their lines and marched in with them. Since I wore a sort of uniform too, although I lacked the "POW' printed on the back, and despite being somewhat smaller than the prisoners, I was hard to detect. A girl could never have done this, I thought. After marching a while, we were ordered to stand at attention. They closed the gates. I would worry about that fact later. Group leaders reported that all men were present then dismissed them. I walked among the POWs asking questions. Some men seemed surprised, some laughed.

"A kid has infiltrated! He's looking for his Dad."

"Where are you from? What is the name again?"

"What organization was he in?"

Many questions, but no answers. "I'm trying to find out if he is still alive. My mother has five children and she is waiting for him to come back from the war. He won't know that we're alive since we moved after being bombed."

"He may not be alive. He could be in another camp or in one of the Vet's hospitals. He might be in any one of them."

As the men went inside they shrugged their shoulders and said they would like to help but no one knew anything to tell. Forlorn and disappointed, I walked slowly toward the gate. The guards saw me and I was taken into an office.

An American, who I later learned was a first sergeant, sat behind his desk and said, "You are in deep trouble boy." I did not understand him but I was worried by the tone of his voice. I told him, in German language, all there was to tell about my search for Papa. With the help of a translator he listened to my story.

"I could hand you over to the German Police!"

I could not hold back the tears. As he spoke to the translator, I was told he had decided to help me.

"Come," he said and led me to an American jeep with open sides. We got in. But I could run if things looked like he would hand me over to police. He drove through the streets and didn't say anything. Occasionally he whistled a tune. I hoped he would not find out who I really was because then he might not help me.

He stopped in front of a civilian apartment building. As he got out, he indicated I should stay in the jeep and that he would be right back. It was getting late and I knew I could not get to Frau Berger's home before curfew time.

Someone whistled. I looked up and saw the American motioning for me to come upstairs. I went up. A German girl stood in the open doorway and said, "Come in, boy. I am Sergeant James' fiancée, Anita. You may sleep on my couch tonight."

She looked at my worn out uniform and boots, shook her head in disapproval that she had to look at such a mess as I walked in and asked, "What's your name, lad?"

"Ortwin" I replied.

They gave me my first American "junk food." I saw and ate American white bread for the first time.

"This is like cake. Do Americans eat cake every day?"

"Don't be silly. It isn't cake, it's bread," she said.

I ate a whole sandwich. The fine grain melted in my mouth. I was excited by everything she gave me-corned beef, candy, chewing gum and chocolate. I inspected each piece as I ate it. "In East Germany, any person caught by the police with items like this that are made in America would get a jail sentence. I have much to tell Mama and my brothers."

They both smiled as I enjoyed the unusual food. Here I was, eating American food and the police did not know about it! Anita acted as though this amazing food was just everyday stuff.

The guard had an "MP" on his uniform along with a lot of bright brass and I thought he must be someone really important. His boots were shined perfectly.

My oversized boots looked shabby and out of place here. I had worn the poorly fitting boots for over two years now. "I hope to have shoes that fit some day," I said more to myself than to my hosts.

He looked so well dressed from head to foot even though the war had made many people into paupers.

"You can find everything under the sun on the West German black market," Anita explained. I wondered what black market she meant when her American friend must have brought everything she needed.

"There are still many people without enough clothing here in West Germany too. Mostly bombed out people or refugees. They come by the thousands and all want to stay here," she continued.

While she put away the dishes, she said, "Some people have relatives in the United States and receive gift packages and some even receive care packages." I had no idea what "care" meant and I was too tired to ask.

When she finished her work she went to sit with her boyfriend and they began hugging and kissing in an open manner. He seemed embarrassed. He looked at me, said something, and then tried to push her away. She kept clinging to him. I was sure he would enjoy her caresses if I had not been there. If she knew I was a girl she would probably kick me out.

"Do you want to smoke?" She interpreted what he said.

"Have one," he said, holding his cigarettes.

"I have never smoked," I replied. "Although I sold our own homegrown tobacco, I had never smoked it. My brothers do that for me to taste if it had the right fermentation and I even saw them. I use diluted homemade sugarbeet syrup diluted to prepare the tobacco."

They thought this was funny. I took a cigarette and watched him as he lit it. I inhaled and gasped! The stinging smoke in my lungs and throat made me cough. They laughed as they watched me try that first puff on a cigarette. "I'll do it later," I explained, laying the cigarette in the ashtray. "I thank you though for your help."

They were friendly and did not press me further. After a night's rest, I again thanked them for my bed and continued on with my search for Papa.

At one of the veteran's hospitals I was shocked to see so much suffering. Many patients had one or both arms or legs missing. I stared at one man's stumps and began to shake. The room felt warm and I took my hat and coat off, unbuttoning the top of my shirt collar.

Startled, I heard, "Hey guys, my bride has come to see me." He roared with laughter, others shouted and whistled.

Scared of any questions, I left quickly. I walked rapidly back to Frau Berger's home. My thoughts were of Mama and of getting home. Frau Berger seemed relieved as she greeted me. "I was so worried about you. I thought they had arrested you. I kept soup on the stove waiting for you."

I thanked her for thinking of me and proceeded to tell her about my activities and my desire to go home. "I doubt that Papa is here and I am needed at home."

"I understand. You are a very brave kid. I'll fix some food for you to eat on your way home."

With her gift of food I left for the railroad station where the Red Cross gave me a ticket to ride to the border. The station was filled with people looking for missing family members. The Red Cross had hundreds of thousands of names on files of missing people. Although I did not know it then, it was to take twenty years or more for some families to be reunited and some have never found each other to this day.

People were talking about the Nuremberg trials, then in progress. I saw black market activities and could not participate. I talked to other travelers about how to cross the border. They were saying, "Don't go here" or "Don't go there." Some towns, they said, were better to go through then others. "Go to Hof and then straight north." I soon knew I'd have to make up my own mind. This time I would be alone with no experienced Czechoslovakians to guide me. Word got around the waiting area that "a kid wants to make it back." Someone found an old map, pieced together with pins.

"Perhaps this will help," said an older man. I thanked him and sat down to study it. I boarded the night train so I would be at the border by dawn. Although the border was not that far, in these days the trains were always delayed. Besides, I wanted to spend a day on the western side near the border trying to find some food to take back home.

After we passed the city of Kronach only a few people were left in the passenger car. As the train sped toward the border I looked out of the window and knew spring was coming. I could smell it in the country air. I wished for lighter shoes and knew I'd be walking a long distance. The heavy boots hurt my feet.

When the train stopped I stepped down from the car and could see that the tracks were actually cut off. The earth had already forgotten that once, right here, trains had run through and fro. Now the ground was covered with a thick growth of grass. Uncertain about where to go, I walked along a road and into a farming area. I needed more directions than the map had provided. I had to be very careful who I asked.

Near the village of Stockheim I saw a woman in front of a farmhouse washing milk cans. I approached her. After explaining my needs, she faced me, put her hands on her hips and looked me up and down for a full minute. Then she said, "Come in the house."

I followed her.

"I am a war widow. I have a sizable farm and my foreign help has gone home. I grow produce and it is hard to get help.

Even the refugees don't want to work. They would rather stay in the camps where they are fed for nothing. No one will work for so little money." She poured me a glass of fresh milk then sat down and watched me drink it.

She looked very serious and said, "How about you? Are you interested in work?"

"I'll have to think about it." I was trying to grasp her situation in relation to my needs. "I need food more than money."

"I would let you go home every second weekend or so."

"But how can I go back and forth safely?"

"I know the forest master well, he may be able to help you."

"I don't see how it could work, I mean, to help you on a continuous basis."

"I'll give you as much food as you can carry."

To get food for Mama was a real temptation. To risk my life crossing the border again was another matter.

I hesitated, then said, "I'll help for a while. Let me think about coming back after I try crossing the border again. It is very dangerous on the other side." She nodded, saying she knew the border well.

I hesitated again, then took the plunge. "I must tell you something you don't know. I am a girl."

Her eyes widened and she looked at me more closely.

"These are the only clothes I have to wear. It is better for me to have people think I am a boy."

She nodded, then a twinkle came into her eyes. "You're okay. A real plucky kid. I admire your courage. My name is Theresa, what is yours?"

"Irene."

"Well, Irene, let's start by talking to the forest master."

As we walked through the village and up to the woods, I wondered why I completely trusted this brown curly haired woman with a round face and hands weathered by too much outside work. I could see she was intent upon having me work for her.

It turned out the forest master was a trusted friend. He agreed to go with me as far as possible to guide me toward and over the border.

The next two weeks were hard work! Theresa gave me some old clothes, skirts and blouses. Now I looked like a farm woman instead of a boy. I really did not care how I looked. My thoughts were on earning food. Up at five o'clock each day, I doused myself with cold water to wake up, then dressed quickly. After rinsing my mouth and combing my hair, I was ready for the day. While Theresa milked the cows I broke up a bale of hay and fed the horses. They nuzzled my sleeves as I fed them and as I pumped water and filled their watering troughs. We strained milk into large cans, then carried them to the front of her property and set them on a wooden rack for the dairy truck to pick up.

After morning chores we went inside and drank milk and ate hearty pieces of bran bread spread with lard and cracklings. After breakfast we cleaned out the stalls and bundled straw from the threshing floor. We climbed up into the hay loft and kicked bales of hay through an opening to the courtyard below. Then we dragged the bales into the stables. We cut them open and distributed them around the animals, but not before we cleaned out the stables from the old dirty stuff which we deposited on a pile outside. This was ready manure for the fields in the spring.

The sun came out every day and melted the snow. Spring came in a rush, drying up puddles on the roads and in the fields. But it was still cold. The farmland would soon be dry enough to till for seeding. I stayed two weeks with Theresa, helping her with all the farm work. I wasn't hungry and the food made me stronger.

When it was time to leave for East Germany she said, "I'll pay you in money rather than food if you prefer."

I told her, "When I get back home, food will be worth much more than money. The Reichsmark isn't worth anything anymore. My family is hungry and food is scarce."

She filled my knapsack and wooden suitcase with smoked sausages, salted bacon, baked goods, flour, butter, hard boiled eggs and many other good things. In this day and age my food supply was worth a fortune and my suitcase felt as heavy as bags of gold.

Early that rainy spring day Theresa walked with me to the forest master. He knew what was expected and picked up my heavy case of food to help me get started on my journey. "I'm afraid you will not come back." Theresa frowned. "I need your help so much."

"I will come back if it can be done," I promised.

The forest master carried the heavy load of food as far as he could toward the border, then stopped and said, "You're on your own from here kid. Be careful. Don't get caught. You know it's very dangerous."

"Thank you for your help, sir," I smiled bravely but my heart knew I feared the miles ahead.

"Stay to the right and you will see a fairly wide road when you get down this hill," said the forest master. "Keep hidden and stay in the brush. When you are sure no one is around, cross the road. Never mind the farm houses, they are probably empty. The East German authorities moved those families away from the border. This is no man's land. Avoid being seen until you see the town of Sonneberg. The train will stop there."

Down the rocky hill I went, stopping often to rest and listen. A gentle rain began falling and all seemed very quiet. I lifted my heavy load and zigzagged through the underbrush. Just as he had said, I saw the wide road at the bottom of the hill. At the least little noise I dropped to the ground and listened, holding my breath. I sat under a bush and looked to my left side, where I detected a narrow path. My action was not a moment too soon. A horde of Russian soldiers on horseback came in silence, riding right by me. They were so close, and I saw their ready-to-shoot rifles glistening in the sun. I was able to see that they were Mongols. The Russian Army had many Mongolian soldiers in its midst. Luckily they did not see me, but I now realized how closely the border was watched. I felt tense and fearful, remembering my recent trip over the border.

Once I was sure they were gone I picked up my gear again.

The hill became very steep just above a flat clearing near the road. I stayed in the bushes as far as possible, then listened a long time before hurrying across the clearing and over the road. I rested in the shelter of some high bushes. I had read Karl May's books about the American Indian putting his ear to the ground to listen for footsteps that were some distance away. I tried it. All seemed quiet.

I struggled on with my heavy load, walking along the edge of the road near the underbrush. It was mid-morning and I hoped to get a train out of Sonneberg. I did not know the train schedule or the terrain between me and the railroad station. The ground was getting soft from the rain so I left the underbrush and walked along the hard road. It was less slippery but much more dangerous since I might be seen.

When I saw the Sonneberg railroad station in the distance, I felt confident and more relaxed. Hopefully, I would reach the station without mishap. I stayed on the road. Suddenly an old World War II car veered into sight! Two men were in it and they stopped. "Hey, kid, hop in. We know where you're coming from."

I gasped, fearing I'd lose everything I had worked for.

"How is it on the other side?"

I stared in amazement. In a real friendly fashion one of them got out and loaded my heavy suitcase into the car. They were Germans and in a hurry to get somewhere.

"We'll outsmart the Russian patrol by picking you up." I sank into the back seat next to my suitcase and asked, "Could you get me a ticket for the train? I have money."

I knew I would be suspected if I went into the station with all my luggage. They drove up to the station and got out. I waited by the car until the younger man returned with my ticket. "Good luck kid, I hope you make it home safe." Suddenly I realized no one really cared much when people returned to East Germany.

As I lifted my heavy suitcase onto the train, a man walking along the tracks said, "We will not roll until afternoon but get on and find a seat."

People were already seated inside the train and some had waited since the day before. I learned there was only one train out of Sonneberg each week.

"You'll be lucky if you are not stopped by the Russians," a man warned me as he eyed my heavy suitcase.

So there would be more Russian control. I checked to see that my ID, with its official looking stamp, was in my pocket. As scheduled, the train left and no Russian patrol had entered to check IDs. It was dark when we arrived in Zwickau and I had to change trains quickly.

Many people were leaving the uranium mines for the weekend. They were crowding into the train, carrying heavy luggage and bumping into fellow travelers. A man tripped against my heavy suitcase. He swore, picked it up and threw it off the train. I jumped down after it. The heavy knapsack on my back buckled me to my knees.

I yelled, "I must have my suitcase!"

"Like hell you do! Look at our shins! There is no room," several men bellowed. We stood there packed in like sardines.

I lifted my suitcase up again and pushed it on the train, then jumped up to get a standing place. The suitcase was kicked off again. Fearing it would break, I screamed. After listening to more cursing, I was in tears.

"Give the kid his suitcase!"

The fight went on until the whistle blew. I was then off the train and my suitcase was on. The train started to roll. Train personnel, keeping a watchful eye to see that people did not cling to the outside of the train, were coming to prevent me from boarding. In desperation I ran and jumped up trying to get in before they closed the doors. A rough hand reached down and jerked me up into the overcrowded car. It took a few stations, till some people got off, before I discovered my suitcase. All the passengers were men working in the uranium mines in Oberscilema, Schneeberg and Aue. This was a restricted area. It was the reason why I saw so many police and Russians were on the platform.

When I changed trains in Glauchau it was much easier than before since I did not have to leave the tracks. I got off and the train and left. The next train pulled up and I boarded with ease. In Chemnitz I stayed at the tracks again and boarded a train to

Niederwiesa. Outside the Chemnitz railroad station I knew only too well, would be the strong police force waiting for "hoarders," and hoping to confiscate foods stuff that people were bringing home under great hardship. Fortunately they didn't give me a second glance.

From Niederwiesa I had to walk about four miles then I would be home. Upon reaching Niederwiesa I half carried and half slid the wooden suitcase into the luggage holding area. After seeing it stored safely on a shelf where it would be under the watchful eyes of the train personnel, I said, "I'll send my brothers for my suitcase." I turned and began walking, then I started to run. I was home at last.

"Irene! Irene! You've really come back." Mama's embrace was a haven of safety and warmth.

Everybody cried with joy. Ortwin and Hartmut left immediately to get the precious food checked at the railroad station. What a story I had to tell. They all listened intently as I told my stories about West Germany.

"Mama, the Americans eat bread as fine and white as cake every day. They never eat that dark bread like ours. They have so much chocolate they want to give it away. They actually asked me if I wanted some! The bakery gave me a whole loaf of bread. Not like here, where we have to fight and beg for a slice of bread. The butcher gave me sausage without my asking for anything. I looked and looked for Papa and I couldn't find him." I was out of breath and very tired.

"Mama, I'll go back to the farm where I worked and bring lots of good food home."

"It's too dangerous. I'm afraid you will be killed!"

I knew we could use the food. Everyone looked so thin and hungry. With great pleasure, I watched their faces when we opened the knapsack and then the suitcase. A large piece of ham, and so much bacon. They had not seen this much meat since before the war.

Late in April I convinced Mama that I should try once more to cross the border. I was rested, my clothes were clean, and Mama had once again cut my hair short. She hugged me as I left, saying, "God be with you Irene. Be careful." Tears streaked her thin worried face.

I planned to get to the border by nightfall. Although the distance could have been traveled in half a day, the zigzag pattern of travel that the Czechoslovakians had taught me would take more time. I traveled west through Glauchau and down to Zwickau, then jumped on a boxcar that took me a little out of my way. I again bought a ticket to Plauen and tried to avoid the restricted area of Aue.

Near the border I saw so many police it seemed like an army. It crossed my mind that the authorities could be concealing the fact that our defeated country had an army again, dressed in police uniform.

By nightfall the train was rolling toward the town of Sonneberg. Before the city came into sight, the train stopped in the middle of nowhere and someone shouted, "Control!"

Police and Russians were boarding to look for unauthorized persons in the border area. By the time the train would arrive in Sonneberg, all arrests would be already made. As they boarded, I jumped off. More police and guards were walking alongside the train with their backs to me. As they walked alongside the train, they shouted that no one was allowed to get off or they would get shot. Both sides of the train were encircled now and I knew I had jumped just in time. I tried to move away from the embankment and into some bushes. I had to find out where I was but it was pitch dark. No moon lit the way. Flattening myself against the ground I listened, hoping the blackness of the night would hide me.

Men were running and voices grew more excited and louder as they moved closer in my direction. They shouted and walked slower.

There must have been a few more people lucky enough to jump off just in time. The Russians, who had machine guns, were shooting into the air, trying to keep everybody else inside. Had they seen me? I didn't know. Slowly I turned my head, keeping most of my face covered. It was so dark I could only see the machine guns reflected by the lanterns. Apparently they were unaware of me.

Several people were taken off the train and lined up. I felt sorry for them. Instead of a trip to the west and freedom it would be jail for years and hard times for them. Presumably, the police were not going to board the train again. This meant we must be within walking distance of Sonneberg.

The train pulled out and the police with their prisoners marched on. I finally found myself alone, walking on the railroad tracks toward town. When the railroad station came into view I knew the direction I must go to cross the border. To avoid unexpected patrols I occasionally paused and listened into the night. I constantly watched for any movement in the darkness. Slowly, quietly, I walked around the town staying near the fields.

I found the road that led me to the boulder strewn hill and climbed into West Germany. It must have been three in the morning when I arrived at Theresa's farmhouse. I sat on a bench in front of her house and fell asleep. Awakened by noises inside the house I knocked on the door. "Irene! You've really come back," Theresa cried. "I'm so glad. I was afraid you would not be able to get through.

"It is very dangerous, Theresa, and now there are so many police. I have been traveling all night and I am very tired."

While Theresa made hot broth and poured it on big chunks over dark bread to make flavored breadsoup, I told her of my trip back home and about my hungry family. "Mama thinks things will soon be better but I see no sign of it. Everyone is hungry. It's a pity if only you could see the people over there. They must fight just for a slice of bread."

"Nothing will ever change over there," said Theresa. "You should consider staying here." Of course she knew the West German authorities would not let me stay and that I would not abandon my family.

After some rest, I picked up where I had left off. Theresa and I worked outside all day, and then Theresa prepared the meals. There was plenty for us to eat.

One day Theresa said, "While you're here I can be a little like your mother." She smiled and patted my shoulder. I was happy for her friendship.

"Our Summer Festival is this weekend," Theresa explained. "What size dress do you wear?"

"Dress? I don't know what size. It's been some time since I had a dress to wear."

I could not picture myself in a pretty dress but I was very curious about her plans. I was sure a new dress in West Germany could only be found on the black market. To my delight, Theresa got me a beautiful dress. The skirt had little flowers on it and the top was black with a collar made from the same material as the skirt. I loved its wide skirt and the petticoat that came with it.

For the first time in years I had a pair of girl's shoes. They were not new but that made no difference. Red shoes, they were sandals. So pretty and perfect and just my size. She gave me some underwear of her own and a string of red beads. As I looked in the mirror, I saw another person. I was a girl again. It felt good. If only Mama and my brothers could see me now. They did not know how good it was to be in West Germany.

"Thank you. Thank you so much, Theresa." I could not keep the tears from my eyes.

"Those stars in your eyes are thanks enough. Come now, after the evening chores we will go to the dance."

At the dance I felt out of place at first. Soon Theresa introduced me to her friends and I learned many of them had already heard about me. I did not know how to dance but I saw that one of the musicians had a button accordion. At intermission I asked if I could play his instrument. He hesitated but then consented half-heartedly. I thanked him and started to play, first two waltzes then two tangos. Soon everyone was singing and tapping their feet. The other instruments followed me and it was one of the happiest times in many years.

Afterwards I sat with Theresa and her friends when a soldier still wearing parts of his uniform, along with civilian clothing, came toward me and said, "I'll teach you to dance if it kills me."

We laughed as he led me by the hand onto the dance floor. The floor was polished and slick and I slipped and tripped my partner. We both fell down. Laughing and joking, we scrambled to our feet. He then took me in a dance position and counted to the music, "One, two, three, four. Watch and step with me." He smiled and I followed. "One two three four and don't hesitate," he prompted.

It didn't take long at all until I could step to the rhythm of the music. First I learned to waltz, then to tango. What fun! After I learned a few steps, other boys asked me to dance. I did not even have time to drink a lemonade. I was getting warm but there was no stopping as I danced with partner after partner.

I felt light on my feet in the pretty red sandals. After learning the dance steps I felt relaxed and talked to my partners. I kidded with the fellows and they gave me tips on how to avoid the guards at the border. Most of them had lived in this area all their lives.

Our table was constantly surrounded by fellows wanting to dance or just talk. Theresa stood up and said pleasantly, "She must go home now, enough is enough. Tomorrow we have much work and church." As we left the fellows called "good night" from the doorway. Theresa and I laughed and talked all the way home.

Two weeks later I left at dawn to make my way back across the border. I left Theresa and the forest master at the top of the hill and descended the rocky slope, slipping often with my heavy load of food. Now and then when I listened for several heartbeats, all I could hear was an occasional bird. At the bottom of the hill I crossed the clearing and the road to hide in the brush. I was breathing heavily from the strain of carrying my heavy knapsack and the old beat up suitcase. Everything was so quiet that I kept going in a hurry, rushing to catch the once-a-week train out of Sonneberg.

Just as I shouldered my heavy load, three riders on horses came silently out of the bushes. We spotted each other almost at the same moment. They whipped their horses to a gallop and were quickly in front of me--all Russians.

"Stoyt!" (Stop) they shouted. Since they were not sure I would understand Russian they started shooting in the air to emphasize that I should stop. They jumped off their horses. Towering over me they shouted in Russian. I knew they were asking questions. I guessed they wanted to know what I was carrying and where I was coming from. I could not understand.

They ripped off my knapsack and grabbed my heavy bags of food. I protested and they laughed and knocked me to the ground. I hoped they would not discover that I was a girl, so I dared not get up as they cursed each other and fought over my food. I thought about Mama. We could have lived for weeks on all that food.

They must have decided to shoot me after taking my things. One of them took a big revolver out of his holster and checked the bullets. I could see he was trying to make himself angry so it would be easy to shoot me. He kicked me on the leg and shot the ground close to my head. I could hear the bullets strike the ground and smell the dust it made. I knew he was going to kill me.

My eyes were wide open and I wondered how it would be to die. Two of them started kicking me and shooting so close at me that I had to quickly move from one side to the other. Each blow from their boots sent sharp pains through my body. My arms and legs felt limp as blow after blow struck my body. The blows came so fierce, suddenly I could not see. I must plead for them to stop, I thought. I felt all three of them worked me over at the same time and I knew I soon would faint and die.

Suddenly I was looking down at myself lying on the ground. I was a spectator and nobody saw me, but I saw the whole scene. A dirty, bloody bundle, lifeless. Although three pair of boots kicked and stepped all over me I felt no pain. I knew instinctively that this was me and I thought, why is this happening? They began playing Russian Roulette. Once they shot close to my head, then directly at it. They laughed as though they were having great fun. One soldier found his gun empty, started reloading and tried to hurry to get into the fun again. Then shots were heard nearby. A man on a horse was galloping toward us and I wondered if he would run his horse's hooves over my body. As he approached he shouted and shot into the air. He whirled his horse to a stop and the men stopped shooting.

Dismounting, he yanked me to my feet with such force that I was conscious of being in my body again. As blackness came over me I felt my bowels move and I filled my pants. It was the last thought I had as I slid to the ground.

I must have lain there for a while before I regained consciousness. I saw the man and my attackers were eating and dividing my possessions.

The man who was in command kept saying something that I understood as "He is a young boy. Let him go."

I opened my eyes to see one of the Russians staring down at me.

"Where do you belong?" He spoke in broken German.

I pointed toward the village I had come from in West Germany. The pain in my body was returning with vengeance and I wasn't sure if I could stand up and walk. I did not dare tell them my home was in Euba. I got on all fours then slowly stood up on my feet. My whole body hurt. All I wanted to do was to go to Theresa's house if I possibly could.

"*Dawey! Dawey!*" They all shouted angrily at me. Pointing toward the village where I came from. They knew without me telling them that I had come from the west. Nobody would have such good and abundant food in the east, but running up a hill in my condition was impossible. I walked, climbed, slipped, stood up and fell, all the while tears running down my face. After a few yards I leaned exhausted on a tree trunk. They started shooting into the air and I stopped for a while. When the shooting stopped I began climbing again. Once I was sure I was out of danger I sat down and rested behind a large rock.

Everything was taken except my ID card and some money I had put in my breast pocket. If they had searched me and discovered I was a girl from East Germany, they would have raped and killed me.

Finally, I reached Theresa's farmhouse. When she opened the door, she looked at me and became hysterical, crying and laughing at the same time.

"My dear girl, what have they done to you?"

"I thought they were going to kill me. When I left I had such beautiful white underclothing and look at me now."

"Come dear, you do need a bath," she said as she hurried to prepare some hot water.

As she gently washed my bruised body, Theresa said, "They worked you over badly. We ought to go get you x-rayed, you might have broken something."

"No I don't think so, my bones are made out of rubber" I joked. "I am alive and that is all that counts."

I hoped that I had not received some serious damage, my insides hurt so badly. "God was with me, Theresa, I know it."

As she bandaged my wounds she said "One thing is for sure, you had a guardian angel that watched over you."

I rested a few days to partially recover from the deep bruises on my body. Theresa pleaded with me to stay with her, saying it was too dangerous to try to go back into East Germany. I wished I could stay. I was tired and things seemed hopeless. But when I thought of Mama I knew I must return.

"My family needs me. They are so thin and hungry. You saw my skinny body. They too are starving and they have no one to help them. So many people are dying from hunger and typhoid. I just can't let this happen to them."

Theresa looked very sad and replied, "You are a brave girl."

"I'll be much more careful next time," I replied.

One week later we got things together again. Friends in the village gave me an old knapsack and Theresa filled this and two cloth sacks, one for each hand. Laden with bacon, flour, butter, cheese, bread, boiled eggs and a bottle of oil. I set out one morning at dawn. By being extra cautious, I made it across the border and got to the railroad station on time. I did not want to risk running into the Russian patrol inside the station so I quickly boarded the train, planning to buy my ticket once I got on board. If questioned I'd say I lost my ticket.

Late that afternoon the train started to roll then stopped after traveling only a short distance. We waited there for hours. People talked quietly about anything except themselves. I surmised many of them were making the same sort of trip as I was. We were all carrying old luggage or sturdy sacks that appeared to contain food or black market wares. Most of us were thin. Our clothes were ill-matched, poorly fitted and dark in color. Few of us were wearing shoes of the right size.

By contrast the people in West Germany had enough to eat to keep a decent amount of flesh on their bones. Their shoes fit, and although their clothes appeared worn, they were pressed far better than anyone I had seen in East Germany. People in the West walked briskly with a sense of purpose in their lives and I saw no gaunt hollow-eyed people with the look of utter despair on their faces. Their faces displayed hope, hope that they would build up again.

American authorities, whether police or guards, were pleasant and courteous when conducting their work. The difference was so great I wasn't sure I could explain it to Mama.

The train started again and the realities of East Germany stood harshly before me. The next stop was Probstzella, not many miles from Sonneberg, but still near the border and it was dark. A guard informed us the train would not run at night and we could not stay on it. This aroused tension and fear about where we were and where we would sleep. Since we were seeking transportation away from the border we considered ourselves somewhat safe among the numerous police guards.

The command to "Find yourself a bed" told me not to expect a room by myself. My knapsack and two bags of food slowed me when I tried to follow the others seeking shelter. I barely managed to keep their shadowy figures in view as I followed. There were no street lights in this border town.

They stopped in front of what appeared to be a large inn.

A sign, lit by a lamp on the wall of the building had the name of the Inn, "Zur Post." The entrance was dark. As we approached, someone opened the door to reveal a lighted interior. We entered the main room. I turned and wanted to leave! The place was totally full with singing and beer-drinking uniformed policemen. I knew I could not find lodging out there in the dark. I had no choice but to go right into the "devil's kitchen."

Timidly, I walked forward. Police were everywhere. They filled every table, laughing, talking, singing and drinking lots and lots of beer. They were off duty and they did not want to notice people with their bags. Smoke filled the room and the man at the counter was busy filling large beer stems with Pils Beer.

Ignoring my pounding heart, I held my head high and walked right up to the bar where a stout looking man handed over the beer to a waitress.

Like the people before and behind me, I asked, "Do you have a room?"

"Do you have a police permit? If not, we cannot give you a place to sleep."

"How do I get one?"

"Follow those people," he pointed. "They're going for permits. They will show you. It's about four blocks away."

As I turned away from the counter I saw the people I had traveled with all day walking toward the door. I followed and we walked out into the night. After my eyes adjusted to the dark I realized I was far behind them again. I caught up with them as they were crossing a square. Worried about getting the permit, I hoped to talk to my fellow travelers about what to say but no one wanted to talk. Finally a man said, "Tell them as little as possible. That is all I can say."

Upon arriving we were told to wait on long benches in a brightly lighted hallway. No one could overhear reasons others gave for requesting lodging since each person entered a specified office, one at a time. I was fearful and uncertain when my turn came to be questioned.

"What is your reason for traveling?" asked the night officer.

"I visited in Sonneberg and I am on my way home, sir. You know how unreliable the trains are, often changing routes without scheduling. We have just arrived after long waits all day. I am stuck in a strange town."

He looked at me and his eyes narrowed. His face took on a new interest as he said, "You visited who in Sonneberg?"

"Some relatives. I'm on my way home." I swung my knapsack off my shoulders and placed it on the floor.

"What is your name?"

I hesitated, adjusting the straps on my knapsack. He got up, came around the desk and ripped the cap off my head. I sensed he thought I was a girl.

"Dein name n bischen dally!" (Your name and be quick about it.)

His face was so close to mine that if I perked my lips I would have kissed him. He shouted and I turned my face away. He grabbed me because he thought I would step back and away from him. I was surprised at that moment to see how ugly a man could be. I was outraged by his power over me. I dared not give my brother's name. I believed if I lied now he wouldn't believe that I had visited relatives in Sonneberg. He would ask me to open my baggage and I would lose all my food again. Prison would be certain.

"Irene," I hurried to add. "I have to travel as a boy. You have no idea what men do to girls. It's much safer to travel as a boy."

"Only if you can get away with it," he smiled as he returned to his desk. 'I'll give you a pass for tonight but never let me catch you again." He was shaking his head, while he wrote out my permit.

'Thank you, sir." I curtsied and walked outside.

Suddenly I felt relaxed and free from tension. A permit to sleep in the hotel! How lucky! I felt as if I was flying as I returned to the Inn. When I got there I walked right into that room full of police.

We were charged a few marks for the night and then were directed upstairs into a large long room containing about forty narrow beds, twenty on each side. Men and women were not separated and the light stayed on all night. Our beds were meticulously clean and narrow like a soldier's bed, with thin mattresses and white sheets. White pillows and field grey blankets completed our sleeping accommodations.

We were checked and permission slips were relinquished. The police counted us again, then counted the slips. Each of us was assigned a bed. I tied my knapsack and two bags of food to the headpiece of the bed. I was not worried someone would steal it unless the smell of the food made someone very hungry. The light in the room was very bright. At the entrance of the long room was a desk where a policeman sat all night, I assumed to keep control over us. Getting into bed with most of my clothes on, I pulled my cap over my forehead to keep the light out of my eyes. Not even the noise from the boisterous policemen downstairs kept me from a deep sleep.

It was still dark outside when we were ordered to get up. The light was still on and we were hurried into a washroom and given a few minutes to use toilets, rinse our teeth and wash up. It was always, "Hurry! Hurry!"

After counting us again we were marched downstairs. I could just imagine the trouble and delay that would occur if there had been one too many of us, or worse, one less. Again, "Hurry! Hurry!" they shouted as we were rushed through the dark to a waiting truck.

I saw Russian guards with those awful machine guns hanging on their backs. Out of the truck and into the train, we had to move fast. Now it was "Dawey! Dawey!" the Russian call for HURRY. It was still dark and I had no idea what time it was. Those with watches kept the time to themselves as it was not wise to show a watch when Russian soldiers were around. They were everywhere, walking up and down the platform impatiently hurrying us on. No one was allowed to stay behind.

"Get on the train immediately!" shouted the police repeatedly. They wanted us all away from the border as quickly as possible. The shouting of orders was continuous and loud. Their departing shout was, "If you come back here you can expect to be under arrest!"

The train was dark and crowded. Men were standing. No one spoke as we jostled for places to sit or stand holding our ungainly bags as close as possible. The train moved then stopped. After this action was repeated several times, we finally pulled out to make our way to Thueringen. When we stopped at Saalfeld several people got off and those of us remaining were able to find a seat. To our dismay, more people got on and the train was once again filled beyond capacity. Many stood between cars and I heard bodies on the roof. I hoped they would not fall when the train went through the tunnels.

I changed trains once, to *Hauptbahnhof* (the mainstation) Chemnitz. The Dresden train stopped in Niederwiesa, and from that station I would walk home.

When I saw Mama's worried face I wept. "I cannot bear to let you go again, Irene. It's too risky."

"I know, Mama, it is very dangerous and right now all I want is some rest." I was too tired to think clearly.

In the days ahead I told Mama about the Russian patrol on horses and how I had gone back to Theresa's farm. I told her of the increasing numbers of police in the border area. We weighed those risks compared to working on the farm for food in East Germany and scouring the country for food by riding the freight cars and bartering in the black market.

"The food you bring makes a big difference but the danger is too great. We need more food than we can get from our work here on the farm. The boys work every hour they are not in school for almost nothing and they are hungry." Mama shook her head and sighed. "Surely this cannot last much longer. If the harvest from our garden would amount to anything, we could dry some stuff for the winter."

Of course I knew Mama was missing all her canning supplies she had lost in the bombing. Now it was impossible to buy these items. I was convinced the risks I took paid off in more than just food for our family and for some unknown reason the adventure of evading the police by traveling like I did was more than a little fascinating.

"The trade schools are not organized yet Mama. Until the schools offer classes again, I think I should try to bring food from West Germany. In a few days I'll go into Chemnitz and see how things really are."

Mama thought this was a good idea. Perhaps she would even relent and approve of my continued trips into West Germany. A few days later I took two raw potatoes and a few ounces of bacon and walked into Chemnitz. I needed money for train fares and the black market would provide me with it.

In Chemnitz changes were coming very slow. Day by day and brick by brick the brave rubble women (*Truemmerfrauen*) were cleaning and sorting the debris from the bombing. With their hands wrapped in rags or old gloves, they pushed their heavily laden lorries on tracks through the streets. Clearing was being done but no construction had begun. There was no evidence of any new materials to repair anything and cardboard still covered the windows.

Nevertheless, as meager as East Germany's efforts were, I knew deep inside me the vigor and industriousness of our people could return. German people are strong and thrifty.

A restaurant in the inner city was trying to reopen, and guests were sitting at tables in the open air with a view of the rubble. Its menu, which hung on a rock outside, announced that by bringing two large potatoes and paying in Reichsmark one could get a bowl of soup. I stood in line after forfeiting my potatoes and five Reichsmark for a slip of paper. After a long wait I was summoned to a table where others were already eating. The waiter, carrying a huge tray of bowls and acting like a military figure of authority, landed a bowl of soup in front of me. No utensils were provided. I ate with a spoon, which I always carried with me like anyone else, in case something eatable could be unexpectedly found.

I looked down at a bowl of watery soup, cabbage I guessed by the aroma plus, some grits and potato pieces. It was seasoned with spices to make it tasty. There was no meat in my serving and I felt sure the kitchen had no meat to serve. It was edible and it filled my stomach. When the waiter saw my bowl was almost empty, he ordered me to eat faster so others could be seated. As I saw him serving others in this same fashion, I thought of how lavish it was before the war and now how humble and timid we had become in our defeat. We were now pitiful creatures struggling to keep alive.

I walked from the restaurant, past the women working in the rubble, to the Schocken Department Store. It was now government property. Advertising merchandise was unheard of and the department stores stood empty and alone. No people were around it even though it was not bombed.

As late as 1948 some flimsy limited amounts of merchandise were seen. The entire store had no more than a dozen shirts, blouses, coats and other assorted clothing. It was sold out in minutes and the people that had waited in line since the day before, some who even slept on the pavement, had to go home with nothing. People living and working outside the city had no chance to buy anything. I walked to the railroad station where most of the black market activities took place. I received 200 Reichsmark for a pound of smoked bacon, more than enough to pay for my train fare to and from West Germany and still leave some money for Mama.

During the early months of 1947 and into the spring of 1948 I made many uneventful trips back and forth across the border between East and West Germany. Each time I made a trip the number of police seemed to be increasing. This was before the land mining intensified along the eastern part of the border. At that time the Communists used heavy police patrols, but many people were still able to slip through the borders. When caught they were sent to the Bautzen Penitentiary where they received eight to ten year sentences, just because they wanted to cross the border. I know this from a distant relative who disappeared and also by reading Walter Kempowski's Book "Im Block". He spent many years in Bautzen.

Winter, though bitter cold, was the safest time for those secretive trips. Russian border guards were not so keen on staying outside for many hours waiting to catch people in this subzero weather. The guards preferred card playing and the warmth of their little "watch houses."

I had learned what trains to catch and how to avoid crowded rail road stations. I studied train schedules constantly to avoid long waits. I learned to act as though I lived in whatever village I was in and to avoid the suspicious eyes of the police. The darkest nights with cloud cover from the moon gave me a feeling of greater safety when traveling in the country. I put my ear to the ground and listened often for the footsteps of men or their horses on patrol. I learned to distinguish noises but sometimes I mistook a running deer for a border patrol guard. It was easier to hear clear sounds during the winter months.

Mama once said I developed a keen sense of hearing and sight since I always heard the faintest whisper and saw the smallest movement in the house. I was not the only one to cross the border repeatedly in search of work and food. Sometimes I saw the same faces as I repeated my dangerous journeys. Some people who crossed the border at other places did not return.

It became easy to identify people approaching the border for the first time. They were apprehensive and some tried to hang on along my trail. Since this increased the danger, I tried to shake them just as the two Czechoslovakians once tried to lose me on my first trip.

Clothing to keep warm was a constant problem. One day a helpful villager in West Germany gave me an Eisenhower jacket. What a combination, the black SS uniform trouser topped by an Eisenhower jacket. It fit just fine. I bought a pair of worn men's shoes--a little large but a welcome change for warm weather. Theresa gave me some dresses but I always left them at her house.

Christmas of 1947 was bleak, but there was enough food to keep us alive. The distance and cold weather kept us from going into Chemnitz to worship. Instead, we attended services in the village church. We slowly realized that Papa might not be alive.

On a winter day early in 1948, I bought my last train ticket at the railroad station in Chemnitz to go toward the border of West Germany. I was hastily stuffing a sandwich into my mouth when a small boy came toward me, his hands outstretched for my food. He looked so starved, his large sad eyes made me stop eating and I gave him the other half of my sandwich. He consumed it immediately. I opened my knapsack and gave him another sandwich I was carrying for a later meal. He did not even smile but his dark hollow eyes were full of thanks as he ate the bread in big bites. I closed my knapsack and walked away with a lump in my throat, thankful to be able to bring food to my family.

In Glauchau I waited hours for another train. Russian soldiers making their rounds spotted me leaning against the wall outside of the station.

"You have wristwatch?"

I shook my head. Three of them closed in around me. Two of them grabbed my arms and rolled up my sleeves, looking for the watch I didn't have. One of them turned me around and twisted my arm high up my back. The intense pain made me feel faint and I buckled down on my knees. There was no one around to help me, as a German would have been much too afraid to interfere. If he breaks my arm, I'll have to go back home, I thought.

One of the soldiers, angry at not finding a watch, started to search my pockets. I flattened myself on the station platform.

He kicked me in the ribs and I doubled up in pain. Then they spotted another victim and left me after one more blow with a boot. I lay there until the pain stopped and thanked God my arm was not broken. The Russians were apparently only looking for watches. They seemed to think every German had a wristwatch. In those days it was better to leave a watch at home.

As the train arrived a compartment opened to reveal two Russians fighting with each other. Plunk! Several boxes fell out and broke open. Cartons of German cigarettes, made in Dresden, tumbled out onto the ground.

I and several others did not hesitate, we each picked up as much as we could, stuffing our pockets full. One girl looked up at me and said, "Oh! I just want to help them get their cigarettes."

"So do I," I said and quickly jumped on the slow moving train. I checked my pockets, twenty some packages of cigarettes. They were made of the finest Bulgarian tobacco, considered to be the best in East Germany. I tucked them into my knapsack and pretended I knew nothing about them.

When I arrived at Theresa's home, a refugee was living with her. It was much better for her to have two people working on her farm and it made it easier for me to tell her that I could not come back again. Schools would be opening soon and I planned to study nursing.

During the final few weeks of work the village people learned that I would not return. They showered me with gifts. I could not carry all of them, shoes, dresses, underwear and generous gifts of food. I mailed several boxes containing clothing, silk stockings, a whole sack of flour and the cigarettes I had picked up in East Germany. All nonperishable foods I could possibly get mailed off and all arrived safely in Euba.

"I'll try to send your family packages in the future," Theresa promised.

The words "thank you" seemed extremely inadequate when it was time to say goodbye to Theresa and to those I had made friends with. On another rainy day I walked, heavily laden with food, down the rocky bill and out of their lives.

My last trip was carefully timed. I was able to avoid the increasing police activity and arrived home under the shelter of darkness as I had done countless times before.

Book III

Iron Curtain Escape

My Journey to

Freedom

1948-1953

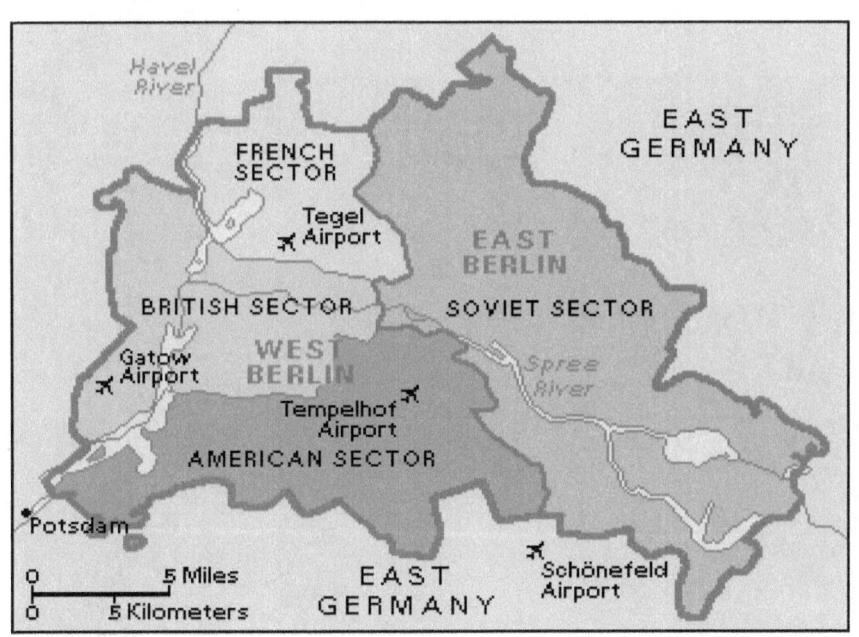

Berlin divided into four occupation zones

Irene and a friend in front of the tooth and jaw clinic

1951 East German staff (Irene front left)

Russian soldier steals a bicycle from East German woman.

Border between West Berlin and Soviet Sector at Potsdam

BUILDING
1948 - 1952

Being a girl again was an exhilarating kind of self renewal. I was almost nineteen and the pretty dresses and shoes Theresa gave me were a source of real pleasure.

Saturday night dances became the highlight of our social activity. They were held in a once fashionable dance hall and restaurant, nestled in the woods near the town of Adelsberg.

Krista and I walked with my brothers and other friends to this weekend event where we were soon caught up in the pleasure of flirtations, laughter and jolly good fun. I had learned how to dance in West Germany and the boys sure noticed me in my pretty clothes.

The Russian Army of Occupation did not interfere with our weekend dances. Although we knew they were near, and they showed themselves now and then, they stayed in the background. They were more disciplined now and we were getting used to the Russian soldiers. Now, we even saw many Russian girls in uniform.

Some German women, young as well and middle aged, still invited Russians into their homes. There they fraternized, even though it was forbidden to do so. Maybe some of them were in love, but Stalin's army punished such human behavior.

To us the Russian soldiers looked forlorn and poor. Their feet were still wrapped in ragged strips of cloth under boots which they aired in the open windows of their barracks. There they fluttered, grey and dingy, where once German soldiers had kept things so shiny and clean. The khaki color of their Cossack shirts did not hide their dingy look. Their winter coats seemed to all have been made in one size. Shorter soldiers simply cut their coats to a usable length and wore them without a hem, giving an unkempt appearance. They sang lively marching songs though, just as the Germans used to do. We often saw details of about 30 men marching and singing in their unhemmed coats.

By contrast, the Russian officers had better living conditions, better tailored uniforms, more food, more privileges and much more freedom.

Due to the Russian desire for theater and ballet, those forms of recreation were revived at the earliest possible date. Russians flocked to these cultural events. Soldiers were brought to the theaters by the bus loads, though they were not allowed to mingle with the German popularity. Much propaganda was made to support the German-Soviet friendship, for which we had to pay monthly dues. Yet the Soviets and the Germans were not even allowed to say "Hello" and "How do you like the German ballet?"

Tall and beautiful, my cousin, Margo, was a ballet dancer. Her never ending need for silk stockings was the chief reason we saw each other often. As soon as Margo heard that we received a box of silk stockings from Theresa, she came with food to trade for them. On one occasion she came in an old black chauffeured Nazi car, creating much curiosity amongst our neighbors. Out of the car stepped a high Russian officer with much brass and many ribbons on his uniform. He turned around and helped Margo out of the car. She was dressed very fashionablely. The chauffeur, a soldier, was told to wait.

Margo and the Russian officer came into our humble home and seemed to feel comfortable with us. Mama exchanged our silk stockings for foods. We learned that Margo was deeply in love with the Russian officer, but we knew that they would never be allowed to marry. Mama saw nothing but heartbreak in their secret love affair. When they learned the apartment above the horse barn was empty, they used those quarters for their rendezvous. Colonel Boris, as we called him, confiscated furniture to provide for their needs.

Since Colonel Boris's rank exceeded that of the village commandant, nothing was reported. When a car was parked near the barn we knew Margo and her Colonel were there.

In April of 1949 I entered a special prep school in Chemnitz to study for entrance tests in the field of nursing. After completing these tests I appeared before the Board of Examiners in order to enter nursing school.

"When you go in, say very little" coached my teacher, "Just answer 'yes' or 'no' to medical questions, but when they ask you political questions talk at great length. They like talkative people when it comes to politics." I did not understand politics well enough to say much and I felt utterly inadequate for the task.

On that important day, four men sat behind a long, high desk covered with a red cloth that hung nearly to the floor. Two of the examiners, who had self-important expressions on their rugged red skinned faces, were the politicians. The other two, whose faces and manners indicated more discipline, were the medical examiners.

The political questions came first. When I could not answer quickly, one of them would bark, "You lost one point there. Hurry it up!"

"How many miles are there in the East German border?"

I did not know how long this hateful border was.

"What kind of government do we have in East Germany?"

I did not know how to explain something so quickly that I did not like. I felt discouraged and we had hardly started. One of the men stood up, towering above me. He looked much taller than an ordinary man. I wanted to talk but I couldn't. I decided to run from the room and turned to leave.

"Come back here! Stand still, Genosse! All right, I will ask you something easier." He looked amused.

"What is the capital of East Germany? Ha ha."

"Berlin."

This was followed by other simple questions. They wanted me to talk about the German-Soviet friendship and whether I would be willing to make donations to this "worthy" cause. I knew I was expected to say "yes."

The medical examiner was courteous but thorough. My head was filled with physiology, anatomy, chemistry and bacteriology. I began to think I'd made it through this part of the examination in good shape. We were given the test results after long hours of anguished waiting.

I passed! Then on to the written tests. Which I also passed. It was exhilarating to succeed in the first steps of my chosen field of work. All that remained was the endless wait for the letter telling me where I could study. It was during this period that Margo came to our home to exchange food and sad news for silk stockings. We sensed a problem since Colonel Boris was not with her.

"Aunt Ella, you know my love for Boris. We cannot marry and I am going to have his child."

Mama was noticeably shocked. I knew mama had always admired Margo, her beauty and grace were as poetry to me.

"Margo, what can I say? I am so sorry." Mama was searching for words. "What will you do?"

"I don't know, Aunt Ella. Here are tickets to the next ballet. Perhaps you and Irene would like to come."

"Could you go to Russia with Colonel Boris?" I asked.

She shook her head. "It would be impossible," she replied. "If the officials knew what was happening they would transfer Boris back to Russia immediately. We would never see each other again. We'll have to keep it a secret as long as possible, then we'll see."

"I wish I could help you Margo." Mama said, and her face looked worried. Margo left with her silk stockings and a great burden in her heart. At that moment I saw the sorrow of illicit love and the anguish it was causing Margo and her mother.

The letter came saying I could attend the Rabenstein School of Nursing in Chemnitz. Rabenstein was considered to be the best and most disciplined school for nursing. Both Mama and I knew that nurses finishing there were always in great demand.

Ortwin, now 16, was attending the technical high school in Chemnitz. His plan was to build motors and "be as good at it as Papa was with radios." Ortwin was taller than me now and looked a little like Papa, with wavy brown hair and blue eyes. He had no more time to work at the farm anymore and this caused a loss of produce.

My classes started and I began the most grueling travel schedule I was ever to endure in my lifetime. Rabenstein Hospital was on the opposite side of Euba and there was no dormitory space available for me at the time. No train schedule could accommodate my need to be in class at eight o'clock each morning. I walked about nine miles in a southerly direction to Gablenz, where I caught a street car. This took me into the central Johannis Square of the city. Here I transferred to another street car out to Siegmar Schoenau. From there a twenty minute walk through Pelzmuehle Park and up a hill put me in class on time each morning.

Following an eight to five class I reversed this long trek to return home each evening. These daily journeys in all kind of weather lasted for almost a year. No one ever seemed to notice how exhausted I was. It was just expected that I would always endure. No one ever thought that I might fail.

Mama would say, "If you are cold, walk faster."

"Think warm thoughts," Hartmut would tease.

I marched on frozen snow and ice, in icy winds, heavy thunderstorms and steady rain. I marched in sunshine and on grey days but there never seemed to be enough sunny days. The last three miles home were the most exhausting part of my day.

Ortwin had the same long trip to Chemnitz but his school was close to the street car line. Hartmut started his training in an agricultural School near Dresden. Hartmut lived at the school and came home on weekends.

Rabenstein Hospital and Nursing School were housed in several large buildings that stood on the crest of a hill and resembled a summer resort, except for the high fence and gate that restricted those who entered or left the grounds. A few smaller buildings, housing, maternity and isolation wards, adjoined a pleasant park where patients and nurses often walked during leisure hours.

Our uniforms were light blue dresses, over which we tied a white apron during working hours or a short cape for street dress. We wore white caps with seven stiff starched pleats. They were not for decoration. We were required to stuff all our hair inside them except for a few curls in front. I remember the heavy starched caps cut my hair off on both sides of my head; the edges were almost as sharp as a knife. My shoes were a delight, comfortable and well fitted for walking. I could never have walked the miles required of me on a daily basis in the poorly fitted military boots. To this day the shape of my feet are not what they would have been if I had always worn well fitting shoes. We were allowed to take baths every day and I felt especially clean in my uniform.

Our studies included pharmacology, chemistry, physiology, anatomy, surgery and neurology. We also studied biology, bacteriology and more. Our instructors were highly qualified doctors and nurses. We studied nutrition and enough mathematics to be able to make our own medicinal solutions. In the pharmacy we were required to smell and taste all medicines so we would know what we were giving patients and so we would avoid making mistakes. We learned the human body inside and out and while we had our little jokes, the emphasis was on learning.

Around the middle of my first year of study, Aunt Martha told us of Margo's tragic death. She danced in the ballet as long as possible, then left the stage to stay at home. Her baby was delivered prematurely with only a midwife present. She died in childbirth, her baby boy living only a few hours. Her lover, the Russian officer, left immediately for Russia. No one in the family ever heard from him again.

Just before spring I was assigned to a dormitory room with three other student nurses. Their roommate had broken the rules and was dismissed from the program. Her leaving was my good fortune--no more walks and rides to and from school each day. I shared a room with Katharina, a Hungarian girl whose father had moved to Brazil after the war. The rest of Katharina's family lived in Germany. Roswita von Warvenstein, whose German parents had to leave a large estate in Poland when borders changed, and Marianne Betzold, a heavyset girl whose parents once owned a farm, were my other two roommates. Now the government owned the farm and Marianne's parents worked there as farmhands. It was the communist way.

We lived under many regulations. Uniforms were worn at all times. My roommates and I never worked in the same ward on the same day. Meals were ruled by "Mother" Oberin. When she sat, we sat. When she ate, we ate. When she stopped eating, we stopped.

Just as in previous schools I found overly strict instructors among our teaching staff. But for fear of losing my opportunity to study I tried my best to get favorable marks.

One day our chief surgeon asked me why I wanted to become a nurse. I replied that it was a suitable profession for a woman and that secretarial work did not appeal to me.

To my surprise he said, "To be a nurse is fine, Irene, but don't leave out finding a good husband. Do you really want to become a career nurse?"

I looked at him in utter disbelief. Seeing my astonishment he went on to say, "Look at those old *dragoners* (battle-axes). Take a closer look at our chief nurses. They have lost much of their femininity. They are like sergeants. They walk like sergeants, talk like sergeants, and order patients around. Don't become one of them."

After his remark I took a more critical look at the head nurses. Many of them really were as he described. Their war experiences made them what they were now. But others were strongly feminine, beautiful, vibrant women doing the work they loved to do. So I dismissed his comments and continued to enjoy my work as a nurse.

Once I worked in the dermatology ward where 42 beds were filled with patients from the uranium mines. Although they were warned of the danger, these men drank the contaminated underground water when they were thirsty. They developed an acne type rash that covered the entire body, even the face, causing intense itching. Doctors instructed us to brush a salve over the patient's entire body. They also gave patients an oral medication, however I doubted its effectiveness. I was often in charge of this ward after the evening meal, between the day and night shifts.

This ward adjoined a lounge in which many patients spent most of their daytime hours. They were allowed to walk around and were expected to make their own beds and keep their area tidy. One evening, while administering medication and counting heads to see that everyone was present, I discovered one patient was missing. If I left the ward to search for him no nurse would be left on the ward and this would be against regulations.

In order to make a search I ordered all patients into their rooms. Although they grumbled, I knew they would stay there. Quickly I started my search. Not finding the patient inside the immediate area, I went through a door marked "emergency" which exited into the park.

Other people were there but my patient was not. I walked deeper into the park. It was getting dark. As I was about to turn around and leave I saw him. Dressed only in his pajamas, he was preparing to hang himself on a tree. Angrily I rushed toward him and grabbed the rope away from his neck. His apparent respect for me kept him from physically taking the rope back, although he was much larger than me. He fell to his knees and cried like a child.

"I cannot go on living with this itching all over my body. Nothing helps. I want to die!"

Taking him by the hand and talking calmly, I led him back into the building. I threw the rope into the greenhouse as we passed and took him to the treatment room and gave him an extra layer of salve on his body. I promised him I would not talk about this incident to anyone, since attempted suicide was punishable by law.

Days later when he said to others in front of me, "Sister Irene, you saved my life," I was very uncomfortable. Since I had not reported the incident, I was relieved when he recovered enough to be sent home.

The medical needs of men from the uranium mines increased and administrative changes were made to accommodate them. Rabenstein Hospital was taken over by Wismut A.G., an organization which was formed after the war by the Russian and German Governments. The purpose of Wismut was to remove ore from the Silver Mountains of the Erzgebirge and its first priority was the uranium.

Working in a hospital owned by Wismut provided us with extra food rations. We bought lavish amounts of food in a special Wismut store while other people were still very hungry.

I saved much of those food ration stamps and Ortwin came by to shop with me and carry the food home. Each time he arrived at the Hospital gate I was notified by the guards. Ortwin, age 17 and tall for his age, explained over and over that he was my brother and not my boyfriend. We secretly laughed about all the fuss and knew we were watched constantly by suspicious eyes when he came to visit.

At the end of my first year of training I was allowed a one month vacation. Wearing my uniform home seemed a bit awkward but people expected it that way. To my amazement, neighbors in the village of Euba came to me for help with minor accidents.

I was now 20 years old. Ortwin was 17; Hartmut 16; Claus, 10; and Christine, 5. Our home was full of merry sounds with much clowning and laughter. I loved to dance and Saturday night dances found me with many dancing partners.

"I never knew we had so many friends until you came home, Irene," Ortwin teased.

Karl-Heinz, my old friend from childhood days in Chemnitz, came to see me. We laughed about the game we called the "dating game" and cried about the loss of Esther and other dear friends. He joined in singing with all our friends as I played my accordion on Krista's porch.

Karl-Heinz came on my days off and we became close friends again. His fond attention brought smiles and knowing looks from friends as they watched us dance. Even Mama soon saw his romantic interest in me.

"He's a handsome young man, Irene," she said. "That dark wavy hair and those deep green eyes could capture any girl's heart. Are you going to finish your training or let marriage come into your life now?"

"Karl-Heinz has several years of training before he will be a qualified draftsman, Mama," I answered. "We've both decided to wait."

We had just finished clearing up the evening meal when Karl-Heinz walked into the room. He surprised me by saying, "I love Irene, Mutter Ella." He hesitated, watching both of us, then continued. "I want Irene to promise she will wait for me until I finish school and get a job."

"It's too soon to plan marriage," we both agreed.

"Things will work out for us," he said, putting his arm around my waist. "It just takes time."

Mama looked relieved by our statements. Taking both our hands in hers she said, "I'm sure you two will do the right thing. Do come see us often, Karl-Heinz."

I promised to wait for Karl-Heinz but neither of us could know the changing winds that would intervene the next year.

My family and I revisited Dresden during my vacation and were dismayed to see the demolished buildings and destroyed bridges. Here again I saw the rubble-women slowly cleaning and salvaging usable bricks. A monument should be built to these brave women. They deserve it much more than any politician.

We took a river boat to Pillnitz Castle. How small the castle seemed now. In my memory it had been much larger. Although the famous restaurant on the hill was closed, we rode the cable car to the top of the hill and sat outside looking down on Dresden, now crushed by war. This is where we said goodbye to Papa for the last time. Mama's sad expression and tears told how deep her grief was in this city where we had once enjoyed much family fun.

We went home feeling sad and empty. Our trip on the train was so different from our happy but bumpy rides in Papa's *dreirad* (three-wheel bike).

HOME

Mama's application to move back into Chemnitz was postponed since she was unable to help with cleaning up rubble. Christine and Claus were too young to leave unattended and this work was a required condition if she moved into the city. As I started my second year of training in the summer of 1950, we heard rumors that the Russians wanted to take over Rabenstein Hospital. At first we only saw a few Russians: women doctors, and some soldiers and officers who performed the duties of occupation.

Just as I began to worry about our school for nursing being closed, the news came. It was all settled. Half of us were to be transferred to Annaberg, the other half to Wiesen. We had no choice about our transfer and if we wanted to earn our degrees we would have to go where they sent us. Even doctors were being transferred. We packed our personal things and climbed into waiting trucks. The canvas sides were rolled down. So our view was blocked but the rain was kept out as we were driven to the town of Wiesen. I had never heard of Wiesen or Wiesenburg, two small towns a good 25 miles distance from Zwickau. Many of those medieval picturesque small towns had no railstop and people walked many miles to Wiesenburg to catch a train into Zwickau. Our hospital, once a home for the elderly, was now renovated to serve patients from the uranium mines. However, there was no school in our new hospital in Wiesen, so we traveled to nearby Schneeberg to finish our nurses' training. Even though our new school of nursing was not as strict as Rabenstein, we still received instruction in Communism along with our classes in nursing. The Communist regime was trying to get a good grip on our people and they were not going to let us be indifferent about it.

Nurses were not housed in the Wiesen Hospital. One of the lucky few, I lived in a two-room apartment above a general store across the street from the Wiesenburg rail road station. I shared this with a student nurse, Gretl. She had come as a refugee from Silesia and somehow got stuck in East Germany.

About twenty years my senior, Gretl had a good sense of humor and enjoyed an excellent professional standing among her fellow nurses. Due to our age difference I came to regard Gretl as an adviser and a little like an older sister. She had clear skin, short brown hair and brown eyes. Her legs were attractive enough that men teased her in a flattering way, and she was very witty to let them know it was all a joke. A boyfriend she had at the time was more like an escort, an actor turned uranium mine worker because of the better pay and food rations. But once an actor, always an actor, and we had great fun when he performed his past roles only for us.

Our landlady, Old Buschin as we called her, was in her late 70's. She wore a wig and we always wondered where she got it from. False teeth were much harder to get so she did not have any. Once wealthy, she lost everything to the new government. She formerly owned an entire building complex and several stores in it. We lived in one of the buildings where she lived. Two sons she lost in the war and her husband died during the conflict in an accident. Now she was alone.

When the state took possession of her store and buildings, she was allowed to live rent-free in only two rooms of her four-room apartment. Gretl and I rented the other two plainly furnished rooms.

The door between our apartments was locked and a couch placed in front of it. The water faucet was outside in the hallway and we shared the bathroom. Frau Buschin's income consisted of our rent plus a few Mark's from her social security. She was resourceful though, she remodeled her upstairs storage room in the attic into living quarters for a middle-age miner called Bruno.

During evening hours we could hear Bruno singing to our landlady and we heard her laughing. It was a good thing for them to spend their evenings together, since life was very dull in those days.

We were given more responsibilities in the hospital as we were expected to be RNs soon anyway since we already had the same duties. I took care of anything that came up in the ward where I worked. I made rounds with the doctors and was very conscientious about my assignments and soon earned compliments from patients. Many patients said that "I had a light hand" when giving shots. In those days, instruments of all kinds had to be sterilized by us as there was no such thing as "throw away supplies."

Doctor I____. said to me "People with blood type B are daredevils, Irene. They'll try things even when they're not sure they can do it. You know, you and I have blood type B."

I laughed at this remark. However, I soon became the right hand to the head nurse in the women's ward, even though I was considered much too young for the job. The women's ward contained female patients who had surgery, gynecological problems, or job-related accidents. On surgery days I was often assigned to help doctors in the operating room. I went more often than duty required, because I wanted to learn as much as I could.

Every second week the police hauled a dozen or so prostitutes into our hospital for examinations. We checked them for gonorrhea and took blood samples for syphilis. Usually four out of twelve were diseased. Those without any sign of disease were taken to a work camp. Those with a disease went into a jail hospital for treatment and then to a work camp.

One day, Doctor Z_____ had to decide to perform an abortion on a pregnant prostitute with syphilis. If she had given birth to this baby, the possibility existed that the child would be born blind. False labor was induced. The girl cried and we worked, pushed and sweated with her for hours until the fetus finally came out.

This must have been an old fashioned procedure, but the girl was too far along to do it any other way. The fetus was a completely formed baby boy. I felt so sad. I turned my head and cried for this lost life.

Our political teachers called venereal diseases the *capitalistic diseases*. Everything they disliked was labeled "capitalistic." On the other hand, all technical achievements were invented by the Russians. We secretly laughed about those foolish claims.

The order came that we must meet once each week to learn how to become better Communists. One-fifth of the hospital personnel now wore party pins. They reminded me of the Nazi pins our school teachers wore. Once seated in a meeting, a list was sent around with instructions to "sign your name." Party authorities checked those who came to the meetings and reprimanded those who did not attend.

Since the village blackboard bulletin at the corner of the hospital grounds was our only link with the world beyond our community, I told Gretl I would love to buy a radio. One day we went to find one and tried many shops in different cities. We were so exhausted, but used all our free time for many weeks until we spotted one. Small and simple, it made sounds and it worked! We bought it, and we took it home with us where it provided news and some music to lighten our study hours. Every Tuesday night I remember we tried to stay home to listen to classical music, and some people who had no radio came to join us.

In the usual way, we began to hear about the "advantages" people would have if the government took over all the farms in East Germany, which they already had in some places. Farmers would become workers on their own farms and receive a salary, but had no more say as to what would be planted. Such decisions were not their concern anymore.

People who owned nice houses were allowed to still live in the homes. If however they wanted to move for any reason, they would lose the house. They were not allowed to sell their house, neither could they will it to their children since it now belonged to the State. Also factories and businesses of all kinds were taken over by the State. Already in effect in 1946 this law called "Volksentscheid" (resolution of the people) expropriated anything that was of value. By 1949 there were not many if any private businesses left. All this was done for the "protection" of the people. People who owned no real estate were told to sign petitions that "the people" demanded that all farms and properties become part of the state and collective farm called "Kolchose."

Near Wiesen was a beautiful little town named Kirschberg. One could feel that this place had lots of history with its medieval buildings, although now it consisted mostly of farmland. I watched this beautiful village being turned into a collective farm, Co-op. All fields became government property and no farmer was allowed to make any decision regarding the land. The farmer would also be punished with jail time should he butcher one of his own chickens or pigs since they no longer belonged to him either. This is how the tentacles of the Communist State encircled village after village and farm after farm into large collectives.

Farmers, as well as the owners of other large enterprises and private businesses, were told that under Communism they would be paid a salary for their work. Savings were no longer needed since the State would provide for them now and when they became old. Pensions would be calculated according to each person's job. There would be a file on every person. All health care and education for children would be provided by the State and the State would select the kind of educational training to be given. "Good workers" and people who were "cooperative" would receive a paid vacation at a popular resort once a year. If they were not productive workers, they should not expect lavish vacations. "The State is generous with the people" was often the subject in our classes on Communism. Many people, myself included, deeply resented the way our lives had become. We felt we were becoming as oppressed under Russian occupation as we had been under Nazis control.

Among our political watchdogs, titled "culture directors," and assigned by the Communist Party, was Rudolf, a little man with feet so quiet he could come up behind you and never make a sound. He delivered many boring lectures on Communism.

On the southern side the hospital had large balconies where we aired beds. One unfortunate day, I sat on one of these balconies with a few nurses and Rudolf. During conversations he always tried to deliver his doctrine to us. I leaned over toward Rudolf and said, "Come on, Rudolf, you yourself can't believe all this nonsense." I leaned closer and said, "Do you really believe what you teach us?"

Two nurses gasped. Rudolf looked me straight in the eye, bit his lower lip and said nothing. I straightened up, still looking at Rudolf and waiting for an answer, but none came. Living with lies day after day, year after year, makes a person physically ill. I always had this nasty feeling about lying. I wanted to shout out what I felt but I knew I should not. I'll never know what made me say it but now that I had I knew I had to live with the consequences.

I suspected that Rudolf's job was to spy and look for people with ideas like mine. He left and did not answer me, but I was warned by my coworkers that he would make me pay for my careless words. After duty hours, I was ordered to come to Rudolf's office. He preached to me about how young I was and that he did not want to ruin my life. If I would say that I was sorry, he might be able to "save" me.

I was ordered to spend my evenings "constructively" by learning how to play chess. Under normal circumstances, people, myself included, would have liked chess. But it was also a favorite Russian game and therefore hated. Nevertheless, it was a mild punishment and I was now forced to spend many evenings after work learning and playing chess. Rudolf's office became a chess tournament room and all individuals with dissident thoughts were regularly assembled. Among those gathered, there were a few nurses and over eighty percent of our doctors. Conversation was not allowed, only the study of chess. Even so, our free evenings were lost.

* * *

My first vacation provided by the State was not to a place where I really wanted to go, but I had to go where I was told. I was sent to Gral Mueritz, a beach resort on the northern shore of East Germany. The more desirable place, the Island of Ruegen, was not available to me.

In spite of the warnings that Gral Mueritz would be a dull place, I wanted to get away and was looking forward to getting a good rest. By going to Gral Mueritz, I could stay six weeks. If I had gone home my leave would have been only twenty-one days. I wanted to see the ocean and this was my only chance.

My new vacation clothes, which were hard to come by, consisted of a bathrobe suitable for beach wear and a two piece beige dress trimmed with brown that felt suspiciously like paper. The sales girl acted as if she had done me a big favor by selling it to me. Since I felt desperate for some new clothes and since the dress did look nice on me, I bought it.

Transportation to Gral Mueritz was on a special train provided just for vacationers. We sat on clean but hard wooden benches, definitely not comfortable. The cars were crowded but there was a seat for everyone. After many hours, when the benches became unbearable, we stood for short periods of time. No food or drink was served. But being excited about going on a vacation, we overlooked our hunger and the other inconveniences. We talked for a while, then, feeling very tired, we closed our eyes. Sleep was difficult as the lights on the train were very glaring and the speakers constantly blared loud music into our ears. Overtired children behaved well enough and parents, happy to get a vacation spot to Gral Mueritz, kept a sharp eye on them.

Our trip should not have taken more than six hours but instead it took us one entire day and one entire night. We knew that many times the whole train was delayed on dead railroad tracks to let more important trains pass. At the end of our journey, with our luggage in hand, we stood in line for lodging in hotels or boarding houses, now all owned by the State. In a vacation house I was assigned to a room with four beds in it. After I plunked down on one of the beds two more girls that I did not know arrived. The three of us would spend the next six weeks together. The rules of the house were that we had to care for our own room ourselves. All the occupants on our floor of six bedrooms shared only one bathroom. We would be allowed to go into the village hotels only when there was entertainment or to use the reading rooms.

I unpacked quickly and rushed to get to the bathroom. After a trip like we had just endured, everyone wanted to take a shower before anything else. There was a long line outside the bathroom door.

I wanted to see the Baltic Sea as soon as possible, so I left the house and ran down to the dunes. I climbed the sandy slopes, which were pegged with pines where buckets were attached to the older trees to draw pungent pine oil for medical and chemical uses.

I could hear the pounding waves. Up one more dune and there it was, rolling forever against Germany's shore--a cold blue-grey sea rippling into surging froth. The white sand lay serene and quiet as this giant of a sea roared toward me and then retreated, spending its energy in eternal motion.

The air was invigorating and rushed through my hair as I ran down the dunes and into the water where cold water flushed around my ankles.

"This is life! This is freedom!"

Nearby I could see the wicker beach baskets. They were six feet high, and inside there was a two seat bench. One could lift up the seat and stuff valuables inside, then lock it up with a padlock to keep things safe when going swimming or on a boat ride. I have nowhere else seen such convenient wicker beach baskets except in Germany. They look like huge hampers, but they serve as combination dressing rooms and shelters in rainy weather for bathers. Judging by the number of vacationers and the available beach baskets, one would have to get up very early to rent one. Each beach basket appeared to be occupied.

Shallow wooden boats were being rowed out from the shoreline. No motors could be heard, just the rush of the sea as it broke on the white sandy shore. Farther out, what looked like a ship's mast stuck out of the water at a crazy angle. No doubt a sunken ship from previous years and now of no apparent interest to anyone.

"There are no sharks to fear," a vacationer said. "The water is too cold. The herring and eel are abundant though."

After breathing deeply of the fresh air, I walked back to my boarding house. There I learned we would be eating all our meals in a dining room located in the largest hotel in the village. We were to have a specific table and strict meal schedules. Our breakfast, the last of three settings, would be from 8:30 to 9:00 a.m.

Our food was the same as what I ate at home, except eel was served more frequently. Ever since I knew that eel feed on dead humans, I did not care much for it. But in a time when food was rationed, I ate it, and it was provided in sufficient amounts. Everyone ate from the same menu, no choices were permitted. There were no sandwiches to take out and no other food available. Those going on all-day trips went without meals. I am sure that when people did not show up at meal time, it was reported.

My roommates, Lone and Linda, were pleasant and we shared some of our activities. We went to a dance one evening where we danced a few times then just sat around. The men seemed dull. An invitation to play soccer on the beach with some boys was fun until our shins got banged up and we quit. We certainly didn't know soccer was such a mean sport. Another day we were able to rent a beach basket and we talked and laughed, built sand castles, then went swimming in the still cold water.

The important thing for me was the sea. Once I walked along the beach a whole day, forgetting both lunch and dinner. I walked where there were no people--just myself and the sea. It seemed so free and it wreathed in rhythmic swells and continually roared a song of freedom. I sang back to it as I walked along its shore.

Die Gedanken sind frei, wer kann sie erraten?
Sie fliehen vorbei, wie naechtliche Schatten.
Kein Mensch kann sie wissen, kein Jaeger sie schiessen,
Es bleibet dabei: Die Gedanken sind frei!

Ich denk' was ich mag und was mich begluecket,
doch alles in der still', und wie es sich schicket.
Mein Wunsch und begehren karin niemand verwehren

Es bleibet dabei, die Gedanken sind frei
(Part of an old German folk song)

English translation:
> My thoughts they are free, no one can ever guess them.
> They flee away, like shadows in the night.
> No human can know, no hunter can shoot,
> I declare to the sea, my thoughts they are free!
>
> I think what I like, and what makes me happy,
> be still my soul, and do what you are told!
> but my wish, my desire, no one can take away,
> I declare to the sea, my thoughts they are free!

Out of nowhere stepped an armed guard. Suddenly I was back in the real world of an armed police State.

"Where are you going, Fraulein? Turn around! Turn around! What are you doing out here? Waiting for a boat that will take you to Denmark, eh?"

"Don't get excited, I am going." *Everything is guarded*, I thought. Always big brother was watching us. It was so depressing. I looked back the way I had come. There was no village in sight, I must have walked several miles. I turned around and started back. A little frightened, I lengthened my stride to put distance between myself and the guard.

As I returned to my room I thought about leaving East Germany. The song "Nun Adieu Du Mein Lieb' Heimatland" kept running through my mind. The wind and the sea caught my song and carried it to somewhere in the future.

"Nun adieu, du mein lieb Heimatland,
Lieb Heimatland adieu!
Es geht jetzt fort zum fremden Strand,
Lieb Heimatland, adieu!
Und so sing ich denn mit frohem Mut
, wie man singet, wenn man wandern tut,
Lieb Heimatland adieu!

Wie du lachst mit deines Himmels blau,
Lieb Heimatland adieu!
Wie du gruessest mich mit Feld und Au,
Lieb Heimatland adieu!
Gott weiss, zu dir steht stets mein Sinn;
Nur etzt zur Ferne muss ich hin,
Lieb Heimatland adieu!

"Begleitest mich, du lieber Fluss,
Lieb Heirnatland adieu!
es ist traurig das ich fort hier muss,
Lieb Heirnatland adieu!
Von moos'gen Stein am wald'gen Tal,
Da gruess ich dich zum letzten Mal,
Lieb Heimatland, adieu!

(Old German folksong)

English translation:

> Now, farewell oh you my Native Land,
> You my Native Land, farewell.
> I am on my way to foreign lands,
> You my Native land, goodbye,
> And so I shall sing a cheerful song,
> as one sings when one is moving on
> You, my Native Land, goodbye!
>
> Oh, how blue your sky does smile at me
> You my Native Land goodbye!
> Fields and meadows are saluting me,
> You my Native Land goodbye!
> God knows, I loved you all my life,
> but away it pulls me with much might.
> You my Native land, goodbye!
>
> You dear river you accompany me,
> You my Native Land goodbye
> Are you mourning that I'm leaving thee,
> You my Native Land, goodbye!
> From the green downstream and stony height,
> I salute you now this final time,
> You my Native Land, goodbye.

One cool day I took my letter writing materials, found a large table in the lounge of one of the big hotels and wrote to Mama, Karl-Heinz and a few friends.

Suddenly a voice over the loudspeaker filled the air. "All persons not employed by Wismut A.G. must leave the resort." We learned that some vacationers had secretly rented some boats in the hope of getting to Denmark. Silently I prayed that those people with children in their boat would reach the safe shores of Denmark and freedom. Many people became angry, saying they all had to suffer because a few had defected. In the confusion, wives and children were being sent home without their husbands. This caused more anger and couples began leaving early, creating vacancies the State had not counted on. Some vacationers were crying from the sheer frustration of it all.

In disgust I left and walked around the resort, now rapidly emptying of vacationers. I walked into the fishing village of Gral, stopping at a gift shop where I bought two rings set with amber, a cigarette holder and a pendant all made out of amber. Amber was big business there. Amber is harvested from the sea, and it is said that once upon a time Germany and the Baltic countries were joined. Only after the Big Flood, they parted and became separate. All the pine forests sank into the Baltic Sea. During the following centuries, the pine trees still bleeding under the water, their sap turned into beautiful amber. A piece of amber with an insect caught in it was exceptionally precious.

When I returned to my quarters I washed my new dress. It turned out to be paper--more disappointment. I had paid half a month's salary for this paper dress.

With two more weeks of vacation left, my roommates and I found little to interest us in Gral Mueritz. We requested permission to leave, but were told that was out of the question. If we left early our vacation would be cut short and we would have to go back to work immediately. If we stayed, we could enjoy two more weeks of the sea, but things were not the same anymore. We got permission to visit a nearby city, Rostock, although we had to promise to sign-in in the evening. Rostock must once have been a very interesting city. Now, however, in the harbor we saw a Russian ship and it sure looked different than the ones I had seen in the Western countries. It was a freighter that had to load up merchandise. Everybody was shouting in Russian. We stopped and watched, thinking that this ship might go to Siberia where all the labor camps were. I always got goose bumps thinking about labor camps.

Hungry and cold, we returned from our outing only to find that in Gral Mueritz the dining room was closed. In Rostock, the few things they had were on ration cards. So that day was without provision. Of course, that made the day not what it should have been.

We plotted how we could get away from it all. With two more weeks vacation left, we wanted to go to Berlin. Only when we promised we would go straight home, was permission given to leave the resort. When we arrived in Berlin we decided to stay in the city. Linda's aunt lived in West Berlin. This knowledge, along with my past adventures in crossing borders, aroused a sense of adventure in me that I could not resist.

We cleaned up in the washroom of the railroad station, checked our suitcases into lockers and found our way to the Brandenburger Gate. The wall was not built yet. East German police with rifles and Russian guards carrying the usual machine guns strapped over their shoulders were walking around watching everyone.

Being very careful to appear nonchalant, we slowly inched our way closer to the big gate. We could see the West German police on the other side.

"Now!" I whispered.

I led and Lorie and Linda followed. We walked boldly toward the gate. Although we could feel eyes on our backs, people were staring at us, no one shouted and no one shot for a long scary minute. We must have caught them by surprise. Their propaganda loudspeakers were going 24 hours a day, telling people to stay in the workers' paradise. Nobody had the courage to just do what we were doing, since everyone was sure the guards would fire. We kept walking, not daring to turn around.

The West German police looked toward us and gestured in a friendly manner to keep going. This was all the encouragement we needed. If we felt uncertain we did not show it. Suddenly we heard shouting and turned to see the East German police shouting at each other and Russian patrols gesturing and waving their weapons about. It was a very angry scene. It must have been about us. The West German police laughed and welcomed us.

Following a policeman's directions, we walked to Charlottenburg where we were welcomed by Linda's aunt and two teenage cousins, Fritz and Kurt.

For several days we enjoyed the freedom of West Berlin. We walked up and down the famous "Kurfuerstendamm," which they called "Ku-Damm," where we feasted our eyes on the colorful merchandise displayed in the shop windows. The drab grays that dominated East Germany were in sharp contrast to this lively scene of action and color.

I was not prepared for the loss I took when I exchanged five East Marks for only one West Mark. That made it seem like I worked for only a fifth of my monthly salary, which was then about 400 East Marks. I learned that for the same job in the West I could make a little more than 450 West Marks a month, which for 1950 was a very good salary, even in West Germany. I exchanged only enough East Marks to buy some post cards and a ticket to a movie.

We later sat in an outdoor coffeehouse and watched people walk by. We learned about travel between East and West. Although hundreds of police guarded the border, Fritz and Kurt found ways to slip by the armed guards on little side streets to attend Saturday dances in East Berlin. Beer was of course cheaper in East Berlin. Linda's aunt said she got her hair fixed only in East Berlin because it cost a fraction of what she would have to pay in West Berlin. I thought about how they came from the West to take advantage of the services in the East and paid very little. Then, with their Western passes, riding the Metro, which they affectionately called the U-Bahn (metro train), they could go back and forth without fear. It was not fair.

Kurt and Fritz said the music and entertainment in East Berlin was alright and the drinks were much cheaper. I felt like everyone wanted the most out of their money. Still, the tightened security of the wall was yet to come.

Friends of Linda's aunt gave us second-hand dresses, nylons and shoes. The bitter experience of washing my paper dress into a pulp seemed less dreadful.

As my vacation came to an end I realized I wanted the freedom of West Germany. The West was then accepting East Germans as refugees, something they could not do when I crossed the border a few years ago near Sonneberg. It seemed to me that it would be easier to get into the West through Berlin. However, I did not want to jeopardize my training just now. A graduate nurse would find it easier in West Germany when seeking employment.

We boarded the U-Bahn, traveled back into East Berlin, picked up our suitcases and caught the train to Leipzig. We traveled on to Zwickau where Lone and Linda lived, and afterwards I caught a train home to Wiesenburg.

BACK TO WORK

When I returned to work I found more people had joined the Communist Party to put themselves in better employment situations. Even Herr Viehstig, a custodian who only had an elementary education at the time, was advanced to be our second Culture Director. He used to go around bringing small bottles of champagne to those who were very seriously ill and were most likely to die. When he left the room he said, "To have a happy ascension." Some people actually laughed and took it as a joke. This unfortunate gesture was very sad for those receiving the gift, though they often wanted more of the bubbling stuff.

It was important to be respectful toward Culture Directors, and now we had two of them. They had the power to send people away for severe punishment and they did. Sister Wally, an RN, and her husband were arrested after her husband was accused of having done some work for the West. Authorities felt Sister Wally must have known about his activities, so she was also arrested. She was a real loss to our nursing staff. We never heard how many years people were sentenced to serve, and I never saw her again.

How strange life can be. When Sister Wally was arrested some people spoke in whispers about what had happened. They tried to look the other way. Sadly, some of those same people got arrested only a few years later. The heavy hand of communism snatched people from our midst just as the Nazis had taken our Jewish neighbors. This had a very sobering effect upon all of us.

Since our hospital existed solely to care for people working in the uranium mines, most of our patients suffered from accidents caused by explosions, falls, or injuries caused when work was pushed at high speed. In spite of these hazards, jobs in the uranium mines remained desirable for several reasons. Following the war, starvation was so great that many people were seeking employment with the Wismut. Since the Wismut was the only place to get more food, many educated men worked right alongside the uneducated. The Wismut provided protective outer clothing to all who signed contracts to work and from then on, everyone looked the same. Workers were paid according to how much and how fast they dug the pitch-blend and ore.

People died from accidents in the mines and our hospital beds were filled to capacity. During the years I worked there, another much larger hospital was built in Erlabrunn closer to the mining area. The wages were good, but most importantly all food rations were better there than in any other place in East Germany.

Doctors worked with insufficient medical supplies. Therefore, many people could not be saved. This frustrated our doctors over the years. I know many of them made it to West Germany.

During the Christmas season in 1950, I played my accordion during some of my off-duty hours to entertain the patients. On Christmas Day a group of male patients, dressed in grey house robes, sat like figures of stone in the lounge. Seeing their despondency, I played my accordion while a few of them sang the old Christmas songs.

Their eyes saw far beyond the room we were in. I knew they were thinking of their families. Some started sobbing loudly and I was sad that I could not comfort them. Plates were passed but all we had to put on them was an apple. These men did not usually reveal their inner feelings but that forlorn apple did it.

Quickly I broke up the Christmas gathering, knowing that it had not been such a good idea. I should not have reminded them of Christmas at all. No clergyman ever visited our hospital but religious services were needed by all of us. I felt anger toward our Culture Directors. Where were they? Couldn't they do more than the useless work for the Communist Party?

Giving permission to leave the lights on longer for reading, I went to my duty room. The entire hospital seemed unusually quiet. Someone knocked softly on the door. I opened it to see a patient standing in the half-darkened hall.

"Yes? What is it?" I asked.

"We thought, well, we just thought--we don't have much to give you. But we made this for you."

I opened the door wider. Two more patients stood there, holding out a small package. I took the package from their outstretched hands but before I could say anything, they turned and hurriedly walked back toward their rooms.

"Thank you and Merry Christmas," I said to a hallway that was empty and quiet again.

I opened the packages to find two wooden carvings, an Erzgebirge angel and an ore miner, made into a candle holder. How beautiful they were. Immediately, they became my most treasured gifts. I thought of my family and how I missed them.

Many patients cried quietly as they went to sleep that Christmas.

During the month of January we started the nursing examinations that would lead to diplomas in April. We learned that further study was available for those wanting to become doctor's assistants. I would have welcomed more studies, but not under those conditions. For the present, being a nurse was enough and very rewarding.

Time flew by, then came the finals. The advice was the same as when I first applied to study nursing, "Speak little and be precise when answering medical questions, but talk at great length when asked political questions."

Finals took three days. Each day, in fresh clean uniforms, we appeared before the examining board to chalk up our points. I experienced a feeling of real achievement when I learned I had passed the State examinations. A small but important freedom we enjoyed as registered nurses was to push our caps back and show more hair. But the cap was starched so stiff that it had already cut off lots of my hair on both sides of my head.

I got vacation leave and went home just in time to help Mama move into Chemnitz. Her apartment was in the same building where Grandma Thekla had lived. People were still cleaning bricks to salvage material to build again some day, although I never saw men doing this backbreaking work. Too many men were killed in the war, and many others had run to the West.

Uncle Albert and Aunt Martha wanted to open a butchery again but they would have to build one from the rubble. This would mean thousands of hours of work before they could open for business. No loans were available to buy new materials. If there would be another butchery, it would most likely belong to the state.

Things seemed so dreary for people trying to earn a livelihood in our destroyed city.

I returned to Wiesen to work on the Surgery and Gynecology wards. Gretl and I continued to share our two-room apartment.

During my off duty hours I continued playing my accordion for patients. Eventually our little radio had stopped playing, and no one could fix it. There were no other radios, no movies, and I never saw a magazine of any kind. There was no entertainment other than propaganda loudspeakers piping some music into the hospital rooms, though it was frequently interrupted with lots of praise for the Soviet Army and talk about the Party.

When the Cultural Directors saw how much patients liked to sing along with me, they promised to arrange for touring groups of entertainers to come to the hospital. Although infrequent, this recreation was welcomed by everyone.

Returning home one evening, we found a large bouquet of flowers in front of our door. No card was enclosed. Since Gretl knew nothing about it, I supposed they were from the patients I had played songs for and thought little more about it. The next day another bouquet awaited our return from work and still no note accompanied the flowers.

Each day for the next two weeks a bouquet arrived. Our two-room apartment began to resemble a flower shop. Since there were no florists in our area and the flowers were the same colors as some blooming in the hospital gardens, our curiosity grew with each bouquet. I asked the hospital gardener about the flowers. He denied knowing about them. I asked the gardener's assistant, who seemed to know something but was reluctant to talk. After bribing him with cigarettes, he told me they were from a patient on the third floor. This was a surprise since neither Gretl nor I worked on this floor.

Seeking the anonymous giver, I walked up to the third floor. On the way I met Doctor W_____, a woman medical intern, whose well known abruptness left her with few close friends among our staff.

"What are you doing up here?" she demanded.

While I was trying to answer her, I noticed a patient behind her began motioning for me to leave indicating that he would contact me later. Confused, and a little surprised, I mumbled something and left.

I entered the nurses' room where patients were not allowed in except by permission. Soon I answered a knock at the door from the male patient I had seen upstairs. I invited him in.

"I did not send you the flowers," he started. "A friend of mine is sending them to you. He is in love with you, and he isn't sure if you will talk to him."

My astonishment left me speechless. He went on to say, "He is a schoolteacher but he works as an *Obersteiger* for the Wismut in Schneeberg."

"I have always made it clear to patients that I will tolerate no nonsense." I knew male patients often became infatuated with nurses, especially when they started to recover. I had seen these flirtations and wanted no association with them. This situation was ridiculous, since I didn't even know the man he was talking about. My visitor was waiting for an answer.

"He must stop sending me flowers. I will tell him so myself." My visitor left, looking downhearted.

During visiting hours I returned to the third floor room. There were at least five people, all patients, in a room with only two beds.

Everyone seemed excited and expectant of my arrival. I was certainly not known to make friendly visits to patients during visiting hours.

Visiting hours were strictly observed and once they were over, visitors who often came from far away, had to depart the hospital grounds. A guard at the grounds' gate saw to it that people would leave.

As I had entered the room, I asked, "Where is the man who sent me flowers?" Everyone motioned to one bed. I turned and looked into the bluest eyes and the reddest boyish face I've ever seen. His flushed face showed embarrassment but his eyes begged me to understand. I had not expected him to be so darn good looking. My resolve began to weaken.

Someone shoved a chair at me and I sat down still looking at those sparkling blue eyes. He could not have been more than five or six years older than I was.

"I don't want you to send me any more flowers," I began as Doctor W_____ came into the room. Doctor W_____ stared at me in disbelief, then turned and ran down the corridor. Puzzled by her behavior and thinking she would report me, I followed her. At the top of the stairs a patient caught up with me, saying, "You must talk to him."

"Not now and not here. Later!" I ran to the duty room. There sat Doctor W_____ crying. She looked up and said, "He is mine!" Then she burst into tears again.

How complicated things had become. I didn't even know the patient's name. Also, why was Doctor W_____ interested in this man when everyone knew the rule never to have an affair with a patient. What was so special about this one?

Doctor W_____ must care for him very much to be so upset, I thought. She probably knew about the flowers? I felt helpless, a little flattered and angry.

"How could you let yourself go on like this for a younger man and a patient at that?" I asked and left, not waiting for her answer.

How ridiculous, I thought. I was now involved in a triangle and it was all his fault. Why did he have to be so handsome? I couldn't forget those blue eyes and his flushed boyish face. I smiled and went on about my work.

As I walked out of the building to go home that evening, the third floor patient, dressed in a robe, was waiting for me beside the door.

As I approached him he said, "I'm sorry if I caused you any problem, but I do want to talk to you."

"Start first by telling me your name."

"Sister Irene, I am Volker Hofmann."

"Yes. Do you have permission to be up and about? What are you in for?"

"Pneumonia. I'm going to be released next week. May I see you?" His face was flushing red again.

Having pneumonia was a four week stay in the hospital in those days. Other illnesses also took much longer to treat than in our day.

"You know nurses cannot mix socially with patients. Walk down that hall and I'll talk to you in a few minutes." I walked away from him, then turned and followed him as he walked toward the hall I had indicated. He was tall, with broad shoulders, muscular, but not thin.

"You sent me flowers?" I asked, looking up into his very blue eyes. "Why me? How did you find out about me?"

"I've heard you play your accordion out on the balcony. I like your music and singing and you have helped everyone to feel better. Even the doctors and nurses join in the singing. I wanted to be your friend."

"I'm not sure, you know it is forbidden that nurses and--"

"I know," he interrupted. "Perhaps I can get a pass from the doctor on your free day and we--"

"Are you able to go out of the hospital now?" I was stalling for time. I shouldn't see him but I did want to know more about him. "Thursday is my free day but where?"

"If I can get a pass, let's meet at the train station. Just one day, please?" His smile was disarming.

I agreed. I don't know how but he got a pass to leave the hospital for a whole day. We boarded the train and went to Zwickau. He wore a blue suit which looked a lot like the old Air Force uniform, a leftover from the war. He, just like everyone else, could not get civilian clothes. People were still in World War II uniforms, only without the markings. Even so, he made a handsome figure. Most people wore ill fitting clothes because that was all there was.

I liked his manners, so gentleman like. It would flatter any woman to be with a man so courteous.

We sat at a table by a large window upstairs in the Ring Kaffee and started to get acquainted.

"During the last year of the war I worked in an office in Berlin. Until I was called into the Air Force I studied at the University of Berlin. Mother and Father lived in Breslau and we became refugees in 1944-1945. They traveled west in a covered wagon and in that cold winter mother died of pneumonia."

"Do you have some Polish blood?" I asked.

"Yes, some."

"So do I. My father is from Galicia."

I began to feel more at ease with this pleasant young man whose blue eyes seemed so eager. We talked all day, telling each other about our families and our experiences during the war. After his mother's death, his father came to Berlin. Now they lived in Schneeberg. His father taught while Volker helped out directing plays at one of the schools there. Volker took a job in the Wismut in order to survive, like everyone else. In the evening, as a band started to play, we danced. His arms trembled when he held me. We circled the floor to many dance rhythms, laughing and feeling the closeness of one another. We drank *Danziger Goldwasser*, a popular liquor, and danced some more. Later, we went downstairs for dinner. The waiter asked for ration stamps first, money was secondary.

Our day was coming to an end. We liked each other and we both knew it. We caught the last train back to Wiesenburg, not sure when we could have another day together.

Gretl was still up reading so I poured myself a cup of chicory.

"Aha, you know you have stolen Doctor W_____'s man. She is going to get you for this," she teased. We laughed.

"Things have become complicated. You know I didn't know who sent all these flowers. What can I do?" I shrugged, smiling. Gretl had put all the flowers out in the hall for the night since the heavy fragrance would bother us sleeping. I went to sleep thinking about Volker's blue eyes.

After Volker was released from the hospital we spent most of our free hours together. It wasn't always easy to make our free days coincide especially when everyone became aware that we were dating. When my supervisor learned that I wanted to keep an appointment to see Volker, the request was often dismissed with "the schedule was already set, cannot make any changes..." I often wondered if Doctor W_____ had influenced my supervisor's decision.

When we were together, Volker often said it was "as if some splendid release from the world swept over us." For a few hours we forgot the difficult problems all around us, the constant propaganda about the Russia-German friendship, the Communist Five Year Plan, the Two Year Plan, and so on, and so on.

Most of our free hours were spent in the one and only restaurant in Oberschlema. We sat at a table by the window. We touched wine glasses, exchanged fond glances, and held hands. We danced when there was a band. Volker's strong arms encircled me with gentleness and warmth. He led me through dances we never wanted to end.

I knew Volker's attention to me was serious and that at some time in the future he would propose marriage. I knew too that to find a place to live together would be difficult. There was no furniture for sale in stores; there were no stores either. To start a home would mean that we would have to find some second hand stuff. Babies that, to continue my nursing career, would have to be raised in the *Kinderhort*. A *Kinderhort* was a State-run childcare center in which children learn from a very early age about Communism and the heroic Red Army. They were also told how bad we Germans were. I didn't want to face that yet. I wasn't ready to give up my independence--and yet I was more than fond of him.

I liked Volker for more than his charm and flattering compliments. There was a certain detachment born of self-control about Volker that distinguished him from other men. He seemed to have a patina of authority that had nothing to do with his position as an Obersteiger for the Wismut. It was somehow related solely to his own self esteem and outlook. This was evident at all times when I was with him: the way he introduced me to his friends, how he ordered our table in the restaurant and even in his conversation with my friends.

I sensed he would never allow himself to become irresponsibly drunk as we were both aware that many men were drinking heavily to deaden the frustrations of the times. Probably these frustrations accounted for Volker's serious nature. The little lines around his eyes and his mouth told me that the war had taken its toll.

When we walked arm in arm in the streets of Zwickau, he must have been pleasantly aware of the glances he received from other women. Secretly I hoped he was not aware of those flirtatious looks. He directed his attention toward me. I thought he was entirely without vanity concerning his good looks.

It was then that I started to fall in love with him. I took great pleasure in his comment that "I was his oasis." The first and last words he always said to me while we dated were, "Remember, I love you."

During warm summer months we walked along the Mulde River. When time permitted we even carried a picnic basket. Volker called me "Reneilienien" and I was thrilled to hear this endearing name.

One evening in August we were sitting on the bank of the Mulde River and there was a growing chorus of frogs in the warm summer air as the stars were beginning to twinkle. Volker took me in his arms and told me again of his love for me.

"Your loveliness had been evident from the first moment I saw you on the balcony playing your accordion. Even then I knew I wanted to be with you." He paused, then put his hand on my shoulder and turned me to look squarely at him.

"I love you, Reneilein. Will you marry me?"

"I've had a feeling for some time that this was coming. I just didn't expect it so soon. We haven't known each other very long. Are you sure?" I asked.

In the twilight the flecks of blue in his eyes were brilliant. I felt helpless when I looked into them.

"I didn't plan to ask you this evening, but now I'm glad I did." He paused because of my silence. "Will you, Renilein? Life will not be easy, it will be very difficult. But I suppose we have to make a new beginning sometime."

His face was close, his eyes so adoring. Suddenly I knew I wanted all the good things life could bring with Volker.

"Yes. Yes, dear Volker. I do love you."

His kiss was tender and possessive and I responded to his loving embrace.

"You make me very happy Renilein. I want to bring you only the good things in life."

He lay on his back, put his hands behind his head and said, "Friedrich Schiller wrote something for this occasion, little Reni--it's from Ode to Joy:

> "Who that height of bliss had proved
> Once a friend of friends to be,

> Who had won a maid beloved
> Join us in our jubilee
> Who so holds a heart in keeping
> One in all the world-his own
> Who has failed, let him with weeping
> From our fellowship begone!
> All the mighty globe containeth
> Homage to compassion pay!
> To the stars she leads the way
> Where, unknown, the God reigneth."

I stretched my hand toward Volker--he held it and kissed my fingertips. "Promise me we shall always be together."

"We can promise each other many things, Volker, but life brings unexpected plans. I want you to know I'd rather be with you than anyone else. I do love you but I need more time."

"I'll be patient because I love you so much. The right time will come for us to marry. In the meantime, you must meet my father. He will love you too. He is very lonely and my love for you has made me understand the loneliness Father feels without my Mother."

I thought of Karl-Heinz and my promise to him. I knew I had to write to him of my decision to marry Volker.

During the rest of the summer I heard many more poems by Schiller since Volker knew them by heart. When we walked along the Mulde River bank to pick wildflowers, he shouted all those beautiful thoughts to me. Oh those were joyous hours together.

Fall came and during October, the month to celebrate the Russian Revolution, a large party was scheduled for hospital personnel. It was to take place in the Wiesen Dance Hall.

The head Nurse assigned me to work on the night of the event. Director Rudolf, however, asked me to play my accordion for group singing during intermission.

"Sorry, I have duty that night. I cannot be there."

He was taken aback, but not for long. "But the hospital will only be staffed for emergency cases that night. Student nurses will be on duty also." He had a list of names on a board. He threw it up toward the ceiling and shouted. "Who said you'll work?"

"Doctor B____."

"I'll see about this. Come with me," he said. I followed.

"Doctor W____. made the duty list," said Doctor B_____. "One RN will be required for each three wards."

"But I thought student nurses would take it that night. I need Irene to play for folk singing."

Doctor B_____ handed Rudolf the phone saying, "You call her."

He took the phone and called Doctor W_____. "Hello Doctor W_____?" He hesitated. "Did you put Schwester (Sister) Irene on duty for October seventh?" He listened impatiently.

"Well, take her off!" He said and then listened.

"What do you mean there is no other nurse available?"

"Fine. Find somebody else." Silence.

"Then you will have to stay on duty yourself. I need Sister Irene." That settled it. I would now be in an even more difficult position with

Doctor W_____: this one not of my making. She would not dare change Rudolf's plans.

The party was within walking distance from the hospital. Volker was my guest. Everyone was there from the hospital, from cooks to gardeners to nurses, doctors and political personnel. Who would dare not come? After the political speeches, the social activities began. We danced to the music of a four-piece band. During intermission I played my accordion and everyone sang.

A poem that had been cleverly written about almost everyone on the staff was sung solo by one of the male nurses. At the end of each verse I played the same little melody while the nurses sang, a pleasant way of poking fun at those in the Party. There is nothing better for people under tension than to sing it all out and we sure did so.

Volker and I danced many dances. Volker thought there was too much alcohol and I was glad he drank only moderately. Later that evening, more people had glassy eyes.

When the party was over, some thought it was too early to go home, especially since the city of Zwickau also celebrated and had a fun fair. In a mischievous mood, we confiscated the student nurses' bus and off we went. We stormed the Ferris wheel, bought tickets and filled it for a few rides. Around and around we wheeled, laughing and singing to the accompaniment of the four-piece band who had joined our party. The people around us thought they ought to join in and pretty soon there was a lot of disorder. I feared the authorities might be called in soon, some people already were talking about it.

When our merry making reached its peak the police arrived. They found out who we were and where we were from and said, "The fireworks are over" and "you must all go home now. Break it up, break it up!" There was some scuffling, but in general it was good natured and peaceful. "We'll file an official complaint with your administration in the morning." Home we went in our shabby old bus, singing all the way.

Two months passed and I spent the Christmas of 1951 with Volker and his father, Herr Rainer Hofmann. They lived in a two-room apartment which they had tidied up all by themselves. Everything was clean and orderly but also nicely decorated. Volker had even brought a Christmas tree. His father was able to buy a few bottles of red wine which we heated with spices. We joked as we decorated the tree. Earlier, they had done some bartering to have a rabbit for our Christmas feast. I helped in the preparations and provided some small trimmings to make our dinner more festive.

It was a bright night as Volker and I walked over fresh fallen snow to church. The stars sparkled in a velvet sky and the snow glistened in pools of light from the lights coming out of the windows of homes. Greetings were exchanged with friends as we entered the church. Both of our faces glowed with happiness. "It's wonderful to have you celebrate Christmas mass with me," he whispered in my ear during the service.

Christmas service was very festive and I was surprised to see such a friendly old pastor conducting the service. Although Volker was of Catholic faith, and though in Saxony almost everyone was Lutheran, he enjoyed the service.

Volker talked about having a special audience with his pastor. "I am worried that I might lose you, Renilein." His face clouded for a moment. "I would like to have his blessing for both of us."

We made an appointment with the Pastor and Volker walked with me to the train station. I only had a four-stop ride to Wiesenburg so I promised to return in the morning to continue our Christmas celebration.

On Christmas day, Volker read poems by his favorite author, Friedrich Schiller. We talked about the poems and stories and he explained those things that I did not understand. I learned many things I could never have known from books alone.

Volker had a very close relationship with his father. They were good friends, not just father and son. Herr Hofmann, with his distinguished white hair and bright friendly eyes, was as handsome as Volker and he seemed to like me right away. Little things seemed to be as important to him as big things. He had a proverb for every situation.

The day after Christmas, Volker and his father escorted me on a friendly walk through town. They exchanged cheery greetings as they lifted their hats to friends. We ended our day in the Rathskeller drinking chicory and beer.

We discussed our future, where we might live and that Father WOULD live with us. His father laughed and said, "Thank you, you two."

"In a few months we'll have to give our *aufgebot*, Reni. You must go with me to make the arrangements. I'll be so proud to declare to the world we intend to marry."

"Too bad my family cannot come to City Hall and read our *aufgebot*," I said. "Can't you just see our names posted in the glass box for everyone to see? Maybe one of your ex-girlfriends will protest," I teased.

We all laughed and made more jokes about it. I loved Volker yet I had a strong feeling of apprehension that I could not understand. Perhaps my fears were a distant echo from the past war or maybe, we might say something to the wrong person and they would stop us. I surely hoped I was wrong.

On New Year's Day, 1952, Volker went home with me to see Mama and the rest of the family. Everyone was there, the boys with their girlfriends and me with Volker.

Mama was obviously pleased with Volker and he loved her too, calling her "Mama" just as I did. The boys all slept together in one room. Mama and I heard their friendly talk and laughter long after we went to bed.

Claus and Christine were anxious to tell me about school. Claus wanted to become a photographer, specializing in portraits and maybe later to even work for a magazine, with a big studio. What a dreamer he was.

"He has plenty of time to dream," Mama said. "But even if we had the money, the stores do not have cameras."

Christine was eager to explain, "We have to keep our desks clean at school. There are no people to clean up after us. We help by cleaning the floors around our desks."

"We get grades for that too," Claus chimed in.

"Yes, Irene, we do everything that Ernst Taehlmann said we must do." Christine, now seven, told me of her new philosophy of life. "We remind each other to do our homework every day and to get everything right."

I knew Ernst Taehlmann was some past leader of the Communist party and his self discipline doctrine was accepted in all ways of life.

He was born in 1886 and died as a political prisoner in a concentration camp in 1944, becoming a Communist hero and martyr.

There was a policy that if a child had a special talent, something that was really outstanding, it must be developed. The child might be an important person later on, for the good and profit of the State, of course.

Christine's statements about school indicated things were orderly and that children wanted to obey their teachers.

"Mama, Claus and Christine are evidently getting good basic education. I can see homework requires concentration but what about politics?"

"They start learning that from kindergarten until they are old. It never stops. There are older children though, who are included in adult planning meetings. They listen to discussions on communism and our country's economic plans. By the time they are 14 and 16 they are working up to 12 hours a week as apprentices on factory assembly lines and other places.

"Children are taught that the work must be done perfectly because everything belongs to the State. If the State loses, everyone loses. That statement is repeated often."

"Why are they pushing such young children into the factories?"

"To replace the adults who were killed in the war and those who ran away into West Germany when they began accepting them over there. They can increase production and save money when they place children in jobs and reward them with grades. Wages are unimportant, money does not buy much here. We still stand in line for everything for our daily needs. Claus is feeling the stress now. Christine is too young to feel it yet."

"But Mama, if the children get this vocational training now, will there be enough jobs for them?"

"Teachers have the responsibility of directing children into jobs the State needs filled. For example, if the State wants more waiters or waitresses for their State-owned restaurants, the teacher must persuade the girl or boy to become just that. When the Five Year Plan demands 100 cooks, 100 boys and girls must become cooks. The five year plan must be fulfilled."

"There is no real educational freedom. They are being completely indoctrinated into Communist philosophy and their relationship to the State." I felt much bitterness about this injustice.

Mama continued, "Every day they must look their teachers straight in the eye and tell them how much they love the socialist State. They are taught to answer 'We must not be influenced by western radio.'"

"I don't like it, we will never be a free people!" I said.

While riding the train back to Wiesen, Volker told me of his frequent hikes along the border near Hirschberg and of going over the border to Hof during the hard years after the war.

"The real freedom is in the West, you and I both know this, Irene. I have helped some of my friends find their way across the border. Their letters tell of much better conditions on the western side."

We both agreed that our families kept us from going into West Germany. Father Hofmann, as I called Volker's father, was much too frail to take a chance like that, and if we were caught, he would never survive a day in prison.

We returned to our separate jobs, seeing each other as often as possible. My resentment towards the Party increased. When the Party decided that extra work must be done they came around with a list for everyone to sign. We called it the "Voluntary Must List."

We were asked to work on our day off each week and to contribute the day's wage to a Culture Palace being built in Chemnitz, near Rabenstein Hospital. Doctors, nurses and other personnel begrudged putting their signatures to this agreement.

Not wanting to sacrifice my free days to this project, I went to the Party Office.

"Ah, Comrade Irene, what brings you here?" I never did like that "comrade" stuff.

"I need my free days--" The man at the desk arose, took me by the shoulders and turned me around before I could say more.

"It was nice seeing you," he said as he walked me toward the door. He whispered, "Don't get yourself into trouble." Then he was louder as he gently pushed me out the door saying, "See you, Comrade."

He knew what I wanted. He also knew that if I objected it could get me into trouble and would ruin my life: no job, no pay, no privileges or rights and eventually a labor camp. It was a ritual that happened all the time.

I signed away my free days.

I must explain our pay days. We were paid once each month and always in cash. We were paid in the dining hall where tables were arranged in a U-pattern. After receiving our pay at one end of the "U" we proceeded along the other tables to pay back to persons representing about six or more different government organizations: *Freie Deutsche Jugeno* in short FDJ, (Free German Youth), *Gewerkschaft*, (Union), Cultural development, German Soviet

Friendship, *Frauenbewegung* (Women's Organizations), and the Communist Party occupied two tables. The latter collected from their members only.

Everybody resented this immediate cash handout and there was no way to avoid them. Needless to say, taxes and other deductions were already taken away. We used to say, payday was like having a whole tree and cutting a little toy out of it, and being given the toy as your pay.

The first day of May is the Workers' Day in East Germany, a day of big parades and programmed demonstrations. Those who parade are the people.

Literally every citizen of both Wiesen and Wiesenburg, from the young school children to the hospital staff, were required to parade. Therefore, there were no onlookers. It always seemed strange to me, whenever we had to get into one of those parades. This was not a dress-up affair; everyone wore their working clothes. Doctors disliked participating in this parade, especially the surgeons. But there could be no excuses, they had to appear and walk.

A few old folks stood on the sidewalk watching us going by, along with some people with drinking water and first aid supplies we saw on the way. I wished they also had first aid people on the other occasions when we had longer parades. We paraded downhill from Wiesen to the railroad station by the Mulde River in Wiesenburg, and back up the hill to Wiesen. It took a few hours. Most of us thought it was senseless. Following this exhibition of the working people, everyone went back to their duties.

BERLIN - 1952

News of the *Jugendfestspiele* (Youth Festival) to be held in East Berlin came to us in the late spring of 1952. As specified by the State, most young people working in our hospital were required to go to Berlin for this event. I had other plans.

"You're asking for trouble, Irene, if you refuse to go," Rudi the Cultural Director said. "We will put you on the list anyway. You are going."

The purpose of amassing the youth of East Germany was to demonstrate to the world the unity and happiness of the Socialist State. I loved my work but I didn't think I should have to march in Berlin to prove it. But I had to go.

Some older workers were very enthusiastic, but they were not in the youth program. They had never been in Berlin, so they alone wanted to participate. They had to pay their own way, and those enthusiastic people who were so happy in Communist East Germany went right into West Berlin and stayed there.

The Youth Festival was scheduled to last for several weeks. Twenty-two nurses from our hospital were assigned to go on different days. The passes came and I knew that I must go. "You'll be going with a large group. Be at the square in Aue at nine in the morning. Go into the town square and wait," I was told.

Since early morning, we had been sitting on top of our bags which held only a toothbrush and enough clothes for a few days. We waited in the square. Hours passed. Slowly the square filled with about 2000 young people, mostly girls, with the exception of a few boys' units. Most of the males had gathered at another town square. Almost all of them were wearing uniforms, black skirts and deep blue blouses, the dress of the FDJ (Free German Youth). *What an ironic name*, I thought.

By late afternoon, though thirsty and hungry, we were told to stand four abreast. After being counted, we marched around the square still carrying our luggage.

We now numbered more than 3000. We were counted again and grouped under leaders. They allowed us to stop marching and rest, but we could not leave the area for any reason. Like a herd of cattle, we stood when they whistled, we sat when they whistled and we sang when they felt we should do so. When we were ordered to march again, we were to sing the Communist songs. I had not learned them and did not know the words. The leaders saw that I was not singing and shouted angrily, "Sing! Sing!" I moved my lips to the songs.

Everyone watched everyone else and the leaders watched all of us. There were no restroom facilities and no food or drink. I wondered how they would move us to Berlin. No train could hold so many. The answer came--we were crowded into boxcars, fifty to each car including luggage.

"This will be a short trip," I heard, and it was.

We arrived in Oberschlema one half hour later and got off the train. Constant whistle-blowing and shouting of orders took me back to the time when I was ten years old and the BDM Hitler Youth marched during the Nazi time. The girls were enthusiastic members of the FDJ. "*Give them some power and they go crazy*," I thought. I had nothing in common with them.

We stood at attention in lines and it took hours to get the 3000 people organized. Roll calls became more frequent. They ordered us to count ourselves and to shout the numbers loudly. Those who were slow got a jab in the ribs. If one turned up missing there was a search and the group leader got minus points which made her unhappy and mean. Those girls could really blow the whistle and bellow orders right into our faces.

We stood at attention and saw the sun go down. Darkness came, and as usual there were no street lights. At the spot where they loaded up many people during the festival, the Party had many large head lights installed on high masts. We still stood, waiting for something.

That day was nothing but military drills and no food or water. It was no use looking for a bathroom, there were none, period. Since we had to sing one song after another and we kept repeating them, I began to pick up some of the songs. When my mouth became very dry I just moved my lips. I longed for a drink of water. I wanted to run away, but there were dozens of leaders watching us under glaring search lights which kept sweeping up and down the lines. Group leaders were watched by other leaders.

Finally some men and women arrived. They were not the FDJ but the Communist Party people. Nobody smiled, no friendly faces, just big mouths shouting orders. Roll call again and again.

It was ridiculous. I thought they were waiting for an order to board the train. Something began to happen-one could sense that some VIP had arrived. Leaders gave their reports.

With no food or water all day, I was not too uncomfortable about the lack of restroom facilities. Some of the girls looked miserable and ready to cry. We were again marched group after group toward the boxcars.

"Anyone needing to go must use the bushes along the tracks. No more than five girls at a time and only with your leaders. Leave your luggage where it is," yelled out group leaders.

Although urgently necessary, the order seemed unbelievable. I imagined three thousand people trying go into the bushes at the same time and felt ill. There was no chance to run away since the searchlights moved constantly along the tracks where we were standing. The bushes were so small and sparse, one did not need glasses to see what was going on.

As this necessary but tiresome episode took place, the odor of urine nauseated me. Again we lined up in front of the boxcars.

Several Russian officers on their way to the train station were watching us. One of them began to curse and make repeated gestures with his hand across his neck as though he wanted to slit our throats. When we had to sing again, he became especially angry. He worked himself into such a frenzy by his cursing that it became obvious to all who saw him how deeply he hated the Germans. The men he was with told him to cool it, but had he been alone, he probably would have crashed into our lines. Some of the girls began to show signs of fear, evidently remembering those times of rape following the war. Group leaders were trying not to show their own fear. They shouted for us to ignore what was taking place and to get into the boxcars. I watched another officer hold his drunken friend back and try to smile at us pretending like his friend's behavior was a joke. It was not. While the Russian officer cursed, we marched past singing about

German-Soviet friendship and how happy we would be to fulfill their next Five-Year Plan.

We climbed into the freight cars again, 50 girls to a car. We sat on a very dirty floor and our legs were stepped on as we struggled to find a place to rest. When we pushed somebody, somebody pushed back. There were absolutely too many of us in such a cramped place. The doors slammed shut. It was suffocating and nauseating. I felt I wouldn't be able to make it until morning.

"I want air! Air!" I screamed. In total darkness I felt nothing but bodies, no wall, nothing to lean on but bodies!

Some girls succeeded in opening the door not more than a foot wide on the other side of the car, letting in some much needed air. Luckily there was an iron bar so no one could be pushed out, but it was attached in such a way that the door could not be opened wider. Since it was the first trip to Berlin for most of the girls, the excitement helped them endure the suffocation and fatigue.

The train was rolling fast now. I figured the trip to Berlin would take about half the night. However, we rolled east to Bautzen, which is the home of the largest penitentiary in East Germany. From there we rolled farther east toward the Polish border. We stopped in stations for hours as more cars were added.

During the entire trip we were allowed to get off once and then only to use the bushes along the train embankment; always we were under the watchful eyes of our leaders. As our fatigue grew we lay like sardines, trying to rest but too tired to complain. I never slept in such a terrible position in my life and it really upset me. I know I slept on top of somebody's body and somebody's head and bodies were lying on top of me. When one person moved the others awoke and moved also.

As daylight came I was lying on the floor wedged tightly between two bodies. I tried to make my way to the door for a breath of fresh air but found others there before me. They were lying on top of one another straining for fresh air.

The cool morning air revived us. We were now at the Polish border. We saw guards all along the train embankment. They wore Russian uniforms and had machine guns strapped on their backs. They looked at us and we looked at them, but nobody made a sound. As we passed small stations, large signs and posters carried the names of the Polish leaders. So much propaganda. We would fulfill the Five Year Plan.

Hours later we arrived at the edge of Berlin. When the first houses came into sight and people appeared on the streets, the entire train full of girls and boys started screaming and singing. If one sings, there is no time to complain or even talk.

The train stopped once or twice to unload passengers. Schools were recessed to provide us with lodging in the classrooms. Around noon we arrived tired, hungry and dirty at our destination. We were unloaded and marched, four abreast, singing every weary foot of the way from the train to the appointed school building.

"After you are assigned a room you may have the rest of the day off. Tomorrow we march," shouted the leader.

Classroom floors were covered with straw for sleeping. We were given a cup of chicory, a piece of salami and one piece of dark sourdough bread. I drank the chicory and put the bread and salami in my suitcase. I wanted to clean up before eating.

Unable to find a washroom in the huge building, I was told to go into the courtyard.

There in the open were about twenty little water faucets along a pipe. Under these was a long shallow trough which was to be our sink. The water was ice cold and I was angry.

"How am I supposed to wash myself? This is crazy!" No one heard me.

I looked up at the numerous windows in the four story school building to see many observers laughing. To my surprise I saw one of the male nurses from Wiesen looking out of the window, enjoying the view. That did it!

"I want the man out of that window immediately! Look at those stupid girls. They have actually undressed to the waist to wash in this place. This makes me sick!"

No one listened. I found an empty marmalade bucket and filled it with water. I looked around and saw at least a dozen outhouses lined up one next to the other. They were homemade with more space inside than the American standard size ones have. The toilet locker was unsatisfactory but gave privacy just the same. After washing I came out, brushed my teeth at a faucet and then went upstairs to eat.

After eating I found the room where the male nurses were ogling the girls below.

"I'll report this stupid behavior when I get back!"

Their arrogant statement of "we are in charge here" brought an immediate argument. What followed convinced each of us the other person was wrong. I left.

My clothes were badly wrinkled and I was told to "iron them at the home of the school custodian across the street."

While waiting my turn for the iron, I listened to the custodian's wife warn us about the evils of West Berlin and West Germany in general.

"If anyone is caught out of line they will be punished severely. Better not go near the West at all. We want you to go and see our war memorials here in Berlin. Here, I'll show you how to get there." She was really laying it on us. The girls, ranging in age from 16 to 24, were smiling and winking.

"Yes, Frau Mueller. No, Frau Mueller. We know, Frau Mueller." To further emphasize her warnings, a loudspeaker in the school courtyard blared continual threats to anyone who might consider going into West Berlin.

In spite of these warnings, I wanted to see West Berlin if at all possible. As I walked toward the U-Bahn station I saw girls crowding around some street-side stands. The girls were walking away with large pieces of red fruit. Curious, I bought some. It was our first taste of watermelon. "They were brought in from Russia for the youth festival," I was told. It sure was a welcome treat to go with our salami and dark bread.

As I approached the dividing line between East and West Berlin, the number of police rapidly increased. Each group of four German policemen was accompanied by two Russian patrolmen with their ever-ready machine guns.

Near the ticket counter by the U-Bahn (metro), a middle aged couple was arguing loudly with two policemen. I and several others watched this argument develop into a scuffle. When the woman attempted to help her husband, a swarm of police hurried to control them.

While they marched this couple away, I walked to the ticket counter, purchased my ticket and boarded the U-Bahn. My heart pounded loudly as I seated myself in the car. I smiled at several people in an effort to hide my fear. Then the door closed and the train moved toward West Berlin.

No one checked my ID when I rose to leave the train in West Berlin. I smiled again at a woman leaving the train with me but did not relax until I arrived at the Amerika Haus (America House), situated near Lehndorf Square. America House was a center where programs, books, magazines and movies told about life in the United States.

During those early days the wall between East and West Berlin was yet to be built. However, the trains were stopped at random intervals every day by East German police and Russian Soldiers intent on seeking out and arresting anyone who did not have their ID with them or who did not give a good enough explanation as to why they were on the train going into West Berlin. If anyone could not prove that they lived in or around Berlin, they were suspected of defecting and were immediately and brutally arrested.

At the Amerika Haus I watched a movie about life in the United States. It was about an hour long and I watched it twice. It showed farmers harvesting wheat with their big machines and I saw their homes, their highways, and the cars they drove. They did not lose their homes in the war. Oh, what a peaceful life it must be. *How lucky people were to be born in the United States*, I thought. I wondered though if they realized it.

I asked the lady who worked at American House how one could go to the United States. She smiled and asked if I had relatives or friends there.

"No," I answered.

"Well," she said. "Then it would be very difficult to get there."

I understood, of course. America seemed like another world.

I spent all afternoon watching movies and daydreaming about people who were my age, living in the USA. As darkness came, I walked along the Ku-Damm, just as I had done on my vacation trip. I was fascinated by the large, lighted letters that rolled from one end of a long sign to the other to display the latest news. Expensive new dresses and shoes were offered for sale in store windows. Outside the Sarotti Chocolate store, the smell of chocolate was intoxicating. Just standing in front of this store and taking it all in was heaven. Stores like that were always full of customers. People were buying the finest chocolate pralines by the pound, yet we back home were not able to buy even one ounce of anything half as good.

Also on display were newspapers, hundreds of different titled magazines, and all kinds of paperback novels which filled multiple Kiosks. It certainly was another world and definitely not a socialist one.

I fervently wished to stay in West Berlin, but everyone I loved was in East Germany. Not only that, but there was no one in the West with whom I could live. I did not have my birth certificate with me, or any other important papers. I was not yet ready to go.

I heard great shouting and singing coming over the loudspeakers from East Berlin. The East and West sometimes had shouting matches. I was certain I recognized the voices coming from East

Berlin. They would be the voices of the demonstration there. *Tomorrow*, I thought, *I will again be a part of it.*

It was dark when I got off the U-Bahn in East Berlin. Street lights were dim and far apart and it was after the hour I was supposed to be in. I entered the school through a back door and slipped into the classroom where I was assigned. The floor was covered with straw. Once again too many girls in one room, and somebody's feet kicked my head when I laid down. Another girl had picked up my food rations for the next day, salami and bread again.

"Everybody has to be asleep early," she whispered as she handed me the food. "We have a long day ahead."

I washed up and was informed that I was being reported. I saw on the paper "possibly been in West Berlin."

"You will be dealt with when you get home," said a leader.

We were awakened at 4 a.m., and we were told to get up and *Schnell! Schnell! (*Hurry! Hurry!). My eyes weren't open yet and my head was ringing from all the orders being given. Outside it was dark. In the building the light was still dim throughout the entire building and everybody was stumbling over everyone else. Luckily I got my teeth brushed, but that was all. Once dressed, we lined up with no time allowed for anything else. We were crowded into old WWII army trucks and even when we thought it was full they kept pushing in more people. Those who had to stand must have had a very hard time. Although I conquered a seat, somebody was sitting on top of me and my legs were cramped. We were driven to some open railroad tracks with no station around and marched into waiting boxcars. We had no idea where we were. As much as it could be seen through holes in the boxcar, we saw the sun rising. Then the train moved, stopped, there were more people loaded, and slowly we moved forward again. We heard orders shouted and a male voice bellowed, "Make those slowpokes move! *Schnell! Schnell!"*

As the sun began to warm us, we ate our bread and salami with nothing to drink to help the salty salami down. Somebody said, "This is the famous Hungarian salami. Enjoy it! You won't see that stuff again."

The train stopped and the unloading began. The leaders were hoarse from shouting and my only wish was to get away. We were marched four abreast for a good mile, then stopped for another roll call. The leaders seemed excited, someone was missing. We stayed in line and waited. Eleven o'clock came, still we stood four abreast in a populated neighborhood. There were apartment buildings, old and used up, and still we saw no pedestrians. "They don't want to have anything to do with us," someone said. We had no watches but it must have been noon when instructions were given to tens of thousands of us on how to march and who to follow into an enormous stadium. The lines of marchers stretched for many blocks.

People arrived wearing uniforms and folk art dresses. They must have been the ones who danced and performed the propaganda words for the movie camera. Television stations were not in our country yet.

An hour before our march began, heavy flagpoles with large red flags were passed out.

"Two girls will share a flag. They are heavy so divide your time," blasted a voice over the loudspeaker. "These flags must be held upright at all times!"

This tops it all, I thought. I sensed we were in for a long walk. Life came into the lines and the front rows began to move. We followed, slowly at first, then faster.

"Don't get behind. Keep up. Take longer steps, hurry."

We took turns carrying those bloody red flags.

"Hold it higher!" my leader barked.

"It's very heavy," we complained.

As we were marching, papers came showering out of the sky. I was sure they were leaflets from the West, but with both hands full and that red flag in front of me flapping in my face, I could not get one. I handed the flag to my neighbor. I just had to have one of those leaflets. They were lying on the ground and we were trampling on them.

"Don't you dare pick them up," warned a loud voice. "Anyone who picks one up gets severe punishment."

One fluttered down in front of me and I grabbed it. There was an immediate scuffle. Raging with anger, the leader burst through the line and ripped it out of my hands.

"You're on the black list now," my fellow flag-bearer said as my name was written down. I still did not know what was written on the paper. I was thinking more about that than the expected punishment I was to get.

We reached the area in front of the big stage where government leaders stood smiling and waving to us. Those in front started their dances as we waved the red flags and marched around the stage. Everybody was singing.

The trumpets blared, red flags billowed back and forth as the inner circle of girls spelled out their propaganda messages of "Love" to the Party officials. It was an enormous demonstration. Some girls seemed to be in a state of ecstasy as they acted out this fantasy of movement and song; others just smiled. All the while there were leaders among us telling us how many steps to take. Go left, go right, move.

We passed the flags to the line behind us, took each others' hands and walked, and then changed our hands to another line. This worked out pretty well and must have looked organized from where the officials were watching us. Tens of thousands of us moved constantly to the shouted orders of leaders. We sang and walked a folk dance. It was a sea of people. I had never seen so many people in one place. I did not know there were so many left after the bloodletting of the war. We were all young and being told, "You are the future of the country."

From the expression on the faces of those reviewing our actions, we were making an impressive presentation.

After a long time we moved toward the exit. Our voices were strong and I was sure this was the sound I heard the day before while I was in West Berlin. As our screams rent the air, mine was not for communism. I screamed in despair to get out of this place and into the sweet freedom of the West. In my mind I saw the golden wheat fields waving in the breeze beneath the blue sky. I saw farmers harvesting grain in the United States of America and wished that my brothers, Mama and Volker with his father could all be on such a farm.

Outside the stadium it was chaos. Nobody knew where they belonged and I had no idea where I was. Where were the leaders? Did they not know that not one of us knew this part of Berlin? I saw streets with rubble on both sides and in between, stands were set up to give out ice-water. We were very thirsty. Much further up the street there were signs telling people which district they belonged to and how to get back to their school. Boxcars were waiting to take us back, but now that everything was less organized, ten horses couldn't get me back into those boxcars. I chose to find my way back on my own and other people had the same idea. Three or four of us went together, still in a festive mood, we walked past entire blocks that had been destroyed by the bombs. As I stopped to get a cup of cold water, I heard my name being called.

"Sister Irene, Schwester Irene!"

I turned around and saw a familiar face from Wiesen. "What school are you in? Now that we are all going home tomorrow, we should see some of Berlin in the evening." I was much too tired to think about going anywhere, although sitting in that schoolhouse listening to orders until tomorrow was not very inviting either.

As I reached my district and eventually my school, it was late afternoon. Most of the girls were out; everybody wanted to see something of Berlin. After all, so far we had seen nothing but the stadium. I met the young people from Wiesen, and off we went. One of them knew her way around, and she led us to a streetcar that took us to a different section of the city. There, the five of us entered a coffee house, elegantly decorated and full of people. A band was playing both popular Eastern and Western music. We found a table and ordered something to drink. I was aghast, *so these are the East Berlin places where the West Germans come to have a good time for little money*. People were well-dressed in comparison to us; for them, money was no object.

I remembered Linda's cousin telling us that they went dancing in East Berlin, because here, they only paid a fifth of what it would cost to go out in West Berlin.

When they saw all of us girls coming in, the music played and one of the West Berliners started an impromptu floor show singing and dancing. Another one followed and he was clowning around our table, making faces while he played the saxophone. We laughed and clapped, calling out "Encore."

They liked this and clowned even more bringing about much laughter. I hadn't laughed so much for a long time. This was good fun and I began to relax after the long and tiring youth demonstration.

A half a dozen husky guys came in and looked things over for a while. They seemed like real bullies to me. Our fun waned.

Suddenly, for no apparent reason, they came across the room like a thunderstorm and towered over our's and other people's tables. The band stopped. Everyone got nervous and the air was tense.

"Is this human culture?" one of the bullies asked us girls. "Aren't those guys humiliating the human body?"

We all felt frightened at seeing his ugly beer-smelling face so close to ours.

"They are the decadent West!" He leaned over the table even more, as if he wanted to strike some of us. Was it because we had clapped so enthusiastically? The young men who had done the clowning were looking sober now. We sensed the tension. One spark and the whole place would be a shambles with someone getting hurt. We didn't want a fight. How unnecessary this all was, but those bullies had come in to start a fight. Stammering something, we all got up and left as quickly as we could walk. Then the fight did start, and we could hear cursing, bodies hitting wood, crashing furniture and shouting. We started to run. Having our fun interrupted, we felt tired and caught a street car back to our school quarters.

I had had enough of all this and hoped to get a few hours of sleep before the long journey started home again. When I went to sleep on the straw that night I vowed to myself I would never go to such an event again.

Long before dawn the next morning whistles pierced the air, and it was "Up and out! On the double!" Another trainload of youth would be arriving soon and the program would repeat itself to puff up the self-important feelings of the State politicians. Once on the train, the girls sang like crazy. They seemed glad to be going home. The leaders, wanting more room in their car, stuffed extra girls in ours. It was unbearable.

I estimated six to eight hours of travel time and again I was wrong. I managed to keep my place near the door, which was opened just a crack for air. It made breathing a little easier. But for some, it was pretty bad. We were given salami and dark bread again, with nothing to drink. Of course, we had no toilet facilities. The salty salami made us all very thirsty.

Long into the night, after the train had been diverted many times, we stopped and were allowed to get off for a drink at the faucets near the tracks on some deserted small railroad station. Several Russian soldiers were guarding the station while others were sitting around on the ground.

When they saw hundreds of girls pouring out of the boxcars, those soldiers got excited at seeing us.

Everyone was headed toward some water faucets and the leaders were shouting at us to hurry. We had to cup our hands to hold a few swallows of water and people dripped over each other.

I boarded the train toward the last so I could keep my place near the door for fresh air. When I reached up to climb into the boxcar, a soldier grabbed me around the waist. I screamed as he clapped his hand over my mouth. His rough hand smelled of garlic, and it suffocated me. Of course, no leaders were in sight. Several girls reached out, got hold of me and pulled while kicking the Russian. He filled the air with curses as I was hauled to safety. The train pulled out and we rolled the rest of the night.

At dawn, the sign "*Zwickau*" was a welcome sight. I grabbed my bag and reported to leave. I was told I would soon hear from the authorities as I left the boxcar.

MISSTEP

I was anxious to tell Volker about West Berlin and my desire to permanently cross the border. On my next day off I met Volker by the Mulde River Bridge. Volker's long embrace told me he had missed me. I had not forgotten how blue his eyes were.

We walked along the grassy farmland and up the gentle slope which soon took us to where no village or farmhouses were in sight.

"It is good to be here with you again, Volker."

"Please don't ever leave me again," he said, holding me in a warm embrace.

"I was only gone five days. But I have so much to tell you."

The summer air was sweet as we walked hand in hand up another slope and came to a pond. Placing our picnic basket and my accordion on the ground, we spread out a blanket and sat down to rest.

"I went into West Berlin, Volker. I saw wonderful things; I learned much about America. I wish we could go there. I want to live in a free country. More than anything else I want to be free. This political pressure depresses me."

He took my hand and looked at me for a long time. "Irene, there is no real future for us here, we both know that. We could plan to leave secretly, but what about your mother and my father? They depend upon us. We have no relatives in West Germany. It will not be easy to leave our families behind."

"I am going to try to get Mama to go but I'm not sure she will leave."

"The time isn't right yet, Irene. We must wait a little longer."

"How long? Until it is too late?" I shouted. "I thought you knew. The Communists have closed off the border between East and West Germany permanently. Roads are cut off and railroad tracks are interrupted. Barbed wire fences are being erected now all along the border. This is only the beginning. Soon, they will lay mines, you know; they shoot to kill at people, we'll never get out. Never!" I cried. But I knew he was right.

We sat there and he tried to comfort me and he tried to make a joke. But my desire for freedom would not be stilled. Instead of talking anymore, we opened the picnic basket and started to eat.

After a while, I picked up my accordion and began to play. We both sang "Nun Adieu Du Mein Lieb' Heimatland."

After the last words ". . . from the green downstream and stony height, I salute you now, this final time, You, my native land, good bye." Volker lay back and said, "If I could embroider that white cloud with wings, I'd spread it under your feet and we'd fly into West Germany right now, my darling."

I loved Volker with all my heart, but I felt like a bird beating my wings against a wire cage trying to get out.

I took a few days leave and went home. Soon after I arrived I asked Mama why she looked so worried.

"I had a terrible dream, Irene. I dreamt that you escaped to the West and we were never able to see each other again."

"Mama, if we are going to leave, now is the time to do it. It is getting more dangerous all the time. The sooner the better."

Ortwin put a newspaper on the table and pointed, "Look, there are articles like this every day about *volksfeinde* (enemies of the people) who try to escape and get caught."

"You have to be bold, look them in the eye and smile," I said. "If we are going to get out, we must do it now. I believe the U-Bahn in Berlin is the safest way to go."

"What about luggage?" Mama asked.

"We could take no luggage. That would only bring suspicion. The train system is under Russian control and if they even suspect someone from East Germany wants to get into West Berlin, they stop the train and check IDs. If you run, they don't hesitate to shoot. People get arrested all the time and are sent to labor camps or Bautzen."

"We cannot risk this for our entire family." Mama said. "It must get better soon. It can't go on like this."

I knew it would be dangerous for all of us to try to go together. We would be much more likely to be stopped. While I had learned enough of the Berlin dialect to purchase a ticket on the U-Bahn. I also knew that the Saxony dialect would be a dead giveaway for every member of the family. I dared not press this matter any further.

The next morning the door bell rang and I opened the door to see Herr Viehstig, our Culture Director, and some other Party people from Wiesen. Shocked, I gestured for them to come in. What in the world could they want? I was soon to find out.

"You behaved disgracefully in Berlin, Irene," Viehstig accused.

The blood drained from my face. I felt cold and shaky. He went on. "You did not know our national anthem and you refused to carry the flag." He went on reading from a list. "You tried to pick up an enemy leaflet and you were seen in West Berlin. Those are very serious accusations and you must be dealt with." I was stricken by these charges which, for the most part, were true. How did they know I had been in West Berlin?

"You are suspended from duty until further notice."

"I cannot go back to work?" It was incredulous.

"Not until we have decided what to do with you. You are to stay here. Report to me in three days." He was pretty sure that I wasn't going anywhere. The whole country was a jail and he knew I would be there in three days. They left.

"There is no chance to go into West Berlin now. You will be watched." Mama was as stunned as I was. I spent three agonizing days in grief and fear. I knew this would now make my file look as if I was a criminal. In a dictatorship there exists a file on every citizen from birth on, and any misstep, however trivial, is recorded and can bring charges with permanent consequences.

I returned to Wiesen and learned I wouldn't be permitted to return to work.

"You shall work at hard labor in the uranium mines." For how long was not clear. Gretl was angry and sad.

I immediately became one of the miners who traveled to Niederschlema and Aue on the train. Wearing a mining suit and rubber boots, the same work was required of both men and women. I first became a *radiometrist*. Carrying a Geiger counter, I walked both along the slope and underground in search of uranium. When the Geiger counter buzzed with rapid clicking, indicating uranium was present, those places were marked for later digging. They would dig for the ore until the Geiger counter could detect no more. This was an easy job, but unfortunately it lasted only a few days and then I was reassigned.

Lorries brought heavy pitchblende out of the mine where they were put onto elevators and raised three or four stories high. There they dumped their contents onto a mountain of black dirt and a chute carried the pitchblende down in stages. The second stage of the chute had an opening where men and women stood on a platform separating large rocks out of the fine dirt with shovels. When the black dirt thundered down in large quantities they could not remove all the rocks quick enough. Another platform, at a lower level, held men and women whose job it was to divert the remaining rocks out of the pitchblende. Chutes then funneled the pitchblende out onto a hill where open freight cars were pulled in to be filled.

I worked inside the freight cars with three others, mostly men. We shoveled the heavy dirt into the corners and sides so the car would fill evenly. Even though we used large shovels, if we did not shovel quickly enough, we would be covered by the pitchblende.

After a car was filled we jumped off quickly because it would roll away and the next car would come into its' place. We climbed swiftly into the next car and repeated the fast shoveling. Full cars left immediately for Russia as everything ordered by Russia was done rapidly and without question.

I worked frantically to keep my corner of the car filled evenly. If one of the work team was slow it brought quick criticism from the others. Workers not completing their work quota were docked on food rations.

Huge blisters formed on my hands the first day, but I kept shoveling the heavy black dirt. Once the supervisor jumped into the car to help me finish my share, then he yelled, "Get off!"

The car was moving before I could recover the shovel he left behind. The car was gaining speed!

"Jump!" someone yelled.

I did and my blistered hands stung as I hit the ground. As I climbed up into the next car I could see that the blisters on my hands had broken.

"Hurry! Hurry! Shovel faster," the workers shouted. "Fill your shovel. They want this train loaded and on the way to Russia today."

It was each man for himself. No help was given. We worked feverishly and there was no time to look anywhere except at the hurtling black dirt. Every second counted.

Russian guards, posted in special watchtowers high above us, watched as we worked. If I had not known that I could go home that night, I would have thought I was already in a hard labor camp. I shoveled as fast as I could though my hands felt raw and I was in great pain. The broken blisters cut deep into the flesh. I felt like a person without hands. How could I go on? They were so pitiful to look at that I cried. No matter how hard I tried I could not keep up with the men. The pain in my hands became intense, beyond bearing, and they still shouted, "Hurry faster, get it done!"

I prayed, *Please, God, take me home. I have nothing more to lose on this ugly planet.*

I tried mightily to keep up my share of the shoveling but could not complete it in time. Jumping from the moving cars hurt my whole body.

Evening finally came. We picked up our special ration coupons and without having a chance to wash up, we walked, sweaty and filthy, down to Niederschlema to catch a train home. Now I understood why the miners sat on top of the train rather than inside the cars. They wanted fresh air, especially those who worked underground.

"Do you get blisters?" I asked the man sitting next to me on the train. He laughed. "Of course, and muscles too." I could see the muscles under the clothes of the people on the train. *They will survive this,* I thought, *but I won't.*

At home I took a bath and went to bed. Gretl brought me some food but I was too tired to eat much of it. She cleaned my hands, spread salve on the raw, open sores, and bandaged them. Without any effort, I fell asleep.

Next morning I felt stiff as a board. Every move hurt. I groaned with pain as I dressed, rode the train to Niederschlema, and walked up to the mines.

My shift changed every week. The mines were operated around the clock and at a back-breaking pace. I hated the night shifts when we pitched the heavy black dirt against the sides of black freight cars. I felt as though I was fighting black devils and they were winning.

I told the supervisor I could not endure the work. "I'll get the whole team behind in their quota."

"I might find you a different job but for now you get with it! We have to keep up this speed to fill the cars on time."

The miners did not talk much, everyone was too exhausted. If any slight break came, we slumped down to get some much needed rest. I was never able to keep up with the other workers, and jumping from rolling freight trains was getting difficult and extremely painful.

One evening Gretl said, "If you stay up there too long you will become sterile from the uranium. You'll never be able to have children." I had no answer for that.

As I tried to keep up, the workers said, "You're soft. Take more on your shovel. Throw faster! Make every move faster!" To me, that black dirt was as heavy as iron.

One evening Volker came to see me. He was visibly shocked to see the weight I had lost. When he saw the difficulty I had standing up straight, he sat me down and took both my hands in his. He looked at the palms of my hands which were crusted with dark calluses.

"Reni, my Reni, what are they doing to you? This is enough. Gretl, we must stop this cruelty."

"We had better get her mother to come and talk to the Party officials," Gretl said. "Irene cannot survive this work."

"You must see a doctor, Renilein," Volker said.

"Seeing a doctor is not easy, Volker. Their waiting rooms are full. You know yourself they often send the sick back to work. There are too many sick people. The doctors at the hospital who know me are afraid to request that I come back to work.

"I'll see what I can do," he said.

Gretl and Volker talked, and then he left. A few days later Gretl and Mama went to the Party officials but they were told that I had to learn my lesson. After many weeks I was assigned to work on a platform sorting rocks out of the pitchblende. The dirt came down with a tremendous noise. I never heard one human voice during the entire eight-hour shift. While the work was far from easy, it was less difficult than shoveling in the freight cars. We were not timed and I had a few minutes between filling boxcars.

Although given extra food ration coupons after each shift, I lost my appetite and ate very little. My arms began to feel numb. I was getting weaker and nothing interested me anymore.

"Please go to a hospital and see a doctor," Gretl begged.

Volker asked Doctor S_____ to come see me. He came one evening and after his examination he said, "You are suffering from total exhaustion. I'm going to talk to the Party people and see what I can do. This work will harm you permanently if you keep it up." Good Doctor S_____. He really wanted to help.

Sometimes I thought that all the people talking on my behalf did more harm than good. *Once winter comes I will die*, I thought. *It was just too much for me.*

One day I came home from the mines to find Father Hofmann waiting for me. He looked sad.

"What's happened?"

"They have arrested Volker."

I was stunned. "What is he accused of?"

"You won't believe this--it started with his school plays when he used to teach school. He did not put enough Party ideology into his work. He has also been accused of helping young people escape into West Germany."

A chill shot through my body as I sat down. "How can I help? What can I do?"

"He is in deep trouble." Volker's father looked beaten. "He wanted you to know."

I felt as though I was in a vice. "I feel so helpless."

"So do I. We'll have to do something, but what?" With that he left a broken man. Volker was all he had left.

Volker's sentence came quickly. He was given no chance to defend himself. There were no open trials like in a free country. No lawyer and no jury. The condemning evidence was a letter from West Germany. A grateful student sent it from West Germany to thank Volker for helping him escape.

I felt sick when I heard the news and could not get out of bed the next morning. I lost all my strength. Even my will to live seemed gone.

Party people, seeking revenge on Volker, would not allow any of us to see him. He got 15 years for spying and being an enemy of the State. In those days, just getting caught crossing the border brought 15 years or more.

A few days later the Culture Director appeared, smiling and showing off his gold tooth, which I wished to knock out. He said, "You have shown us that you can endure punishment. If you promise to behave, we will reinstate you as a nurse again. You will not work in the main hospital but in the Annex."

I was too sick to even feel relief. I showed no emotion at all but after they left, I cried because I could not talk with Volker. I remembered the blessing Volker had insisted we get in church last Christmas. I remembered how he held my hand during that blessing and how he wanted us to be together forever. It was not meant to be. Was this going to be the answer to my uneasy feelings about our love? No! I could not accept this!

I rested a few more days, then went back to work. It was good to wear a clean uniform again, but with Volker gone from my life, I felt little enthusiasm for anything.

The Annex where I was to work was located halfway down the hill between the hospital building and the railroad station. The pharmacy was located in the basement. The first floor held patients with internal illnesses. Food was delivered to patients from the main hospital.

As I approached the hospital entrance on my first day back, two of the male nurses came out of the building carrying a dead body wrapped loosely in a sheet. They threw it like a piece of wood onto a four wheeled hand wagon.

In answer to my look of surprise, one of them said, "He died one hour ago. A bad heart. We are taking him to the morgue."

"But you don't have to throw the body," I gasped.

"He doesn't feel a thing now."

"But that is not the idea." Aghast at their callousness, I said, "Don't you have any respect for the dead?"

"Wait until you are dead, Irene. They are going to use your head for a bowling ball," they said laughing. A wave of nausea filled me.

I liked working in the Annex because Party officials seldom came around, which suited me just fine. I was actually more on my own than before. After my experience in the mines I felt much more compassion toward the sick miners.

One night two miner's trains collided and we were told to expect the worst. The trains were filled to capacity and many workers were sleeping at the time of the crash. Gretl and I were asleep in our apartment. They aroused us and all the personnel living around the area. Along with other nurses and doctors, we were rushed to the scene of the accident in old beat up Army trucks.

On the way the head nurses handed out bandage material and other supplies for first aid. Trucks and ambulances from other hospitals were arriving on the scene when we got there.

The darkness made it hard to see how bad the situation was until they brought some emergency lights. Many of the injured were moaning and crying. Some had to be cut from under twisted steel. One man's head was sticking out from under a metal piece that had pinned his entire body down. He was still alive! Broken glass caused many serious wounds. I worked on one person, then another, searching with my first aid kit hanging around my shoulders. I left the dead behind and tried to help where it was needed. Those we could move we carried to the trucks. The one from our hospital filled quickly. One doctor drove back with them to the hospital where nurses were getting the operating table ready. It was almost dawn when we returned to the hospital to help with patients that were still in need of care and a bed.

Not until morning were we able to change our bloodstained clothing, take a shower, and get a few hours of sleep. We had worked to exhaustion but by midmorning things were under control and all those who had gotten hurt were taken care of.

The Railroad Minister from East Germany came early the next day to visit the accident victims. He brought flowers, candy, and champagne. He went to great lengths apologizing and expressing the hope that they would recover soon. After thanking the personnel who had worked all night, he went on to other hospitals where other injured people were being cared for.

After a few weeks some of the injured were able to go home. Some still needed care, which they would get in their hometowns. The satisfaction of helping, and seeing the results of healing, lifted my spirits and life again seemed worthwhile.

To fill my lonely hours on free days, I often visited Father Hofmann. I was always hopeful for some news about Volker. Father Hofmann wanted to visit Volker in the penitentiary in Bautzen where he thought Volker was held. They told him, "No visits, no gifts." He said he only wanted to leave a small pound cake for Volker at the jail but that the guards had taken the cake and smashed it, as if they thought there was something hidden in it. Father Hoffman became very depressed because he did not get to see Volker. Even though he was glad to see me, our visits were very sad.

Carrying food obtained from my Wismut ration cards and little gifts for everyone, I took Father Hoffman home with me for part of my Christmas holiday. Members of the family called him Uncle Hofmann, which seemed to please him. He responded to every question with long detailed answers. He was well read and educated; it was a pleasure to have him around. Best of all for me was the news that Volker's sentence was reduced from 15 to 8 years. But eight years still seemed like a lifetime to me. Mama's home was now directly across the street from the church and a small park about two blocks large surrounded the church. When she looked out of the window she could see senior citizens walking and sitting on benches in the summer. The house was warm and the snow made our Christmas beautiful. Ortwin and Hartmut were entertaining their girlfriends for the holidays but there was still enough food for everyone. No Christmas *stollen*, but a cake just the same.

As we attended the Christmas service, I thought of Volker and our Christmas the year before. The past year had brought so much happiness, and yet even greater sorrow. I cried silently. I felt so empty as Father Hoffman and I traveled back to work.

January of 1953 brought a severe flu epidemic. Many seriously ill people died a short time after being admitted to the hospital. One night, I was on special duty with patients needing shots every hour to keep their hearts pounding. I stood by the bed of one patient and held his blue hand as he gasped for air.

"You have survived the night," I said. "It is morning it will be easier now."

He held my hand and nodded, then fell back and died. I could not hold back the tears. That morning, five patients passed away. People were being admitted in such advanced stages of illness that medical care was ineffective. Those few patients we were able to nurse through the epidemic were our only reward for many of those sleepless nights.

A severe winter left the hospital grounds in need of much cleanup and repair. Since all the custodians were now big Party VIPs, who did the custodial work? The nurses! The doctors were also asked to do their share, but they flatly refused. The Party bosses fumed but that was all.

In February I joined other nurses in sweeping snow off the sidewalks. The flu epidemic had subsided and we were back to our regular nursing activities. Our free time was used to work on the hospital grounds, clean around shrubs, and to do general outside work. When I watched the way some of the nurses handled a broom, I had to laugh, which resulted in very little work being done.

This continued for a while until another event came to change the course of my life.

It happened quickly. Our hospital was ordered by the Russians to become a tuberculosis sanatorium. All patients in our hospital were transferred to the new and larger Erlabrunn Hospital.

Tuberculosis patients came, spitting into little cups they carried around with them. The first patients were ambulatory, followed by those with more advanced stages of the disease.

All nurses under 25 years of age were told to look for another place to work since we could more easily contract TB. The prospect of more rest and better food seemed to outweigh the risks to Gretl, she stayed. So did other nurses I had become good friends with. As specialists on tuberculosis came, our doctors left.

I sent resumes to the hospitals in Chemnitz and Potsdam, both near Berlin, and received prompt answers from both. I could start immediately in either hospital. I rushed home and begged Mama to approve of my going to Potsdam City Hospital.

"Mama, I cannot stand the Communist ways anymore. One of these days they're going to get me too, just like they got Volker. I've seen the West and I want to go there and work."

Potsdam was still East Germany but was also a gateway to the West.

Mama and Christine cried.

"Mama, as much as I want to live near you and the family, the Communist ways never made any sense to me. I don't believe they want us to live better, ever. All they do is promise us things. For years only promises and Party doctrine. I am tired of it. I hate it."

"But Irene, you have always loved Chemnitz. Here you would be with all the family."

"I am sick to death of this political indoctrination. Every week we have to listen to more political speeches. See what they have done to Volker? I want to be free of all this!"

As I spoke I realized how strong my desire for freedom had become. My brothers had their own interests in Chemnitz, including plans to marry. Since they did not know how life could be in the West, their longings for freedom were not as strong as mine, for they loved that old town Chemnitz too much.

We all shed tears when I left for Potsdam. Ortwin clung to me as if he knew we would never see each other again.

FLIGHT- 1953

In Potsdam, a city of about 136,000 inhabitants, I rented a furnished room in the Weinbergstrasse, which was only walking distance from Sanssouci Castle and Gardens. The Sanssouci Castle was built by Knobelsdorff according to plans by Friedrich II from 1745 to 1747.

The Park of Sanssouci's area is about three square kilometers. It had its beginning in 1744 and was enlarged by Garden Director P.J. Lenne under the reign of Friedrich Whilhelm III and Friedrich Wilhelm IV. It has marvelous parks with carpet-like beds, borders, circular flowerbeds and fountains decorated with sculptures.

It also was eight blocks from the hospital. My windows faced toward a small front yard, and then the street as was customary in the old Potsdam area.

I liked my landlady and we often sat in her kitchen and talked. I trusted her and we became good friends.

Across the hall lived an old informer from Nazi days. Now she did the same thing for the Communist Party. Frau Loose was so curious she would burst into the hall whenever she heard the slightest movement in the building. Sometimes I turned my key very slowly to avoid alerting this overzealous woman of my presence. I seldom succeeded.

I worked eight-hour shifts at the hospital, six days a week. When I reported for work the first day, the nurse major looked at me for a full minute, then said, "We are happy to hire you but we hope you did not come here only to run to the West."

After being introduced to all the wards, they assigned me to surgery. Potsdam Hospital was much larger than both the Wiesen and Rabenstein hospitals put together. It took me a while to learn how to get around in that large building complex.

My free afternoons were spent in the famous Sanssouci Castle and Gardens. At the time I was there, the Castle was getting restored to its original glamour and tourists were rare. In the future, I knew, I wouldn't be able to sit there in private with my books. Things would change and too many people would invade the gardens, the orangery and all my secret places.

As I walked to and from work, I passed the Russian's command post close to the gate of the castle gardens. Their loud march music drummed in people's ears, day and night. After dark their building blazed with lights, spot-lighting the big red star high on the roof. In front a large red flag was displayed. The whole building reminded me of the Commandantura in Riesa, where Krista and I were in a wet prison cell. When I passed that building I wondered how many prisoners were now held there. Most people I knew avoided coming anywhere near there.

I lived near the best of Germany's past, the castle and gardens, and the worst of her present, the Communist rule that lay like a choking mantle over our country.

Shortly after I started my work in Potsdam, Hartmut got married, but I was not given leave to go home for his wedding. Ortwin's wedding soon followed. On a long weekend I was able to buy him a pair of shoes that Ortwin needed so badly. Thus, I headed home carrying a small suitcase and a sack of potatoes, which was more welcome than flowers. Carrying all these things on the train was nothing unusual since there were still many people who traveled into the country in the hope of finding food to stretch their meager food rations. Before returning to Potsdam, we talked about where Ortwin and his bride would live.

"It's going to be a while before we can have our own place. Until then we will live with Herta's mother because she has more room for us than Mama. They are beginning to build apartments soon and we will register for one next week. It might take five to eight years but we must be on the list. We also must help with the construction in our spare time."

Since there was a shortage of men to work in construction, every family who wanted a new apartment had to put in thousands of working hours after working a job in the day. In the evening they labored as construction workers with the hope that they would one day move into one of those apartments. For this backbreaking work there was no pay. Only credit for each hour they worked. There were no extra food rations for this either.

As I traveled back to Potsdam I longed to see Volker. I wondered if we would ever have the chance to live in an apartment as Ortwin and Herta were hoping to do. All my letters I wrote to the jail came back. He was not allowed to receive mail. I knew he must feel terrible and I prayed for him that he would be strong enough to endure his unfair punishment.

While walking to work one day, I saw a guard standing in front of a photo studio and a policeman posting a sign saying, *ZUTRITT VERBOTEN* (OFF LIMITS). My landlady explained in a hushed voice that the owner had been arrested. But the police spread the rumor that the owner had escaped to the West, leaving all his expensive equipment behind. A few days later the same thing happened at several other stores. One day they are open for business, the next day the store was guarded by police. People were disappearing.

One of the apartment buildings was converted into a prison and Russian soldiers, together with German guards, put up barbed wire around the building. In many windows the glass was broken and iron bars were put on them. I grieved for every poor soul that was imprisoned in there. Of course I heard many rumors, especially when I stood in line for a few soup bones from the butchery located near the prison building. If it was true, what they were saying, I felt a chill through my bones.

I wrote to Mama, urging her to come with Claus and Christine. Her answer convinced me she would never leave Chemnitz.

"An old woman is like an old tree. You cannot transplant it. Now that the boys have married I am busy helping them. Hartmut has a job on the government farm and lives in an old beat up house, you ought to see it. But they make it livable. Their first child is on the way. I will be a grandmother soon. Ortwin has a job in the city."

Holding the letter that told me no matter what they had to go through, they loved their homeland and they would stay no matter what was happening, I felt very lonely. I knew there were people who felt this way about their birthplace. But I never thought my family would be among them.

Most of our patients in Wiesen Hospital were young miners. Here in Potsdam people of all ages came to be treated and I became acquainted with the more serious diseases of cancer, diabetes, and many other serious ailments. Many patients with cancer of the colon came to our ward. Although they survived the operation, not enough had been done for them to survive for too long afterward. The treatment was not as modern as it is today.

A three month old boy with leukemia was brought to our ward. Everybody just loved him. He needed many blood transfusions and after each time he would revive and be quite lively, only to become listless again in a few days. He would lie as though he were dead. He had type B blood, the same as mine. I volunteered to give blood. I was so happy for him, to be revived with my blood. But each day he would lapse further toward death and in spite of a series of treatments, he passed away. The doctors did not know what to do other than give him transfusions and study his blood.

We had our humorous experiences too. One of our smaller wards was occupied by a Party member who had lost one of her eyes. It had been replaced with a glass one. One day I washed her glass eye and set it in wrong.

When the doctor made his rounds, her glass eye was looking in a different direction while the other eye looked at him. It looked so weird that instead of helping her, the nurses laughed like crazy. Of course they did not tell her what I had done. Later, after everyone had left, I corrected my mistake. This was a very commanding person and she always tried to get people in trouble, so we played little tricks on her.

One night I wheeled a deceased patient to the morgue in the basement of the hospital. Bodies of all ages lay next to each other on different long wooden tables, covered with stainless steel sheeting.

Some of them were covered completely, others had their upper bodies uncovered. Their names and information about their deaths was written on little cards fastened to their big toes.

"They use some of these bodies to make autopsies when teaching," explained a nurse. She chuckled, then continued, "Once they picked up several bodies. One was a woman with an unborn child. When they sewed her up again they were in such a hurry, they forgot to put the infant in her. When they finished with the next, a male body, they stuffed the little one in his belly just to get rid of it. Who would know or care?" She sighed.

I shuddered and left, glad to be healthy and alive. I surely did not want to die here!

In our hospital a Party official was assigned to each ward. They found this the best way to control everyone in such a large building complex. One afternoon, just prior to our weekly political lecture, I excused myself to go to the restroom. Our Political Officer, a male nurse, followed me into the ladies room and waited for me outside the toilet booth.

"Of all the nerve---why do you come in here?" I asked very angry and in disgust.

"We have nurses that jump out of the window to avoid coming to the meeting," he replied with a sneer.

"Through a third floor window?" I laughed sarcastically.

"Yes. They jump to that balcony."

"I see," I replied walking over to the window. "That makes good sense."

Angrily, I pushed him aside as I left the room, saying, "Maybe I'll try it some time."

The food allowance in Potsdam was much less than I had received in Wiesen. Ration cards ranged from A, the most, to E, the least. Mine was a D card. I could only afford 300 grams of meat in one *decade* (ten days) and I often stood in line for a full hour at the butchery only to see the meat bone supply run out before my turn came. I was never able to buy meat itself, only bones with some meat on them. My total rations would never be enough to even buy a steak. I ate my main meal in the hospital dining room each day in exchange for some of my ration coupons and money. Those meals were always meatless, usually sauerkraut and peeled potatoes or grits cooked in milk.

In this hospital dining room I became friends with Lottie Buchner, a nurse with five years experience. She was a pretty girl, about my age, and just a little shorter in height then I. She was always full of energy. Her boyfriend worked for a newspaper. One day she came by my home and wanted me to meet her attractive, curly-haired, tall fiancée. They were a nice, interesting couple and I liked them both.

After I served tea and we talked briefly, he asked, "How would you like to work for the Americans?"

Amazed that they trusted me enough to reveal their political activities in such an open way, I asked, "What in the world could they want to know?"

"I am sure you have all kinds of information from the uranium mines. They will contact you."

"This is silly. I think this is a trap."

"No trap," he said. "They will tell you what they want to know and you will be well paid."

I thought of Volker. I certainly did not want to risk being sent to a labor camp, nor had I forgotten my back-breaking experience in the uranium mines.

"We felt you could be trusted. Think about it," said Lottie, "but say nothing to anyone."

"You can be sure of that. With my luck, I would only get in trouble with the Party people. It so happens we have one informer right across the hall."

"We are trying to save enough money to get married," he said.

"I hope on the Western side. I cannot picture you two living here the rest of your lives. I admire your courage."

When they left I was still uncommitted to such a dangerous mission. For now I needed time to make my own plans.

When exploration of the Sanssouci castle and gardens, which were just in walking distance, ceased to hold my interest, I began riding the electric U-Bahn. Although controlled entirely by East Germany, the U-Bahn traveled from Potsdam, through West Berlin, and into East Berlin again. Each time I rode the U-Bahn I watched and I learned.

Many people got off the U-Bahn in West Berlin. At all train stops on the East side, people were spot checked by armed Russian border guards. We always held our IDs high so they could read them quickly. Without a proper ID, one could not get through the barrier at the station. We had to show where we lived and worked and give a reasonable explanation for our travel.

After Russian guards separated out suspected persons for further checking, the German police mustered them into a large room that served as a police station. People caught in a search raid had to put their purchases on a long table and handbags were searched. They ran their hands over the body on the outside of the clothes to determine if things might be concealed.

Persons in possession of forbidden Western items were transferred to another police station in the city. Each case was punished according to the degree of the offense. Even foodstuff and soaps were forbidden. We had such bad soap powder that it could only be called sand. Western soaps of any kind were welcomed articles for the black market.

Confiscated items were sold in a store run by the government in Potsdam. I and others often crowded in front of those store windows to see dream items such as shoes, ski boots, ladies' lace negligees, sheer colorful gowns, dresses, coats and cameras. All items were of high quality and prices were even higher. Few people could afford them. The exchange rate was still five East Mark to one West Mark and four West Mark to one American Dollar. That gives one an idea of how little East German marks were worth. Next to nothing.

Persons caught trying to escape from East Germany were usually sentenced for ten to twenty years at hard labor. I knew the prisons were full because buildings other than the regular prison were now being used to hold the prisoners. I could see the barbed wire strung over windows of these makeshift prisons and guards were often seen standing in front of buildings that looked deserted. Yet in spite of the danger, many people were escaping to the West.

The West Berlin radio station, RIAS, followed each news broadcast with the warning "If you escape into West Berlin, go immediately to Kuno Fischer Strasse. Do not talk to anyone but a West Berlin Policeman. Trust nobody."

RIAS broadcasted a program on Saturday nights called "The Islanders," an appropriate title since West Berlin was an island in East Germany. I liked the way they made fun of the East Berlin way of life because it always was true. People flocked to the radios to hear RIAS, although it was officially forbidden. Sometimes, the old man Adenauer would speak. In a fatherly voice he said, "We are all Germans, we are one people." He made us feel as if he had compassion for our situation and that he would like to help if he only could.

A letter came from Gretl. As I opened it the East German radio broadcasted their daily warnings again of the penalties if caught going into West Berlin. The only exception was if one was lucky enough to have a job in the West, but people who worked in the West and lived in the East got harassed by getting searched on border crossings. Trains were often stopped so they usually came to work late. Then in the evenings at rush hour, people again had a hard time coming back home since the trains would not run at all hours. This was nothing but harassment but people had no other means of transportation at the time. They just had to live with the nuisance. Many scuffles occurred and many tears were shed, and not just by women. The East German authorities hoped that by harassing people like that, they would give up their jobs in the West and start working in East Germany where they lived. Every time I heard those threats on the radio I turned it off in disgust.

I sat down to read Gretl's letter. Another letter was enclosed and addressed to her boyfriend, Ottokar Mangold, in West Berlin. He had escaped and wanted her to come to him. She was afraid to risk it.

Gretl wanted me to hand-deliver the letter to him at one of the refugee camps. In spite of the danger I decided to try.

On my next free day I placed the letter in a hidden pocket fastened inside my skirt. I bought a ticket from Potsdam to Henningsdorf. Such a ticket was easy to obtain since Henningsdorf was opposite from Potsdam and still in East Germany, but one had to pass through West Berlin. This way, I gave the impression that I would take a ride through West Berlin without stepping off the train in the West. When I got on the train again coming back, nobody would even know where I had been. My ID would verify where I lived and worked and on my way to see Ottokar, I was careful to appear unconcerned by reading an East German newspaper. As I rode the U-Bahn, I watched those who got on and off at each station. I looked for police and guards. The closer I came to my stop, the more tense I became.

The train slowed for the stop. I folded my newspaper, placed it on the seat and rose to leave. I stepped off the train and walked briskly toward the steps that led up to the street. As I reached the street, a great flood of relief filled my body. I had made it! I was safe!

I located the refugee camp in a huge building that was evidently a converted factory. The whole area was surrounded by a six-foot high chain-linked fence. Large trash cans full of garbage were stacked behind the gate.

At the entrance I showed my passport, my ID from the hospital, and a passport photo. After recording my ID information they sent me to another office where they recorded the information again. Then they called Ottokar over the loudspeaker. In a short time he came, almost running. He thought his papers had come through with his clearance to leave Berlin and go into West Germany.

"Irene!" he called in surprise, "How happy I am to see you."

He told the officials he was willing to talk to me, then said, "They are always on guard against infiltrators and people often get kidnapped."

Taking both my hands in his, he seemed excited and on the verge of tears. "This waiting to get processed gets to you."

We walked into the yard and sat on an empty box. As we talked, Ottokar turned his head a couple of times to hide his tears. I gave him Gretl's letter. As he read it, he kept shaking his head, "Why? Oh, why is she so frightened? She could be here with me right now. You could help her get across to the West, couldn't you?"

"Yes I could," I assured him.

It was plain to see he was disheartened by the letter. I gave him a chance to change the subject by asking, "How are you managing? There must be many people here."

"This camp is crowded, as you can see. We are all waiting for our papers to be processed. A few leave every week to go into West Germany. Those that have been discovered as spies are sent back to East Germany. Although this is a temporary shelter, it is well organized. Hundreds of thousands have already come this year and they just keep pouring in. The authorities don't know where to put them all but they let them come anyway."

I explained to him how lucky those people are now that West Germany is accepting people from East Germany. "Yes, no one wants to live under the Russians. My family is not happy there either but when it was easier to cross the border some years ago, the West did not accept people from the Russian Zone. They would have sent us back and then we would have all landed in jail or in a deathcamp built by the NKVD called "*Internierungslager*." It was like the one *Fuenfeichen* and others. There Stalin committed mass murder on German soil and after the war, thousands of Germans of all kinds. Those mass graves were discovered after the Berlin Wall came down.

"Some families are lucky enough to have escaped together, although too many have left loved ones behind. I am one of those," Ottokar sobbed.

I put my hand on his shoulder trying to comfort him. "I left everything I owned," he said. "And I will have to start from the bottom. But I know I can make it, Irene. Gretl could too. I love her and she wants me to forget her and start a new life without her." Tears poured down his face and he held my hand tightly.

"I'm so sorry, Ottokar. It's the same with Mama. She is so intimidated by radio broadcasts and informers everywhere that she too is afraid to leave."

"Once I get cleared, I hope to go to Canada and start a nutria farm." Saying this he looked more hopeful.

"What about your acting career?" I asked.

"I will first make enough money from acting to buy a nutria farm." He laughed.

Dreams, I thought. *Everyone must have dreams*. "How is it with the other refugees?" I asked.

"I don't know anyone and it's better that way. From the moment I walked into Kuno Fischer Strasse it was absolute silence to everyone. Those big signs posted around the walls high above our heads did it. They read:

PST, DO NOT SPEAK
DO NOT TELL, ANYONE BUT AUTHORITIES YOUR NAME
DO NOT TRUST ANYONE

There must have been a thousand people standing inside the small courtyard. Not a word was spoken, not even a sound from the children.

"It isn't even safe here in West Berlin?" I was aghast.

"One man who talked, told me he saw someone kidnapped off the street. A man was pulled into a car and they drove off. He figured it was someone East Germany wanted back."

"But how could they?" I asked.

"Think about it, Irene. The West has no border guards. They are all in the East. The Police State begins when you enter East Berlin. They are kidnapping people regularly."

"You will never regret leaving, Ottokar, but the price of freedom is high."

"I try to look on the bright side, Irene. Remembering your courage, I'll make it. I have to."

The ease with which I had gotten into West Berlin and out once more quickened my interest in trying it again. I learned that nurses who worked with me in the hospital also went many times into West Berlin. They gathered their antiques and went into the West to sell them. When they came back the nurses and doctors showed off their nylons, pretty shoes, and fancy underwear and other items.

The Charlottenburg Youth Center in West Berlin became my favorite haunt. Youth from both East and West met there to enjoy games and reading material. Occasionally they took us to a movie theater. Although I felt conspicuous walking in the streets three abreast with a large group of teenagers, my desire to see a western movie was stronger than any embarrassment I felt. The free meal served late in the afternoon was also an attraction for me. People trying to escape into West Berlin without maps and no understanding of police procedures usually stumbled into a well organized net. Many were shot and killed. The seriously injured were brought to our hospital for treatment.

A young boy from Leipzig, a couple from Frankenberg, two teenage boys from Dresden, and an 18-year old girl from Halle all lay in isolation rooms under 24-hour guard. No one was allowed near them except doctors and occasionally a nurse. Nurses and doctors had to sign in and out to treat the wounded.

One day Doctor R_____ walked into the nurses' duty room and said, "That dumb kid, why didn't he get more information before he tried to escape. Those kids never think of the consequences if they're caught. I feel so sorry for him. Have you seen any of them, Schwester Irene?"

"I saw the couple from Frankenberg. Their heavy Erzgebirge dialect puts them under suspicion the minute they open their mouths. I think they have a brother living in West Germany who is waiting for them. They thought it would be so easy to go through Berlin, but they arrived at night and missed the last U-Bahn. Since they had no idea where to cross, they found a room for the night in a small hotel. After they registered, the hotel owner reported them to the police. Before they were ready for bed the police were there knocking on their door. When they tried to jump out of the window they were shot at. They have been interrogated and were apparently caught in a lie. They were huddled together in their room like two frightened rabbits. It's heartbreaking, Doctor R_____"

Shaking his head, the doctor left the room.

A group of young boys tried to escape by running along the Babelsberg Bridge. They swung themselves up to catch the U-Bahn and must have panicked when they saw Russian guards with their machine guns at the ticket entrance. They thought they could cross the bridge and get back on the train. Some of them were caught without being shot; others must have gotten on the train. When the guards saw them running they stopped the train. While the guards were checking IDs one young boy jumped off the train and ran. They shot him. Two bullets were removed, one from his shoulder blade and one from his kidney area. He said there were others arrested with him who were not part of his group. It was just their misfortune to be on that train at that time. Had they been on another train they probably would have made it.

He was just a baby, trying to escape to freedom. When the other nurses and I saw what they had done to this boy, we felt very sad. Doctor R_____ was doing his best to keep the boy in the hospital as long as possible. Guards, stationed outside the hospital rooms constantly reminded us "to give prisoners necessities only." When prisoners were able to travel they were taken to a prison hospital.

* * *

I sat in the Sanssouci Gardens reading a letter from Mama. *The propaganda machine must be pounding louder in Chemnitz than in*

East Berlin, I thought. She wanted to see me but was afraid to come near Berlin.

"...People are constantly warned to expect 25 years of hard labor if caught trying to escape. Ortwin's brother-in-law, only 17 years old, was caught at the East-West border and is now in Bautzen Prison."

It wasn't fair, a 17-year old sentenced to 25 years of hard labor; I had heard that this happened in Russia, but now it was happening in Germany too? Her letter continued.

"Now that Stalin is dead, it must get better. The Russians produced Tschaikowsky and Tolstoy and their dancers are world famous. We'll just have to make the best of it and live with them."

Mama was frightened. I wanted to go home, to see everyone again. I knew they were finding it hard to accept the idea of my working in Potsdam.

ARRESTED

I visited the Charlottenburg Youth Center and read about Stalin's death. It was as if the world celebrated this terrible man's death. I was amazed to read that some Russians actually cried when Stalin died. My landlady commented, "Even the devil has followers."

I now spent my free time in the West Berlin Youth Center, reading books and magazines, along with all the literature forbidden in East Germany.

"Could I borrow some of these? I'll bring them back." They smiled and said, "Of course, but be careful. Don't get caught with them."

I was about to leave when someone announced that an American movie was going to be shown. I just could not pass it up. They put a group of people, mostly East Berliners, together and we left immediately for the movie theater. Some of this movie is still in my mind; it was the first time that I realized how people from the USA had also suffered because of the war. The title was: "The Five Sullivans." When we left the movie theater, most people were wiping their eyes.

After the show I boarded the U-Bahn for Potsdam. It was pitch dark and when the train rode through East Berlin, and I was already dreading the walk from the station home. Since the streetlights were so far apart, women often got molested in the dark spots.

The train was filled to capacity. As I gave my ticket to the German employee, I noticed that because of the large crowd, the

Russian Guards were holding about 20 people, and then letting a hundred go by before separating out the next 20 or so. This time I was stopped. I had never been searched before. Suddenly I remembered the Western literature. Ice cold fear gripped my body. There was no place to discard my borrowed material.

We were all ushered into the interrogation room at the Potsdam U-Bahn Station. The woman ahead of me was carrying a bag full of eggs. Although the woman was crying and pleading, the Russian took them out of her hands. After writing down what he had taken, he picked up the eggs to take them away. She became very angry and, in great desperation, grabbed the bag. He had not expected this and resisted only partly. She ripped the bag open and started screaming. Then she quickly threw the eggs down to the floor and trampled on them. She cursed in German. He cursed in Russian. The rest of the people cheered for a minute but were commanded to keep quiet. It was a big mess. In the scuffle, I threw my magazines on the floor hoping no one would see where they came from.

Too many police and Russians were watching. Everyone saw me! I was signaled to move away from the rest of the people. It was amazing how many people they arrested for having such little things as soap, food, or small amounts of Western money in their possession.

I was immediately labeled a dangerous spy, as the papers were considered propaganda material from the West. They treated me as if I was their enemy. I was held at the police station all that night. Early the next morning, I complained of extreme pain in my stomach and said that I had been pushed when they arrested me.

After they made several phone calls, they took me to the Potsdam City Hospital where I worked. This was just what I had hoped for. Perhaps someone here would be able to help me.

Under guard I was taken to an examining room. I knew the guard was standing outside my door and no one would be allowed to come near except by permission of the police. My watch and other valuables had been taken away but I knew it was almost noon when Doctor R_____ came in to check out my stomach complaint.

Obviously, rumors that a nurse from this hospital had been arrested had spread like wildfire.

"Schwester Irene! What have you done, you foolish kid?" he whispered. "You of all people should have known how careful you must be."

"I know. I've made a serious stupid mistake." I explained to him why I was arrested. "Have you heard what they have decided?"

"An emergency conference has been called and people you work with are being questioned."

"About what, Doctor R_____?"

"The usual. Are you attending regular political lectures? What you said? Who you talked with? How many trips you made to West Berlin? Why this, why that? I can tell you, they are not interested to know if you are a good or bad nurse. They only want to know how you think politically. That is all that is important to them."

I covered my face with my hands and the weight of the world a came crashing down on my emotions. Doctor R_____ took my hands away from my face and looked squarely at me. "I can tell you that those who know you in the administration office are insisting that you are not as bad as the Party people are trying to make you appear.

But you know how vengeful Party people can be and they usually have the last word."

He walked toward the door, then turned and said, "They said they are contacting Wiesen. They want any file Wiesen has on you. As you know, everyone has a file and it stays with you until death. I'll come back if I can get in. The excuse will be to see how the medication is working."

He left and I waited. I knew when they learned about my work in the uranium mines they would find my present acts serious enough for a long jail sentence, probably 25 years. *My life is over*, I thought.

The hours ticked away. Then the key turned and I heard Doctor R_____'s voice. I waited tensely as he entered the room.

"Well, you foolish girl, how could you do such a dumb thing?" He put his hand on my shoulder and continued. "Things look very bad, Irene. You will get a long prison sentence at least. You know as well as I do the labor camps always have space for people making mistakes."

I felt the blood drain from my face and I trembled. He looked concerned, but I knew he was angry. He looked at me and his eyes narrowed in thought.

"There is only one thing you can do, Irene. Get out that window and run as fast as you can. I will stall them as long as possible. Pick up your birth certificate and other important papers. No, wait. I don't know if you have enough time. Go straight to the U-Bahn and into West Berlin. Here are two marks for a ticket. The guard will see that you are in bed when I go out. Let him lock the door, then run!"

He unlocked the window with the master key and leaned it together again. The window had two wings that opened inward.

"Dress and get into bed. I can only wait a minute. Hurry!"

Quickly, I put my clothes on, even my shoes. He kissed my cheek and whispered, "I'll stall them as long as I can. May God be with you. Hurry!"

He knocked on the door, indicating to the guard that he was finished with me. Seeing that I was in bed, the guard locked the door after Doctor R_____ went out.

I threw the covers off and ran to the window. I pulled it open, sat on the sill, and swung my legs out, then jumped about two yards down from a first floor window. I stumbled briefly from the drop, but quickly ran. I was gasping for air when I reached home.

In my panic I pulled drawers out onto the floor while looking for my birth certificate. I grabbed my only good dress, some other small items, and a few eating utensils. The thought flashed through my mind that Ottokar said eating utensils are important to have. I packed underwear and other things I don't even remember. I was too nervous to search for anything I might need for the coming weeks. Listening for a knock on the door, my breathing sounded very loud and the tension made my neck muscles cramp. I was not thinking rationally. I changed into my nursing uniform thinking maybe that would help me get by the guards.

I stuffed things into a small suitcase and snapped the lid shut. Why hadn't I planned this better? I could have mailed some of my things to Mama and had her send them to me later. I was sure I had taken too much time. As I opened the door, I dropped my suitcase. The informer heard me trying to lock my door and came out of her apartment like a pistol shot. She saw my suitcase but I didn't wait for her questions.

"I have a couple of days off and want to spend them with my mother," I said. "I have to hurry to catch the train."

She smiled slyly and I knew that is what she would report. I ran down the street, three blocks to the next street car stop. Once inside, I thought everyone in the coach must be looking at me and know where I was headed. My head throbbed. I felt sick.

If I need to, I thought, *I'll leave my suitcase in the streetcar and run*. I thought of the young boy shot twice and still in the hospital under guard. Yesterday, I would never have dreamed that today I would be the one being hunted.

I stepped down from the streetcar and walked across the road from the Potsdam U-Bahn station. Suddenly I stopped, frozen with fear. So many police--they were swarming around much more than usual. I was sure they were waiting just for me. They must have already been to my home. This was not the place to board the U-Bahn.

Turning my back, I moved quickly to conceal myself in the crowd and wait for another streetcar. Within minutes I boarded a car for Babelsberg, further into Berlin. I never thought this kind of situation would arise. I always thought there would be plenty of time. Why didn't I have a better plan? Now I felt like a frightened rabbit darting about in utter panic.

There were fewer police at the Babelsberg stop. I left the streetcar, entered the U-Bahn station and bought a ticket with a return since the U-Bahn enters West Berlin nearby. A return ticket was above suspicion. As I walked up to the barrier, a Russian soldier with the usual machine gun and an East German policeman were checking tickets and people were holding their IDs up.

They let me go through, even with my suitcase. I sensed that my nursing uniform was helping me get by. They had even smiled. Two very young guards stood by with dangerous guns in their hands, ready to shoot on command. If someone died they would say, "I only did my duty." Had they been older, they would have been more experienced and more suspicious. They would not have smiled.

I walked along the platform, trying to stay behind a pillar, and acting as though I was reading the train schedule.

The U-Bahn arrived. I got on, still not sure if I could make it. If they thought I was on this train, they could always stop it. Even now someone could be inside searching for me. A family sat across from me in the coach, a husband, wife, and two children. They were well dressed and must have been "somebody" in East Germany.

The husband was drinking heavily. He stood up and asked silly questions of everyone. His wife sat there crying and the children seemed just as frightened as I was. He shouted out loud, "Life is only bearable by being drunk." Other people looked embarrassed and tried not to answer him. He did not listen to his wife and finally she gave up. Everyone sensed that this family was about to escape. I was very frightened and I was sure that this fool would get us all into trouble.

He looked at me and asked me what I thought of him. When I could not ignore him any longer I said, much too loudly, "*Setzen Sie sich*" (sit down). I surprised even myself by the tone of my voice. He was aghast for a moment and actually sat down quietly until a few minutes later when he started all over again.

Dear God, let me leave this place safely.

As I saw the Charlottenburg sign the U-Bahn slowed. I walked off the train and down the platform to the steps, still carrying my suitcase. No policemen were in sight. I walked up a few steps and onto a sunny street.

The impact of it all suddenly engulfed me. Trembling, I put my suitcase down and sat on it. There on the sidewalk of West Berlin I wept uncontrollably. My body jerked with sobs and the tears washed down my face, wetting my hands and dress. People rushed by me and no one stopped. Finally, when the stream of tears ceased, a great emptiness came over me. Less than an hour before only tension and fear had gripped my body.

Why should anyone stop? They probably saw this scene every day at this same place. I was about to pick up my little suitcase in one hand and was drying my eyes with the other, when a policeman saw me and walked towards me.

"Now, now. Things will get better," he promised in a soothing voice. This only made me break out in tears again. He picked up my suitcase and carried it almost up to Kuno Fischer Strasse. I thanked him and he warned me not to speak to anyone but the authorities.

"There are many agents from the East around here and kidnapping is an everyday event. If they want you back in East Germany, they will come over here and get you. Please be careful. Above all, do not give your name or where you come from to anyone but an official." He handed me my suitcase. "They'll take care of you in there. Expect to wait in long lines but be patient. Today you are free."

On that warm day in May of 1953, I began the long and tedious task of being processed through the refugee camp. Unprepared for the human flood that reached for freedom rather than live under Russia's oppressive hand, West Germany and the allied governments struggled mightily to sort out and care for the millions who came seeking freedom.

Two months later, after establishing an address, I received my first letter from Mama. Anxiously, I read:

July 1953

Dearest Irene,

Thank God you are safe. I have much to tell you about the police search. The day after you left Potsdam a noisy motorcade pulled up in front of our building here in Chemnitz. Everyone was so excited they ran out of the building or stuck their heads out of the windows. Others who were hiding could only worry what it was all about. They all wanted to see what was going on and hoped it would be the other guy who would be arrested. As you know, that is always the case. I looked out of the window and saw two cars, one civilian and one police, led by four motorcycles. They all had grim faces and were, of course, in uniform.

It never occurred to me that they were coming to see us. I saw one of the girls from downstairs go across the street and into the church. I thought she was trying to get away from the police. I knew the police saw her, but they came into our building instead. Imagine my shock when they rang our doorbell and pounded on the door.

I was so frightened. I didn't know what had happened. They were so sure you were here they burst into the apartment and looked through all the rooms and closets. Some ran up the staircase probably looking at the roof. Then they asked for you. They must have thought you were a dangerous spy or something. When they said "Irene" I knew I must stall for time. I was not sure if you were safe in West Berlin or exactly where you were.

I said I didn't know where you were but that you had left the house. Then I thought of the girl crossing the street and said, "You must have seen her." I couldn't imagine why they sent two cars and four police on motorcycles to arrest just one person, but they must have had their orders from Berlin and that meant high priority. After they questioned me in a very unfriendly way, I told them you might have left to go to Euba to visit some friends.

They also asked all the neighbors if they had seen you. I learned later that they had searched the main road all the way to Euba. They even found Krista's family. Someone must have told them you and Krista were friends. You know how her brothers like to trick the police. They said you must be coming through the fields and that you never took the main road. They ran their motorcycles right through the plowed fields at the government farm looking for you. I am sure they did not like to see that, their motorcycles were full of mud but they sure went through a lot of trouble trying to find you. They searched for hours. Krista said they heard the motorcycle noise for the longest time even in the dark. When they returned to Chemnitz, they were very irritated and exhausted.

They were angry and warned me that when you came home, day or night, I must report you to the police or face arrest myself. Apparently many people in the neighborhood were alerted to keep an eye out for you and report anything to the police. The police watched this building for days. So you see my dear, they really did not know where you were.

The first letter I received was not intercepted but they seized the second one. They knew then that you had escaped. Still, they could not get any definite information on where you were in the refugee camps and the search was called off.

I hope you get this letter before you move again. I know you would not have left unless it was absolutely necessary.

Take care of yourself, Irene, and remember we all love you very much.

Mama

As I put the letter aside I closed my eyes and thanked God for my freedom from the unbearable restriction of Communism. I thought of Volker. If he survived the eight years in Bautzen, I would hear from him through Mama. Mama was where she had to be and I had to learn to accept that. Thousands of families were kept apart because of the division of the country. I was not alone.

At age 23 I could now live my life with the freedom I had wanted for so long.

I was one of 331,000 people who escaped to freedom in West Berlin in 1953.

EPILOGUE

For years after the war, there was so much chaos in Germany. Small towns that were not bombed sometimes owned a castle or fortress with large rooms. They were used for quarters for homeless and jobless people. The West German government did a tremendous job, over just a few years, to create housing and find work for all those people. After all that was set up, they has to make room again for thousands of German prisoners of war that came home from the USA and some trains full of POW's from Russia.

I saw trains rolling into the railroad stations with POW's wearing horrible wooden shoes and ripped uniforms, and some with no shoes at all. Also everyone who left Russia had to go through a Disinfectant Station because of lice. A joke made the rounds that Germany was not a civilized country because they had no Disinfection Stations.

POW's who came from the USA were well fed and wore clean clothes and shoes. They had duffle bags full of their belongings. Many Germans came from Silesia, Pommern, what is now Poland. Also Sudeten Gau, which became Czechoslovakia, and from other border countries. The French still recruited men for the Foreign Legion, and was told they fed the German POW's very poorly. They made barbeque in front of the prisoners to make them so hungry that they would sign themselves up for the Foreign Legion.

Many families never found each other even after many years. The Red Cross worked with them and was always searching to bring families together again.

In 1953 I made it to West Berlin. Since so many people arrived daily, we, about 40 girls under 25 years old, were flown from then Templehof Airport in Berlin to Hannover, and from there by bus to Westertimke, near Hannover.

It took about three to four weeks to be processed to receive our West German Passport and to be allowed to stay in the West. Not everybody was that lucky. Some were sent back into the DDR (Deutsch Democratic Republic) if they were found to be spies.

We also received job assignments. Some lucky girls had relatives in West Germany; others were assigned to domestic jobs since they had no other education. I was sent to Koblenz where I was offered a job in their city hospital or another job in Mainz. I chose Mainz. Although Koblenz is a very charming city with much history, I wanted Mainz since it is like a sister city to Wiesbaden. And I liked that area.

I had a very enjoyable week in Koblenz and learned all about the history of the lovely town. During all this time I lived with nuns in a row house and slept in one room with ten beds. I ate and slept there and I was grateful that they gave me my first shelter in West Germany.

I was on my way to Mainz. The *Zahn & Kieferklinik* Tooth and Jaw Clinic was located directly inside the Johannes Gutenberg University and was run by Professor Doctor Hermann.

According to the nurses uphill in the Mainzer City Hospital, I was very lucky to land this job. Our patients were mostly from France, Monaco and German business people with money. Germany was still recovering after that devastated war.

Those were private patients with private rooms, and they did not leave until their dentures were completed. For the first time in my life I realized big money has power. It was not like in East Germany where everybody was poor and the daily life was "fight for what you need." Here the stores were so full of things that I had to get used to it.

With my first monthly pay I wanted to buy myself a pair of good shoes. It was a pleasure to have such a big selection in the stores. I wanted to write about everything to my mother and I hoped she would believe me. From then on I also sent many care packages East. Chocolate, coffee, nonperishables, some old clothes, umbrellas, for instance, were the type of things my family could not get in East Germany. My letters went to the police first, and then they were delivered to my mother.

Now I lived inside the clinic. Some rooms were for patients and the same type of rooms were used for us. I shared with other one nurse, my friend in the office. We were encouraged to take courses in medical fields at the university and we ate in the Mensa (student cafeteria) where all students ate.

"*Fasching time*" (Mardi Gras) was unforgettably crazy and full of irresponsibility. Students hired river boats and cruised up and down the Rhine River. They partied until Ash Wednesday. Then things got back to normal and many people started again to save money for next year's party.

In the clinic, we often fixed broken jaws from motorbike accidents. But most of all older well-to-do people from Monaco and Nizza came to get new dentures because our clinic was known for perfect fits.

I loved that job and enjoyed it all the more because we got more free time than the nurses up the hill in the city hospital. I explored the city of Mainz and the Rhine River, everything was new to me. Every butcher and dry cleaners seemed to be called Emmerich (my maiden name). But they did not want to admit to being related to a poor refugee girl.

The nurses I worked with were mostly also from East Germany. They had come earlier. I made very good friends and I stayed there for several years. Meanwhile the wall went up in East Berlin, and they were shooting their own people who tried to cross. Our newspaper showed us pictures of the people shot.

One day we got an American patient; he was an Army Colonel stationed in Mainz. He was the liveliest and funniest soldier, not at all a stiff person like some of the other patients. I picked up English very well. I had to pay for a class to learn English with some other nurses. People wanted to be able to talk to the Americans. They were glad they were there and that they received American patients too. He always had friends visiting and a few times a real hunk of a man came to visit. His name was Walter and he was a long time friend of our patient. He came often and not only to see the Colonel. After I had some pleasant conversations with him, he asked me out and we started dating.

Walter was a real gentleman. He took me to the best places to eat. At that time, a little outside of town, butcheries had small restaurants with really good food. Mainz and Wiesbaden (sister cities) were also very close so we went out to both. When I had gotten this job, the union had given yellow tickets, and one time there was a show with Hungarian dance groups. Before, Walter hadn't wanted to use my tickets, but then he was fascinated and we started going to shows with my tickets. We also went to gatherings with American families.

For two years we dated and tried to get married, but the paper war was unbelievable. They wanted my mother's marriage certificate from East Germany, for instance. It took us so long. Every time we brought a new document to the American authorities they were asking for something else, in threefold and in both the English and German languages. Only this one translator was acceptable. He had an office with papers stacked to the ceiling. We had to beg him to do our translation. We already had a huge folder of documents together when Walter was transferred to Munich down in Bavaria. It was impossible for me to move there, and I was sure we would never see each other again. I thought everything would fall apart.

But I underestimated the man who was to become my husband. He continued to work on those wedding papers. Walter secured an American apartment in Munich while I still lived in Mainz. Quarters could only be kept for so long or someone else would move in. He made an appointment with the *Standesamt* (Marriage Office for Germans marrying foreigners) in City Hall, and I had to pack my belongings in a jiffy to come to take the train to Munich. I wore whatever I could find and I had no bouquet. I wanted one, so he gave me some marks to go into the flower store. I asked for something green and quick, but she said no, it must be full and nice. Walter was waiting. He had to run for two witnesses and though everyone worked on Tuesday, he found them. Downstairs was the marriage office, and upstairs the judge put on his robe and called people in to get married. They did very it nicely, and even had an organ playing.

Walter was so emotional tears came down his face. He had been so anxious to make things happen so fast. It was the last day for the apartment. And then we went to eat. He started to carry me across the threshold. I didn't know what he wanted. We had put our stuff down and he turned to me. What did he want now? It was so unexpected.

The City of Munich was closed to newcomers, because the city was filled to capacity with refugees. Living space was nowhere to be found. Germany then had a system that any person who wanted to live in Munich had to get permission from the *Einwohnermeldeamt* (Office for Habitants) in the city. I don't think there is a right word in English. They still have a system that when you move from one place to another, you have to fill out a form for the police. It may not be the police now though.

Walter already had work for me waiting. I signed in for the job, working as a teletype operator in an American facility. I transcribed and wrote up letters and paperwork and messages that came in from maneuvers. It was a poking machine that poured out long thin strips of paper from the side. It had to be correct and they were usually in code.

Luckily I knew how to type. It was so different-the work, the life in Munich, and the wedding. It had to be quick because the apartment could not be held any longer. They finally had pity on us and let us get married but not before I had to spend one whole day at the American Embassy for examination. They administered a physical examination to see if I was sick and also a mental exam and saw how much English I spoke.

We suddenly got permission and in Munich we married. We moved into our beautiful new apartment and were finally able to live a normal life together. The wedding was hilariously funny, with witnesses quickly found. We celebrated in a restaurant close to the English Garden. It was truly a whirlwind-wedding, and the apartment was now ours.

My mother was happy to hear the news. We never heard from Volker and his Father had died earlier that year. My brothers got married in East Germany. They had to live their life and I lived mine. Although I searched for my Papa, he never came back and must have died somewhere in Russia. At one time he wrote to us that heavy fighting was going on at the Caucasus mountains because of the oil there. My father, on the other hand I only know he was driving red cross trucks with wounded away from the front. In those days not many people knew how to drive a car. All that luxury came later. Trucks of wounded were also attacked during the war. Father perished and never came back, so we guess that he got killed somewhere on the road. I still sent care packages to my family. I made enough money to save and do this. Also, my husband felt it was a good thing to do. He proposed to me by saying "Marry me, and I'll show you the world."

He meant every word. After enjoying Munich and the annual Oktoberfest, the city, the mountains, and the many lakes, we were transferred to Lawton, Oklahoma. There, I applied for a nursing job in a beautiful new hospital in Lawton. To my surprise, many of the nurses that I met there were German. So many Germans in Oklahoma? What a surprise. I was looking very much forward to working there in my real profession with all those nice people. We were only there for one year. The green cards laid out in the post office in a stack. Walter said you have to fill out your green card, but nobody wanted them. I said what for?

Then my husband got a new assignment, this time in Ethiopia, Africa. We spent three years in Eritrea. His job was communications and he ran a signal tower in the mountains. One time we were invited by the King of Ethiopia, Haile Selassy, to his castle in Massaua and discovered he had all "Made in USA" appliances and furniture. The King of Ethiopia was married to the Queen who made him King through marriage. She died while we were living there.

We enjoyed Africa, and went on safaris and fishing trips. They had huge shrimp. I never ate so many shrimp as I did during those three years. They also had mushrooms as big as a steak that we picked ourselves, had a friend check if they were good, and then fried. The Italian butcherie was so good and there I learned to make a good roast.

We visited schools and gave gifts to Eritrean children. We women were very much involved in helping Eritrean people. The weather was always an even 75, never more than 80 degrees. Winter was the rainy season, and it started every day at the same time.

There were also many beggars. Parents mutilated their children in order to encourage people, mostly foreigners, to give them more money. Nice clothes were not wanted. The nicer the clothes the less pity people had for them. So our gifts were small. I had a permanent beggar who came every day at the same time and same place for food and a few pennies. Children were sold, but it was strictly forbidden in the Army for us to get involved, otherwise I know we would have taken some of those poor children home with us.

We also made, with many other people, a trip to Israel. In those early days Israel did not have a big hotel so we slept in a *kabbutz* (a youth hostel) for two nights, sharing a room. Then we went to Egypt, and I never ate more oranges in my life then in Cairo. Orange juice places were all over Egypt's capital city. Cairo had big wide avenues with orange juice sellers everywhere, and men sitting smoking pipes. We saw the sphinx and pyramids and other marvelous things like that.

There was a story about a wife who went into a shop and disappeared while her husband waited outside. Over a 100 girls disappeared every year in those Arabian countries (they told us later in Paris).

I saw American merchant ships. Young healthy boys, sailors, going with girls of the night into dark places. *No wonder they came back with diseases*, I thought. We learned that merchant marines would often buy a girl from their families for a cow or camel, which the sailor could buy cheap. The American dollar was very high then. They would keep the girl for as long as they were in the harbor, then leave the girl behind. She could not go back home, because she was considered as being married to that merchant marine. The family pride forbade them to take her back, because she belonged to whoever bought her. But he was gone and from then on those girls became the girls of the night. Nobody inspected them for their health.

Americans were liked by the people of Ethiopia and Eritrea, but Italians, who lived there permanently, were often in danger of being killed by the natives. Sometimes they were intercepted going from home to the airport and were killed. But Americans went out to the villages with milk, toys, and food. I even baked cakes. There was a big cemetery for soldiers, one for Italians and one for Ethiopians. Many things happened there, too numerous to mention.

I enjoyed that country and the Red Sea where we spent many weekends. Since Asmara, the town where we lived, was so high in the mountains, the air we breathed was very thin. So we had to leave the mountains once in a while to breathe normal atmosphere. Ethiopia then had wild herds of baboon monkeys. They often crossed the roads and were very protective of their mates and their young, so we kept our distance.

When our time in Ethiopia came to an end, we were assigned immediately to Paris, France. Before our quarters were ready we stayed three months in a hotel, giving me plenty of time to learn all about Paris with the help of Germans who were once soldiers in the Foreign Legion. They showed us the night life in Paris. They were beautiful shows, but too wild for us. We then moved into wonderful quarters, a house beyond the city in Feucherolls, a few miles outside of Versailles.

While my husband worked at the Blockhouse, near the Champs Elysees, I explored the city of Paris. I was amazed at how many French people spoke German. At midday I met my husband at the Rue de Marbeuf for lunch and took newly arrived American families for a tour, either to the Sacré Coeur, the Eiffel Tower, the Bois de Boulogne, or wherever they wanted to go. I took them there. We lived right in the block near the George V Hotel. I stood on Champs Elysees and people thought I was a local and took my pictures.

Here I also met former German POW's who had joined the French Legion years before but now lived and worked in Paris. They spoke French very well and worked in the tourist business. They also told us stories, and everybody who fought in the Foreign Legion now received a modest pension from the French government, but only if they stayed in France. If they would go to live in Germany, they would lose that income.

My best friend from Munich came to visit us with her son. Her son and I went up the Eiffel Tower and felt, at the peak, the Tower swaying in the wind. There was real old antique furniture up there in a small place. Although it was off limits to ordinary people, Wolfgang spoke such polished French that the Tower Keeper bowed and allowed us to go up there. I never forgot it, but Wolfgang, my friends' son, spoke to this man and I never knew what was said. I found myself high up at the Eiffel Tower.

Every weekend my husband and I and the many friends we made at the time went up the hill to Sacré Coeur where we found all the international painters on Butte Montmartre. It was a wonderful time. I watched them paint and we bought a paper-cutting of my profile with my glasses by Claude Marin. I still have it. It was close to the hotel where Elizabeth Taylor, Richard Burton and Errol Flynn stayed.

We were in Paris when President Kennedy was assassinated. It was a terrible blow to people and we were very sad. To think that something like that could happen in our modern time.

From Paris we were assigned to Stuttgart, Germany. In 1965 all retirees were allowed to come free from East to West Germany, and my mother came after all those years. She had much, so very much, to tell me. But she also was very ill. In East Germany she was told she had arthritis and had to live with it. In West Germany I took her to a specialist. We were told that she had kidney cancer and would not live very much longer.

Since this was her first visit to West Germany ever, we went to the supermarket, where she saw a mountain of oranges. She said, "They must be phony. They cannot be real." So we bought some. I also wanted her to have a good pair of shoes. She was so astounded that the first store we went in had just the right shoes for her and that when we left the sales girl opened the door for us. Mom was overwhelmed.

Many other things she saw and wondered about. I saw her writing letters to my brothers. I asked, "Are you writing everything you see Mom?"

"Oh no, I cannot," she said. "They would think you brain washed me. They won't believe me."

I was so happy to have my mother with us, and we wanted to take her along to the Good Olde USA, but it was not to be. She passed away while she was with us after only two months.

Now my husband was homesick. Walter had had enough of Europe and wanted to go back to the USA. We were lucky to get tickets on the big USS United States, a ship as big and long as a city block. I had a wonderful time and gained 12 pounds, which I lost rapidly once we were in Pennsylvania where we visited family till our house was ready. We moved into an apartment, an Army place in Prince Georges' County, Maryland.

I loved my husband's family in Pennsylvania. They were such wonderful people and took me in as if I was an American. And I gladly thanked them for it. We made many visits later on when we lived in Maryland, and I enjoyed it and wished we could live there. My husband also inherited some property there that he wanted to use for future plans.

For many years we lived in Maryland where my husband eventually retired, and we bought a newly built house in Gambrills. "Our first house," he said. Later on we would buy a bigger one, we said. It never happened, but we were very happy in our little house and if two people really love each other, they are happy in the smallest hut.

Walter retired from the Army and worked for a while at NASA until he was able to get a government job where he worked until total retirement. Unfortunately, he died in 2009.

Now I am left behind with my dog, a Lab named Rusty. Age wears on me and I no longer use all the ceramic molds in my backyard artisan cottage. Over the years I've enjoyed knitting, macramé, making lace and other crafts which I often give to friends or were used as small table gifts for special occasions. I also treasure the fourteen years I taught German in the local schools and my many years of volunteer work with Army Community Services at Fort George G. Meade

I am still active in our local Lutheran church and sing in the choir. I am also a member of the LA Fitness near my home with a pool, and I continue in the German-American Club near the post. My last battles were not in East Germany and included a fight against breast cancer which I overcame several years ago.

* * *

I began writing these pages nearly twenty years ago. The memories of my life in Germany before World War Two, the fear after the war, my dangerous crossings into West Germany and my life under the oppressive Communists are as vivid and real today as ever.

It is said that everyone has a story and this is part of mine. People tell me it is remarkable, and maybe it is, but I know it is not unique. Millions of people were caught behind the Iron Curtain against their will and suffered terribly. Countless thousands died senselessly and tragically. I came close to dying many times. The only reason I escaped was because of the kindness of others and the protection of God.

Freedom is a different sort of thing. When you have it and grow up with it, it might be the last thing you think about. When you don't, it seems as far away as a dream. I am thankful for the freedom I have and the country that has opened its arms to me and allowed me to enjoy that freedom. I also remember enjoying freedom as a small child in Germany before the Nazis took over. We should never take freedom for granted because it can disappear so very quickly if we let it.

I have lived in many places in my life. Some were places of hiding and others of comfort. Dwellings filled with fear and those of love, a refuge from what is dark and evil. All my life I strive for my home. A place without tears or sorrow or pain. I have not found it yet.

Soon a day will come when I will leave this world as we all must. On that wonderful day I will meet my Jesus and see my beloved Walter again. On that day I will feel the arms of my mother around me. On that day I will weep in joy to see all those lost and yet alive again.

On that day, I will finally, after all this time, be home.

Mrs. Walter Kucholick, left, one of the Army Community Service "Very Important Volunteers," will have her name attached to the plaque displayed here by Mrs. Kucholick and Mrs. Jack Dunham, ACS volunteer supervisor. Mrs. Kucholick is one of the four volunteers who have contributed more than 1000 hours to the ACS program. She is chairman of the German Wives group here. [Photo by Howard]

One of Irene's awards over 14 years of Army volunteer work

Picture of Berlin Wall checkpoint Heinrich-Heine Strasse

Irene teaches German in US.

German-American Club (Irene 2nd from Left)

Walter P. Kucholick

Irene in America

Irene plays her accordion for students.

Key Dates

January 30, 1933 - Adolf Hitler is appointed Chancellor of Germany.

February 22, 1933 - 40,000 SA and SS men are sworn in as auxiliary police.

February 27, 1933 - Nazis burn Reichstag Building to create crisis atmosphere.

February 28, 1933 - Emergency powers granted to Hitler as a result of the Reichstag fire.

March 22, 1933 - Nazis open Dachau concentration camp near Munich, to be followed by Buchenwald near Weimar in central Germany, Sachsenhausen near Berlin in northern Germany, and Ravensbrück for women.

March 24, 1933 - German Parliament passes Enabling Act giving Hitler dictatorial powers.

April 26, 1933 - The Gestapo is born, created by Hermann Göring in the German state of Prussia.

August 2, 1934 - German President von Hindenburg dies. Hitler becomes Führer.

March 7, 1936 - Germany occupies the Rhineland.

June 17, 1936 - Heinrich Himmler is appointed chief of the German Police.

August 1, 1936 - Olympic Games begin in Berlin.

March 12 - 13, 1938 - German troops enter Austria. Hitler announces *Anschluss* (union) with Austria.

September 29, 1938 - Germany, Italy, Great Britain, and France sign the Munich agreement which forces the Czechoslovak Republic to cede the Sudetenland, including the key Czechoslovak military defense positions, to Nazi Germany.

October 15, 1938 - German troops occupy the Sudetenland.

November 9 - 10, 1938 - *Kristallnacht* - The Night of Broken Glass.

March 15 - 16, 1939 - German troops seize Czechoslovakia.

March 31, 1939 France and Great Britain guarantee the integrity of the borders of the Polish state.

August 23, 1939 Nazi Germany and the Soviet Union sign a nonaggression agreement and a secret codicil dividing eastern Europe into spheres of influence.

September 1, 1939 - Germany invades Poland.

September 3, 1939 - Great Britain and France declare war on Germany.

September 17, 1939 - Soviet troops invade eastern Poland.

September 27, 1939 - Poland surrenders.

September 29, 1939 - Nazis and Soviets divide up Poland between them.

April 9, 1940 - Germany invades Denmark and Norway.

May 10, 1940 - Germany invades France, Belgium, Holland, and Luxembourg.

June 14, 1940 - Paris is occupied by the Nazis.

June 22, 1940 - France signs an armistice with Hitler.

September 27, 1940 - Tripartite (Axis) Pact signed by Germany, Italy and Japan.

October 7, 1940 - Germany invades Romania.

November, 1940 - Hungary, Romania, and Slovakia become German Allies.

March 2, 1941 - Germany occupies Bulgaria.

April 6, 1941 - Germany invades Yugoslavia and Greece.

June 22, 1941 - Germany invades the Soviet Union.

September 1, 1941 - German Jews ordered to wear yellow stars.

September 17, 1941 - Beginning of general deportation of German Jews.

December 7, 1941 - Japanese attack United States at Pearl Harbor. The next day the U.S. and Great Britain declare war on Japan.

December 11, 1941 - Hitler declares war on the United States. President Roosevelt then asks Congress for and receives a declaration of war on Germany.

February 2, 1943 - Germans surrender to Russian troops at Stalingrad in the first big defeat of Hitler's armies.

May 13, 1943 - German and Italian troops in North Africa surrender to Allies.

May 19, 1943 - Nazis declare Berlin to be Judenfrei (cleansed of Jews).

June 11, 1943 - Himmler orders liquidation of all Jewish ghettos in occupied Poland.

July 9 - 10, 1943 - Allied troops land in Sicily.

January 3, 1944 - Russian troops reach former Polish border.

March 19, 1944 - Germany occupies Hungary.

June 6, 1944 - D-Day: Allied landings in Normandy on the coast of northern France.

January 14, 1945 - Invasion of eastern Germany by Russian troops.

January 17, 1945 - Liberation of Warsaw by the Russians.

January 27, 1945 - Russian troops liberate Auschwitz. By this time, an estimated 2,000,000 persons, including 1,500,000 Jews, have been murdered there.

April 4, 1945 - Ohrdruf camp is liberated, later visited by General Eisenhower.

April 10, 1945 - Allies liberate Buchenwald.

April 15, 1945 - Approximately 40,000 prisoners freed at Bergen-Belsen by the British.

April 23, 1945 - Berlin is reached by Russian troops.

April 29, 1945 - U.S. 7th Army liberates Dachau.

April 30, 1945 - Hitler commits suicide in his Berlin bunker.

April 30, 1945 - Americans free 33,000 inmates from concentration camps.

May 5, 1945 - Mauthausen liberated.

May 7, 1945 - Unconditional German surrender signed by General Alfred Jodl at Reims.

July 1, 1945 - Germany is divided into four occupation zones: American, British, French, and Soviet. Soviets begin establishment of the Inner German Border which was later to expand and be referred to as the Iron Curtain.

July 12 - 2 August - Potsdam Conference.

February 1948 - Soviets officially impose travel restrictions into West Berlin and other occupied zones.

March 7, 1948 - Americans, British, and French agree to merge their respective zones into one country.

June 12-24, 1948 - Soviets close all autobahn and rail links into West Berlin.

May 23, 1948 - Federal Republic of Germany (West Germany) formed.

June, 1948 - Soviets blockage Berlin. Americans initiate the Berlin Airlift to keep the Allied sectors of the city supplied.

October 11, 1948 - German Democratic Republic (East Germany) formed.

May, 1948 - Soviets lift Berlin blockade.

1951 - First Five Year Plan for East Germany instituted by the Soviets.

March 1953 - Stalin dies.

August, 1961 - Berlin Wall goes up, cutting off East and West Berlin.

19 August, 1989 - Hungary dismantles its fortified border with Austria resulting in a huge flood of East Germans into Austria.

September, 1989 - Large scale protests begin in East Germany.

4 November, 1989 - Over 500,000 East Berliners gather at Alexanderplatz in a massive protest against the Berlin Wall.

November, 1989 - Czechoslovakia eases its western borders allowing persons to flee into Hungary.

9 November, 1989 - East Germany announces that the next day they will allow persons to travel between East and West Berlin through official gates. East Berliners began gathering at the wall in massive numbers almost immediately after the radio broadcast.

10:45 PM, 9 November, 1989 - Unwilling to use lethal force to hold back the increasingly insistent East Berliners, the East German soldiers were ordered to open the gates separating East and West Berlin. West Berliners met East Berliners with champagne and flowers and groups from both sides stood on the top of the wall in celebration.

December, 1989 - Communist governments in Czechoslovakia, Bulgaria, and Romania fall as a result of events in East Germany.

1 July, 1990 - All borders controls between East and West Germany end.

3 October, 1990 - The official dissolution of East Germany and its reunification with West Germany into a united country.

September 1991 - Dissolution of the Soviet Union.

www.ingramcontent.com/pod-product-compliance
Lightning Source LLC
Chambersburg PA
CBHW020937180426
43194CB00038B/211